MAKING THE
MOST OF
YOUR MONEY

Ray Linder

VICTOR BOOKS

A DIVISION OF SCRIPTURE PRESS PUBLICATIONS INC.
USA   CANADA   ENGLAND

Unless otherwise indicated, all Scripture references are from the
Holy Bible, New International Version®. Copyright © 1973, 1978, 1984
by International Bible Society. Used by permission of
Zondervan Publishing House. All rights reserved; other quotations
are from the *Authorized (King James) Version* (KJV).

Copyediting: Jerry Yamamoto; Barbara Williams
Cover Design: Scott Rattray

Library of Congress Cataloging-in-Publication Data

Linder, Ray.
   Making the most of your money / by Ray Linder.
     p.   cm.
   Includes bibliographical references.
   ISBN 1-56476-389-7
   1. Finance, Personal. 2. Investments. I. Title.
HG179.L513 1995
332.024 – dc20   94-33606
                                                    CIP

To my wife, Christine
"Her children arise and call her blessed; her husband also, and he praises her: 'Many women do noble things but you surpass them all' " (Prov. 31:28-29);

And to my girls, Diandra and Cassandra,
"I write to you, dear children, because your sins have been forgiven on account of His name" (1 John 2:12).

Contents

Acknowledgments

I am one of those people who actually enjoys the long thank-you speeches at award shows. I read movie credits and album liner notes. Nothing worthwhile gets accomplished without many people. Here are thank-yous to the people involved:

George Escobar and Dave Nicholson, whose personal testimonies challenged me to examine my finances.

Scott, pastor, mentor, and dear friend, who knows how to get the most out of his pupils. Who could guess that my asking you for Bible verses on money would eventually turn into a book?

My Bible study class that helped shape some rough guidelines into something that may actually make some sense.

Oakbrook Church, Reston, Virginia — I'm proud to be part of this small but mighty band of spiritual warriors.

Nelson Keener for introducing me to Victor Books.

Bob Anderson, who made my introduction to Nelson possible. Thanks for giving me confidence to act on my vision.

Dave Horton at Victor Books who helped make the process of publishing a book a lot of fun.

Todd Rivetti and my mom for their very thorough critiques of the original manuscript. Moms are definitely kinder and gentler than opinionated friends but not necessarily more valuable.

Dave Merrill for his excellent(!) graphics.

My wife for being a Proverbs 31 woman while her husband chased a dream, now a reality.

The Holy Spirit, the real author of this book.

Introduction

Why does Satan's work always have sufficient funds to move quickly, yet lack of financial resources often slows God's work? The answer lies in two passages of Scripture — one dealing with attitude, the other with aptitude.

In the Parable of the Shrewd Manager (Luke 16:1-13), Jesus told the disciples that "the people of this world are more shrewd in dealing with their own kind than are the people of the light" (v. 8). The church has historically had an aversion to money because of its worldly connotations: hedonism, greed, abuse, and so on. Therefore, as Christians we've become indoctrinated not to allow ourselves to think unnecessarily about money. Our attitude has been to ignore, hate, or feel guilty about having financial wealth.

Jesus, however, said that "the people of this world are more shrewd . . . than are the people of the light." The word "shrewd" is from the Greek word *phronimos*, which means thoughtful, sagacious, or discreet — all godly attributes. They imply a cautious, covert means to achieve a particular end. Thoughtfulness and discretion are not natural to greedy, abusive behavior, which is more emotional and irrational. The parable is making the point that while money can serve evil ends, it can still be used with godly means. Jesus is teaching us that Satan's followers are superior to Christians at using money to achieve specific goals. Furthermore, He exhorts us to make shrewd use of money for godly ends.

9

Our denial of the importance of money is an incorrect attitude that is born from a natural desire to please God, but it is exactly this attitude that is displeasing to God. In the Parable of the Talents, we see that it was the servant who hid his money who was rebuked for being wicked. He knew his master was a "hard man" and the servant was fearful of losing his master's money. Yet the servants who skillfully multiplied their master's assets were praised as being "good and faithful."

I believe the correct biblical attitude toward wealth is not denial but desire. Desire not as an end in itself—that is idolatry—but a desire for the greatest godly use of money—giving. I have come to the indisputable conclusion that the ultimate manifestation of Christian stewardship is loving, sacrificial giving. How much are we to give? Just as God did, we must give all that we have. But our ability to give is limited by our ability to get. Until we become more skillful in our use of money, our "all" will not amount to much, and the enemy's work will continue to flourish because we cannot match his funds.

Making the Most of Your Money is about how those who believe that the Bible is God's Word can increase their ability to fund the work of God's kingdom. This book will teach how to control, manage, and multiply resources according to godly principles to meet godly objectives. It is written for the typical individual who does not have a great understanding of financial terms and matters. It will show readers how easy successful money management is. It requires little knowledge, little money, and little time to substantially increase one's financial wealth.

This book will also introduce a model of Christian stewardship based on wisdom, skill, and faith, and prove that all are required to be considered a good steward. We need wisdom to know the difference between right and wrong. We need to have skill, for biblical wisdom is useless without an understanding of the secular activities to which wisdom is applied. Finally, without faith, our knowledge and ability will never bear fruit. As with the unfaithful servant, our "talents" are as good as hidden. *Making the Most of Your Money* will provide the wisdom and skills necessary for people of the light to become as shrewd as the people of this world and become good and faithful servants.

Chapter One

YOUR DESIRE FOR MONEY MUST BE TRANSLATED INTO ACTION

THEREFORE, PREPARE YOUR MINDS
FOR ACTION
(1 PETER 1:13)

> Steve is having trouble making ends meet. Things were always tight, but with a new baby and Mom working only part-time, even a large raise failed to help. There are so many things he could do, though not all of them are easy. Frozen by the fear of making the wrong choice, he does nothing and instead hopes that something in the future will change their situation for the better. What he fails to realize is that his inactivity is only making the problem worse.

We must realize that we do not own "our money." What is our proper role in the handling of money? The key concept in God's view of money is *stewardship*. In biblical times a steward was one who managed another's property. The steward did not own the property but was personally accountable to the owner. It is apparent that right from the beginning of the world people were charged with the duty of managing God's property. It would be easy, but faulty, to assume that "man-made" things such as money belong to us alone.

However, our creations are actually His creations. This would include our ability to produce wealth. "But remember the Lord your God, for it is He who gives you the ability to produce

11

wealth" (Deut. 8:18). "For who makes you different from anyone else? What do you have that you did not receive? And if you did receive it, why do you boast as though you did not?" (1 Cor. 4:7)

Stewardship Requires Action

Our goal as stewards should be to receive the praise given by the master in Matthew 25:21: "Well done, good and faithful servant!" Therefore, we must learn how to go about stewardship in an effective manner. Often the best way to learn is to emulate those in positions of authority over us. For instance, employees can sometimes learn good job skills by observing their supervisors. More importantly, we can find a critical element in good stewardship by studying God Himself.

"In the beginning God created the heavens and the earth" (Gen. 1:1).

The Bible is the authoritative Word of the one true God— His revelation of Himself to the world. It would be presumptuous to make any claim regarding the relative importance of one part of God's Word over another. However, I find it highly significant that the first thing that God revealed about Himself is that He creates. In other words, He is a God of *action.* Moreover, He is a God of *creative action.* Our initial insight into the character of God is not one of maintaining, although He obviously maintains and sustains the existence of the world. Nor did we first see Him as a God of consumption, although we also recognize that part of His character. Therefore, if we are to be good and faithful in the management of God's creation, then we must also be people of creative action.[1]

A Biblical Model of Creative Financial Action

Creative action as the key ingredient to good stewardship is clearly demonstrated in the Parable of the Talents in Matthew 25. This parable is one model of creative stewardship in action. It describes the correct attitude that we should have as managers of God's creation. It also describes God's attitudes toward our results.

God has entrusted each of us with a portion of His creation

to manage. What He has given us charge of is in proportion to the unique skills and abilities He has given us. "Again, it will be like a man going on a journey, who called his servants and entrusted his property to them. To one he gave five talents of money, to another two talents, and to another one talent, each according to his ability" (v. 14).

The purpose of our stewardship is not to maintain but to expand God's kingdom. Good stewards understand that time is of the essence and that we are not to delay in carrying out the work we have been called to do. "The man who had received the five talents went at once and put his money to work" (v. 16). However, God will never force us to do His work against our will. "But the man who had received the one talent went off, dug a hole in the ground and hid his master's money" (v. 18).

While we do have the freedom to choose our actions or inactions, we will be held accountable for what we did with the resources we were given to manage and the extent to which we used our God-given skills. "After a long time the master of those servants returned and settled accounts with them" (v. 19).

This parable tells us that two of the three servants were successful in adding to the resources under their management.[2] To each one the master replied, "Well done, good and faithful servant! You have been faithful with a few things; I will put you in charge of many things. Come and share your master's happiness" (v. 21). There is a key point here that cannot be missed. The servant who earned two talents was as equally praiseworthy as the one earning five. Each one added to his master's wealth in proportion to the resources he had been given to accomplish his task.

We may not be given much to be in charge of for the Lord. This is for God to choose.[3] The amount we've been given is not what makes us great in God's eyes. It's what we do with the resources we are given that makes us good and faithful servants, and what we are called to do is be occupied with creative action.

The result of the third servant's stewardship was quite different. "I was afraid and went out and hid your talent in the ground. See, here is what belongs to you" (Matt. 25:25). Likewise, the master's response to his actions was different than his response to the other servants. "His master replied, 'You wicked, lazy servant. . . . Take the talent from him and . . . throw that worthless servant outside, into the darkness, where there will be weeping and gnashing of teeth' " (vv. 26, 28, 30).

The servant hoped to play it safe and protect himself from failure. This attitude was self-centered and disobedient as it related to his will and not the master's. We cannot allow our fears to be barriers to accomplishing God's will. Thank God that Jesus didn't let His fear stop Him from going to the cross in our behalf.[4]

In God's plan, mere maintenance of His resources is not enough. Even though the disobedient steward's one talent was returned intact, it was considered wasted as it failed to grow as it should have. What is small in our eyes is actually an integral part of God's master plan, of which a major component is creative action.

A Second Model of Financial Action: The Parable of the Shrewd Manager

The Parable of the Talents is often used as the prototype of good financial stewardship. Yet while it tells us what our attitudes and goals should be, it tells us nothing about how to accomplish those goals. Conversely, the Parable of the Shrewd Manager in Luke 16 is generally used as a model for bad stewardship. However, a detailed look into this parable reveals many of the qualities of good financial stewardship.

Jesus told this parable to His disciples. A disciple is a pupil or learner. The implication is that the truths in the parable are for those learning to be like the Master. That, presumably, would be us.

"Jesus told His disciples: 'There was a rich man whose manager was accused of wasting his possessions' " (v. 1). This is in direct violation of the creative aspects of stewardship. Not only that, the steward's actions show a total disregard for the value of the master's possessions. They were not consumed according to a plan for the owner's benefit. They were simply wasted.

"So he called him in and asked him, 'What is this I hear about you? Give an account of your management, because you cannot be manager any longer' " (v. 2). Stewards are accountable since they are not their own boss. Their highest loyalty is not to themselves—but to the one to whom the assets belong.

By not challenging his master's accusation, even the poor steward recognizes his accountability. Nevertheless, he now becomes active. He assesses his present situation and lays out the facts (vv. 3-4).

Based on the facts of the present, he makes his plans for how he can take care of himself in the future.

"So he called in each one of his master's debtors. He asked the first, 'How much do you owe my master?' " (v. 5) He immediately takes action according to his plans. " 'Eight hundred gallons of olive oil,' he replied. The manager told him, 'Take your bill, sit down *quickly*, and make it four hundred.' Then he asked the second, 'And how much do you owe?' 'A thousand bushels of wheat,' he replied. He told him, 'Take your bill and make it eight hundred' " (vv. 6-7, italics added). Expedience is the order of the day. He does not procrastinate, nor does he hope everything will work out. He is taking quick, decisive *action*. Notice that he is not using the debts incurred by others as a reason for his poor stewardship. He recognizes that he is fully to blame and that no excuses will be acceptable to his master. It is the steps in this process, rather than the motives that are worth noting. First, there is the recognition and assessment of a problem. The assessment is based on facts, not hopes or emotions. Next, rather than ignore or run away from the situation, the manager immediately puts together a plan to deal with the problem. Notice that the solution is—in his mind—a long-term solution. He is not merely trying to get out of trouble but to make the problem somehow work out to his advantage. Finally, as noted above, he takes quick decisive *action*. In reality, he is active at every step.

"The master commended the dishonest manager because he had acted *shrewdly*. For the people of this world are more shrewd in dealing with their own kind than are the people of the light" (v. 8, italics added). The word shrewdly describes the essence of skillful stewardship. It is the Greek word *phronimos* meaning thoughtful, sagacious, or discreet, implying a cautious character. Significantly, there are two other New Testament Greek words that could translate into "shrewd" or "wise" that were not used. *Sophos* denotes skill or acumen; *sunetos* indicates intelligence. This would imply that lack of skill or intelligence in financial matters is not a valid excuse for poor stewardship. We are to use whatever skills we have been given (see Deut. 8:18; Matt. 25:14) and achieve results commensurate with those skills.

Being thoughtful, sagacious (wise), and discreet are clearly godly attributes. They imply a cautious, covert means to achieve a particular end. Jesus was making the point that the people of this world are more shrewd in dealing with their own kind (here He is referring to money, rather than other people) than the people of the light. By commending the shrewd manager, Jesus was praising not his self-serving ends, but his godly means. Sadly, He is also saying that the people of the world are superior to Christians at using money to achieve their goals. Ironically, the greedy do get what they deserve—they get rich! They have turned their desire for money into action.

Christians too should have a desire for money, but not as an end to itself. Jesus tells us exactly what our desire for money should be for. "I tell you, use worldly wealth to gain friends for yourselves, so that when it is gone, you will be welcomed into eternal dwellings" (v. 9). Jesus plainly stated the goal of financial stewardship. As with the shrewd manager, Jesus wants us to invest now for future goals, but our goal is to invest money in others that will welcome us into heaven. Doesn't it make your heart shout for joy when you are praised for your generosity, and when others testify to how your goodness made a difference in their lives? How much more will it be when you find out that the use of your money was the reason for someone being in heaven? Surely, they will be waiting to greet you with open arms! Could this be what Jesus referred to when He said, "But store up for yourselves treasures in heaven, where moth and rust do not destroy, and where thieves do not break in and steal"? (Matt. 6:20)

By contrast, the shrewd manager was trying to gain earthly friends for himself. He was able to cut deals by getting debtors to go along with reducing their indebtedness. This violates a biblical financial principal, that of not paying your debts.[5]

This was obviously stealing by the debtors, since they legitimately owed more money than they were intending to pay back. The steward was willing to use any means possible to assure his earthly salvation. His eyes were not looking toward heavenly objectives. As Christians, however, we must strive to find moral financial solutions with eternal consequences.

It is also fascinating that Jesus exhorted His followers to use worldly wealth to accomplish the task of making heavenly friends. The King James translation has a superior expression: "mammon of unrighteousness." Mammon is from the Greek word *mammonas* meaning wealth personified or avarice deified. The mammon of unrighteousness is the evil deification of wealth. It means making money into an idol and greed into a form of worship. Mammon doesn't need money to exert influence. Adam and Eve had everything they needed, including daily fellowship with God; yet they sinned because they had to have more.

There are two points to be made here. First, worldly wealth is to be mastered for kingdom purposes. We will be held accountable for how well we have achieved this objective, and to achieve this goal we must be active with our financial resources.[6]

The second point here is the temporal nature of worldly wealth. Regarding worldly wealth, Jesus said without reservation, *"When* it is gone," meaning worldy wealth does not last. All that lasts is money's use for the kingdom. The manager acted shrewdly but unwisely by investing in activities that will someday be lost forever.

"No servant can serve two masters," said Jesus. "Either he will hate the one and love the other, or he will be devoted to the one and despise the other. You cannot serve both God and Money" (Luke 16:13).

Poor stewardship—that is, not furthering the kingdom—is a symptom of a potentially devastating spiritual disease. *Serve* in this context means to be in slavery or bondage. To be a slave is to be another's property. Once again, the point of stewardship is made, but in very strong language: Failure to be a good steward with our financial resources implies that we belong to Money—or *Mammonas* in the original Greek—rather than God. This suggests that we serve an idol.

Wisdom

Wisdom is the starting point for good stewardship. Why? Because, first we need a definition of "good." Good stewardship, as opposed to any other form of stewardship, is obviously important to God. The Parable of the Talents tells us that the master responded to the efforts of two servants with the reply, "Well done, good and faithful servant!" (v. 21) If we are going to do something good, we need to know what the standards are.

From the story of Adam and Eve we see that wisdom is the knowledge of right and wrong, or *good* and evil. Therefore, to be a *good* servant, we must be *wise*.

Wisdom is also the primary property of stewardship because to properly please any figure of authority, we must understand how they think and act. Simply knowing the rules and following them out of blind obedience is pleasing only up to a point. We must obey them as if they were our own. This will not only force our own obedience but also influence the behavior of others too.

Being wise unquestionably puts us on the path to good stewardship, for if we are wise, we are so in tune with God's desires that we cannot help but be good in carrying out His commands.

Skill

Unfortunately, automatically knowing what God wants isn't enough. We need to have the ability to perform His requests and carry on His work. Knowing what is right and what is wrong in a particular situation is completely useless if you do not have the skill to implement your superior insight.

The church has correctly focused its energies on teaching biblical guidelines as the only way to approach day-to-day situations. However, these guidelines are not enough. We need to have skills in the secular activities to which wisdom is applied. ("Secular" here refers to its traditional meaning of any activity not specifically related to institutional church activities.) In fact, the Bible gives us the ends but not the means.

We know that skills are important to God because the Parable of the Talents says that His servants are "entrusted His property . . . each according to his ability" (Matt. 25:14-15). The Bible further verifies that we indeed have been given specific abilities with which to serve God.[7] These gifts or skills are critical because God gave each of us a unique set of abilities to manage our portion of His world. In return *for* these skills God expects a return *on* these skills. A good return is one that is proportional to the skills given to us. To merely give back intact what God gave us is not good.

We can see that the first two properties of stewardship complement each other. "Good" not only refers to the wisdom applied by a "good and faithful servant," it also refers to the skills applied to stewardship. The two stewards were rewarded because they produced good results in accordance with the skills they were given.[8]

Faith

Interestingly, as commanding a figure as Moses tried to plead with God to excuse him from his mission. He was willing to allow his substantial leadership skills to lie dormant because he thought he lacked the talent.[9] He was afraid to fail God. This was the story of the bad steward in the Parable of the Talents. The "bad" servant was not willing to apply his individual skills on behalf of another. His primary concern was self-preservation by not being a failure. This really amounts to a concern for self rather than God.

The problem was not a lack of skills but a lack of faith. He didn't believe he had been given the resources to be successful. The Bible tells us that this wasn't the case. The bad steward was given "one talent . . . according to his ability" (Matt. 25:15). Since little was given, little was expected, although little should not be confused with nothing.

Lack of faith is completely unacceptable to God. To the unproductive steward "his master replied, 'You wicked, lazy servant!' " (v. 26) Lack of faith occurs when we accept our limitations as God's limitations. In the words of German philosopher

Arthur Schopenhauer, "Every man takes the limits of his own field of vision for the limits of the world."

The stewardship process is grounded in faith. Faith is the catalyst and the active ingredient of good stewardship. Without faith, we can do nothing. Many Christians have wisdom and skill but bury their talents due to lack of faith. They accept their limitations as God's limitations. This is a great Christian tragedy, for that lack of faith not only affects us, its harmful effects are felt by others as well. David could have saved his life by not fighting Goliath, but his people would have become captives of the Philistines. The disciples were willing to keep their food to themselves, but Jesus believed their few loaves of bread could feed thousands of hungry people. Where would *we* be if Jesus hadn't believed God would raise Him from the dead and forgive our sins?

To the obedient stewards the master replied, "Well done, good and *faithful* servant! You have been *faithful* with a few things" (Matt. 25:21, italics added). With faith, the third property in place, we can see how all the attributes work together to accomplish the will of God. According to the master in the parable, to be an effective steward we need to be good, in that we have the *wisdom* to know what is the right thing to do. We also need to be faithful by not allowing our perceived limitations to prevent us from using our *skills* to carry out God's wishes. But the more we know about God, which is the beginning of wisdom, the more *faith* we are going to have.

The final lesson of stewardship is that its quality is measured in the heart. God deplores acts that glorify the actor. Stewardship is a matter of obedience. Its duties are carried out in a manner that glorifies God. It is not done to seek the praises of men and women nor to receive blessings from God.

Jesus said,

Be careful not to do your "acts of righteousness" before men, to be seen by them. If you do, you will have no reward from your Father in heaven. So when you give to the needy, do not announce it with trumpets, as the hypocrites do in the synagogues and on the streets, to be honored by men. I tell you the truth, they have received their reward in full. But when you give to the needy, do not let your left hand know what your right hand is doing, so that your giving may be in secret. Then your Father, who sees what is done in secret, will reward you (Matt. 6:1-4).

Summary
1. God has appointed each of us to manage a portion of His creation.
2. Christians are to be active in our stewardship, particularly in activities that expand the kingdom.
3. Christians need to develop worldly skills in the handling of money.
4. Poor stewardship is a symptom of potential spiritual disease.
5. Good stewardship = wisdom + skill + faith.

Notes
1. *1 Peter 1:13*
2. *Matthew 25:16*
3. *Romans 9:21*
4. *Luke 22:42*
5. *Psalm 37:21*
6. *James 2:14-24*
7. *Romans 12:6; 1 Peter 4:10*
8. *Matthew 25:16-17*
9. *Exodus 4:10, 13*

Chapter Two

YOU MUST SEEK
WISDOM BEFORE YOU
SEEK MONEY

BLESSED IS THE MAN WHO FINDS WISDOM,
THE MAN WHO GAINS UNDERSTANDING,
FOR SHE IS MORE PROFITABLE THAN SILVER
AND YIELDS BETTER RETURNS THAN GOLD
(PROVERBS 3:13-14)

> Jim is a bright young MBA, rising up the ladder of a major corporation. Still, he just can't seem to get ahead financially. None of his broker's "can't miss" stocks ever seem to pan out. Reading the financial papers and magazines hasn't done any good either. His substantial income is growing and he's done everything the experts have recommended but is still struggling to get ahead. If he can't make it, who can?

Whoever can be trusted with very little can also be trusted with much, and whoever is dishonest with very little will also be dishonest with much" (Luke 16:10). Hudson Taylor said, "A little thing is a little thing; but faithfulness in a little thing is a great thing."

Quite often people think that the answer to their financial problems is more money. Unfortunately that's rarely the case. If you are unable to successfully handle what you've been given, why should you be able to handle more? More money would actually have disastrous consequences. This is a biblical principle taught in the Parable of the Talents (Matt. 25). We each are given resources according to our own abilities. Our standard is not what we could have accomplished if we had been given more, but our accomplishments relative to what we have been given. If we are unable to handle what we currently have, we cannot be trusted with more.[1]

The real, permanent answer to financial problems is to learn how to make correct decisions. This is a crucial matter, for all of our resources are God's. Therefore, every financial decision has spiritual consequences. What we need as opposed to more money is the ability to make wise financial decisions. Since we are managing God's resources, it would seem that the best course of action would be to do so in a godly manner. Therefore, we must learn how to exercise godly wisdom.

Webster's dictionary defines wisdom as follows:

Wisdom, *n* 1 a: accumulated philosophic or scientific learning: knowledge b: ability to discern inner qualities and relationships: insight c: good sense: judgment 2: a wise attitude or course of action 3: the teachings of ancient wise men

This is the world's definition of wisdom according to *Webster's Ninth New Collegiate Dictionary*. What is extremely fascinating about this definition is that we can find these attitudes on display in the story of Job. Each of Job's three friends believed he had the best reasons for why God had seemingly abandoned Job. Eliphaz based his reasons upon his years of observation and experience. Bildad's analysis came from knowledge handed down from the past. Zophar simply felt that he had special insight and discernment. While these methods do provide elements of truth, they are far from complete.[2] In the end, their worldly wisdom was rebuked. What more needs to be added to gain a fuller understanding of the concept of wisdom?

What Is Wisdom?

It is folly to try to fully characterize any of God's attributes. However, there are two basic properties of wisdom that we should seek to understand. Both of these properties work together. First, wisdom is the knowledge of right and wrong, or

Making the Most of Your Money

more directly stated, good and evil. We know this from the Book of Genesis, which tells us that in the Garden of Eden there was a "tree of the knowledge of good and evil" (Gen. 2:9, 16). The fruit of this tree was "desirable for gaining wisdom" (3:6).

However, what is right and wrong can be determined relative only to an action's effect upon others rather than ourselves. The intent of the Bible is not to regulate morality by dictating specific behaviors. Jesus said there are only two commandments: "Love the Lord your God with all your heart and with all your soul and with all your mind" and "Love your neighbor as yourself" (Matt. 22:37, 39). According to the Apostle Paul, " 'Everything is permissible'—but not everything is beneficial. 'Everything is permissible'—but not everything is constructive. Nobody should seek his own good, but the good of others' " (1 Cor. 10:23-24). What the Bible is saying is that right actions are those that first, glorify God and that second, benefit others. Any act that seeks our good before the glory of God and the good of others is wrong and evil. Therefore, it is unwise. This is why giving is so important to our financial stewardship. Giving is a wise financial act because it puts others' interests before our own.

The world may think that the source of wisdom is limited to the accumulated teachings of wise men, but Job correctly concluded that "it cannot be found in the land of the living" and that God "alone knows where it dwells" (Job 28:13, 23). Not only is it true that "to God belong wisdom and power" (12:13), but also He is its only source, "for the Lord gives wisdom" (Prov. 2:6). That being the case, we must learn how to get God's wisdom.

Receiving Wisdom

There are three steps to receiving true wisdom: First, we must fear the Lord.[3] This does not mean we should be afraid of God. Rather, it means that we should respect and revere God. This reverence is shown in our willingness to be obedient to God and to worship God. Faithful financial stewardship requires that we recognize that we are accountable to God as caretakers of His

24

resources. Financial wisdom begins, therefore, not in a text-book, seminar, or advice from a friend, but with a deeper under-standing of who God is. This unlocks the door to God's infinite storehouse of knowledge.

Second, we must ask for wisdom. Remember from chapter 1 that we must be proactive in our stewardship. Answers to difficult financial issues will not come by hoping things turn out all right. They will not go away by ignoring them. Christians do not have to stumble blindly in financial darkness. God is waiting to give us the right answer in all of our individual circumstances.[4]

If as faithful stewards we know who God is and what He can and desires to do for us, then we have no reason to doubt that He will keep His promises. This, in fact, is the test God applies to our requests for wisdom.[5] He will test whether or not we really believe that He will meet us at our point of need.[6]

Does this mean that we can get wisdom anytime we want? Will God truly solve all of our financial questions? This depends upon the purpose of the request. In other words, what is the problem that we are seeking wisdom to resolve? The final step in receiving true wisdom is that the request must ultimately please and glorify God. "To the man who pleases Him, God gives wisdom" (Ecc. 2:26). When we pray, we must pray with God's interests as our priority. This is the way Jesus prayed, and His prayers were *always* answered to His satisfaction. God is willing to give us wisdom, but this wisdom must be for God-centered motives, not self-centered motives. "When you ask, you do not receive, because you ask with wrong motives, that you may spend what you get on your pleasures" (James 4:3). Our prayers for financial wisdom are meant to assist us as we faithfully manage God's resources under our stewardship.

Fearing God and asking God for wisdom are necessary but not sufficient conditions to receiving wisdom. Your desire for wisdom must result in actions that are pleasing to God. Without that desire, your prayers are empty. Financially, the consequences can be devastating. We know that God gives wisdom to those who please Him, "but to the sinner He gives the task of gathering and storing up wealth to hand it over *to the one who pleases God*" (Ecc. 2:26, italics added). It is through our pleasing actions that we demonstrate that we have successfully acquired godly wisdom.

Chapter 3 of the Book of James describes two kinds of wisdom: "Who is wise and understanding among you? Let him show it by his good life, *by deeds done in the humility that comes from wisdom,*" and heavenly wisdom is "pure . . . peace-loving, considerate, submissive, full of mercy and good fruit, impartial and sincere" (James 3:13, 17, italics added). These are all attributes that clearly place the welfare of others ahead of our own. Such righteous actions are obviously pleasing to God. On the other hand, there is worldly wisdom, the kind demonstrated by Job's friends. Earthly wisdom is that whose source is selfish ambition. Earthly wisdom ultimately seeks to promote our own desires first. This is why there are so many financial experts. Their primary goal is not the financial success of those that take their advice. Rather, their objective is to be viewed as being financially wise.

The Wisdom of Solomon

The story of Solomon is highly instructive in the application of these principles. It is no accident that God gave wisdom to the wisest and wealthiest man who ever lived, not because he needed wealth to govern God's people but because he asked for wisdom to govern God's people. (That's something to think about whenever political leaders want to raise taxes in order to provide better government!) In fact, God told Solomon to "ask for whatever you want Me to give to you" (1 Kings 3:5). Ever the faithful steward, Solomon responded, "Give Your servant a discerning heart to govern Your people and to distinguish between right and wrong" (v. 9). What was God's answer to this request? Because the Lord was pleased that Solomon had asked for wisdom, God said to him, "Since you have asked for this and not for long life or wealth for yourself, nor have asked for the death of your enemies but for discernment in administering justice, I will do what you have asked. I will give you a wise and discerning heart" (vv. 11-12).

What Solomon understood about money is what we must never forget—more money is *never* the solution to your financial issues. The pursuit of wisdom must precede the pursuit of money if we are to be faithful financial stewards. Who has ever known more about the relationship of wisdom to money than Solomon? It is impossible to ignore Solomon's timeless advice and be successful in handling our money. We must listen when he said, "Choose [wisdom] instead of silver, knowledge rather than choice gold, for wisdom is more precious than rubies" (Prov. 8:10-11); "Blessed is the man who finds wisdom, the man who gains understanding, for [wisdom] is more profitable than silver and yields better returns than gold" (3:13-14).

It would be easy (easy, but foolish) to dismiss Solomon's instructions as inapplicable to us since he was so wealthy. It is easy to be pious and give self-important advice when things are going so well. This was the trap Job's friends fell into. It was easy for Solomon to seek wisdom since he never had financial hardship. But just as Solomon was the wealthiest man who ever lived, who has ever suffered more financial and personal hardship than Job? Job was the wealthiest man of his day, and in the blink of an eye, he was penniless.

In terms of material and earthly comfort, Job and Solomon were poles apart. Yet they shared a common understanding of wisdom.[7] And like Solomon, Job knew how to find wisdom. "It cannot be found in the land of the living. . . . The fear of the Lord—that is wisdom" (vv. 13, 28). God ultimately made Job "prosperous again and gave him twice as much as he had before" (42:10).

For his part, Solomon, the wisest of all men, tried for a time to live without God's wisdom. What was the result? He in his wealth learned what Job learned in his poverty: "Wisdom is a shelter as money is a shelter, but the advantage of knowledge is this: that wisdom preserves the life of its possessor" (Ecc. 7:12).

How to Apply Wisdom in Your Finances
The act of seeking wisdom before seeking money as a basic tenet of sound financial stewardship cannot be emphasized strongly enough. Most financial difficulties eventually find their roots in lack of wisdom. To this point I have stressed the importance of seeking godly wisdom in making financial decisions. If wisdom is known by its actions, then how can wisdom be

applied on a day-to-day basis? There are several key ways, all of which contradict conventional, worldly applications. Above all, remember once again that more money is never the solution to your financial problems. If you have not handled what you've been given to this point, then it is unreasonable to expect that you will handle more money any better. In fact, you will probably do more damage than you did before.

The starting point of applying wisdom is to recognize the importance of independent thinking. *You must realize that if the majority were right, the majority would be rich.* It is human nature to want to do what everybody else is doing. We draw comfort by being like everybody else. Likewise, we feel extremely uncomfortable when we feel different from others. Therefore, we tend to adopt behaviors that are viewed as being acceptable by whatever group of people that we regularly associate with. This can be dangerous. For just as it is human nature to seek the approval of others, it is also natural to want something for nothing. The path of the majority tends to be the easiest path to travel on. Indeed, Jesus said, "Enter through the narrow gate. For wide is the gate and broad is the road that leads to destruction, and many enter through it. But small is the gate and narrow is the road that leads to life, and only a few find it" (7:13-14). Jesus, of course, was referring to the gates that lead to either eternal life or destruction. He may as well have been alluding to money management. What everybody else is doing with their money cannot by definition be right, for again, *if the majority were right, the majority would be rich!* The majority opinion, the easy way, is never the right way to handle our finances.

After Solomon, probably the wealthiest man who ever lived was oil baron J. Paul Getty. While Getty admitted that being in the right place at the right time certainly helped him begin to amass a fortune, he also had another secret. This secret probably explained why he was in the right place at the right time. This secret will help you too. In Getty's famous words, "Buy when everyone else is selling, and hold until everyone else is buying. This is more than just a catchy slogan. It is the very essence of successful investment" (J. Paul Getty, *How to Be Rich*). In other

28

words, if you want to make money, you must do what no one else is doing. You have to master the art of contrary thinking.

Contrary thinking is the art of independent thinking. It is not trying to be intentionally argumentative or disagreeable. It is developing your own opinions and money management strategies that often are in conflict with the majority view. At its core is the belief that the best opportunities are found when and where the prevailing wisdom is looking elsewhere. Things are always the cheapest when nobody wants them and they are the most expensive when everybody wants them. Therefore, contrary thinking is the simplest method of buying low and selling high.

Being a contrarian investor consistently works because human nature is, has been, and always will be the same. This is itself a principle that we see acted out throughout the Bible. Most people would rather play "Follow the Leader" rather than "Lead the Follower." People tend to wait to see what everybody else is doing before taking their own action. The tendency is to buy only after others are buying and not to sell until others are selling. This is easy to do because it makes us comfortable. Unfortunately, this is exactly the opposite of Getty's rule of doing what nobody else is doing. What we need to do is to become comfortable being in the minority rather than the majority. We need to seek the narrow gate, financially speaking, that is like the heavenly gate so few find. On a more basic level, it is the early bird that gets the worm.

Generous, sacrificial giving is one of the best ways to practice contrary thinking in money management. On the surface, it doesn't seem to make much sense to give away money if you're trying to accumulate money. Yet most givers have few financial worries. Being a generous giver clearly will place you in the minority. When your giving represents a sacrifice you are obviously taking the hard, narrow road. Yet this financial principle works because it is an investment that is found in a place that is overlooked by the majority.

Along the same lines as avoiding the majority view by being a contrary thinker is the knowledge that predictions are useless. Rather than follow the consensus view, many people try to outsmart their peers by seeking the opinion of an "expert." This could be an economist, stockbroker, financial planner, or other professionals (including authors!). Everybody would love to have someone accurately divine the future for them. The truth is that anyone who thinks he or she can consistently predict the future is arrogant and a fool. Therefore, people who blindly follow forecasts and forecasters are foolhardy. Even a broken watch is right twice a day. So it goes with economic and investment predictions. If you hear enough of them, you're bound to find one or two who are right at some point in time. However, successful money management is built upon a foundation of consistency, and predicting is anything but consistent.

It is hard enough to make sense out of known facts. However, the real problem with predictions is that it is generally unpredictable events that move markets the most. Who knew that the Iron Curtain would be torn, ending the Cold War and creating an entirely new global economic landscape? Who in 1990 would have predicted an invasion of Kuwait, which created havoc for months in world financial markets? In January of 1992, how many were predicting a Democratic president? Even if they were, who thought at the time that it would be Bill Clinton? Not only are experts often wrong, but also they are incapable of foreseeing those events that will ultimately most affect the economic environment.

Instead of relying on predictions, wise stewards prepare for possibilities. The best way to use forecasts is to generate ideas of the trends that could have a broad impact on either the overall economy or specific economic sectors. Successful investors are rarely the ones with the most accurate outlooks. They are, on the other hand, the ones least often surprised. Their lack of surprise comes from having envisioned what may occur rather than deciding what should occur. Understanding possibilities makes forecasting unnecessary. Unless you are gambling and not investing, predicting is an intellectual, not a financial exercise.

Wisdom in Dealing with Financial Professionals
The third way to apply wisdom in finances is to properly understand the role of financial services professionals. The relation-

ship between a stockbroker, financial planner, or life insurance agent is often misunderstood. There are a number of key facts that you must understand to properly deal with financial services professionals.

How Much Their Service Will Cost You

Your adviser should tell you how he or she is being compensated each time you buy any service. Don't deal with anyone who doesn't. Nobody sells something for nothing. It's your job to know, although a reputable adviser will tell you. This is not to suggest that you price shop to find the lowest cost adviser. The most economical adviser is the one who is charging you a fair price relative to what your needs are. Those who intend to do little or no work on their own behalf should be willing to pay more for quality advice. Investors who have the time and knowledge to do some research on their own should attempt to pay less as long as they are comfortable that they are capable of doing good work on their own behalf. In all cases, price is not a measure of quality. So while it is crucial that you know what you are paying, there are other considerations that must go into the decision to hire a financial professional. Among them are experience, background, quality of the company and its products, and your degree of comfort with the individual.

Potential Conflicts of Interest

Brokers and planners get paid for their (sales) performance not your (financial) performance. What do you think gets recommended the most, the investment product with high commissions or ones with low commissions? Or how about the products that win advisers expensive vacations or other nice gifts? It is commonplace throughout the financial industry for companies to find creative incentives to sell more products. This is not to say that every investment recommendation made carries a nice bonus for the salesperson. However, even an ethical planner often struggles with the conflicting goals of good advice and good compensation.

The industry will counter this conflict-of-interest issue with the argument that they can't stay in business by pushing bad products and creating dissatisfied customers. They'll say that a salesperson won't last long by taking bonuses in the short run without being cognizant of the long-term effect this will have on his or her career.

Unfortunately, this argument doesn't stand up. First, while companies tell customers they are interested in their long-term well being, they push their salespeople extremely hard for sales in the short run. That's why incentives exist in the first place. Moreover, poor producers are usually fired. Second, the products with the best incentives are those that carry the most profit for the company or those that are the toughest to sell. Finally, the success of the salesperson's long-run career means nothing to you if you were coaxed into buying something that hurt you in the short run.

You will rarely, if ever, be told that the salesperson is receiving a bonus for a product that he or she is recommending. Therefore, to protect yourself you need to ask a lot of questions to become completely comfortable that you are receiving the best possible advice for your individual circumstances. This will require that you gain a minimal level of knowledge prior to making an investment decision.

Biased toward Certain Investments

Financial markets are too big for anyone to be expert in everything. Yet planners and brokers sell it all: stocks, bonds, municipal bonds, mutual funds, limited partnerships, options, commodities, real estate, insurance, and on and on. The natural inclination is to sell what they know best, which may not necessarily be best for you. Even if they don't know much about an area, there will be a natural tendency to sell whatever pays them the most as we saw above.

This is especially true if a firm is trying to expand its product line and offer customers a wider array of investment choices. Know your adviser's background and areas of expertise and match that against what he or she is recommending. Don't be afraid to ask them what expertise or training they have in the area they are suggesting to you. It would also help if you familiarized yourself with the basics of the investment ideas that you are considering.

Training and Competence as a Broker/Planner

The exams for certification as a financial planner or broker are comprehensive, but not particularly difficult. The knowledge required consists of textbook, definition-type knowledge, rather than competence in financial markets. To pass the licensing exams, a professional needs to know the difference between a stock and a bond but does not have to know the difference between a good stock and a good bond. Therefore a person can know 100 percent of all the rules, regulations, and definitions but 0 percent about what it takes for their clients to make money. There is no college-degree training in these fields, and courses focus on theoretical rather than practical knowledge of investments. Furthermore, on-the-job training stresses sales techniques rather than investment expertise. A professor I know has his students call local brokers and ask in-depth questions beyond the type necessary to pass a licensing exam. It is safe to say his students are far more expert in investing than the typical planner or broker.

Time Spent Looking for New Clients vs. Monitoring Your Finances

Most financial services people are professional salespeople. Depending on how they get compensated, a financial professional may need hundreds of clients to be able to make a decent living. Since there are only so many hours in a day, you cannot be assured that your finances will get daily monitoring. In fact, unless you are a particularly large and influential client, you can probably be assured that you will not. Many professionals are capable of doing a thorough review only on an annual basis. This is because they have so many clients and spend much of their time trying to get more. That's how they get themselves a raise. You can't blame them for trying to make a living, but you shouldn't delude yourself into thinking that you're getting frequent, personal attention.

Scare Tactics

Professionals call it "hurt and response," and according to one stockbroker it is the favored sales tactic of the financial services industry. The idea is to create fear in your mind about your finances and then offer a solution. In the initial meeting, the salesperson will attempt to show you how needy you are by showing you how your present financial situation does not have adequate insurance, retirement, and college tuition investments, tax shelters, and so on. The fact that you are seeking assistance indicates that you suspect that you do have certain financial needs that are not being met. Naturally, they have all of the answers to meet these needs. To protect yourself from meeting a need you actually don't have, have a firm idea of what your immediate and future goals are before you get talked into something.

Unhappy Former Clients

You can find just how unhappy by calling your state securities commission and asking for the Central Depository printout on your financial professional. You can check out your stockbroker by calling the National Association of Securities Dealers (NASD) at 1-800-289-9999. Get references—it's your money! If your adviser has sold you stocks or bonds, he or she should be affiliated with the NASD. This means that you can take them to arbitration if you have a complaint. About half the complaints are decided in favor of investors. Call 212-480-4881 to ask for an arbitration kit.

Learn to Do This Job Yourself

The financial services industry makes investing seem hard. This is their basic marketing strategy. The wife of the head of a successful financial planning firm once told me that her husband's greatest ability was "making people think that they need him." In reality most people don't need a financial professional despite their seeming lack of knowledge, experience, or money. Ironically, it is the person with knowledge, experience, and money who needs a professional the most. A person with a lot of money has financial needs well beyond the average person. Their finances are potentially very complicated and may even require legal assistance. People with less money—most of us— have limited financial choices. The complexity of these choices is rarely beyond anyone's ability. The knowledge and experience required to make these limited choices is minimal. If you apply the same effort to your money as you apply to buying a car, a stereo, furniture, or whatever, you'll do just fine with little outside advice.

In the next chapter we'll talk more about planning, but I want to prove this point with an example. If you've ever done grocery shopping, then you have the skills necessary to be a successful money manager. First, you'll assess your needs by checking what you have and what you don't have. Based on this list of needs, you'll put together a plan of where to go to fill these needs. Where you end up going will be determined by your own knowledge and research either through past experience, asking others who have done grocery shopping before, or reading ads. Finally, you'll make your purchasing decisions, hopefully resisting the internal and external temptations to deviate from the list of your predetermined needs. After a period of time, you will repeat the process. Periodically monitoring your results and making improvements and changes when necessary will improve the process.

Anyone who has ever done this (although you probably never thought about the process of grocery shopping) already has most of the skills required to make sound investments and other financial decisions. All that is necessary is to add some specific knowledge of the financial activities in question.

At this point I'm sure that financial professionals reading this book are in a highly agitated state. I don't want them or their clients to misunderstand me. The preceding points are not meant to be an attack upon the financial services industry (although, if the shoe fits . . .). The best firms and individuals recognize the preceding points to be problems in their industry and have personally taken steps to address them with their clients. In fact, one of the biggest changes in the financial services industry is the move to compensate professionals with salaries or flat fee percentages rather than sales of individual products. Unfortunately, many of the quality firms I talk to admit that they would make more money if they had lower ethical standards. This is an admission that bad sales practices, incompetent salespeople, and the other dangers I've warned against do exist.

Why You Should Be Your Own Money Manager

Good financial advice, regardless of its source, is literally worth its weight in gold. However, I strongly feel that anyone will benefit from a do-it-yourself mentality in handling his or her finances. The degree of independence should be determined by your own individual needs. Remember, though, that faithful financial stewards recognize their accountability to God for the management of the assets placed in their control. If others are handling your money for you, they are accountable to you.

Therefore, you must have enough knowledge to properly assess how well they are doing on your behalf in meeting your stated goals and objectives. Poor performance on their part will not excuse you from accountability. To acquire the knowledge necessary to review your adviser's performance may require effort on your part. This effort is not optional. Once you put yourself in a position to review another's performance, you may find it just as easy and much more satisfying to handle your finances yourself. I can think of four good reasons to do this:

Nobody Knows YOU as Well as YOU

You are a unique individual with likes, dislikes, goals, and skills unlike anyone else. A superior personal investment plan accounts for an investor's financial objectives and their tolerance and ability to handle risk. No matter how you try to articulate this information to another individual, they are bound to filter this data with their own particular biases. In too many cases, commissioned salespeople will ignore your wishes and steer you into an inappropriate investment that pays them a generous commission. Making money starts with the *investor*, not with the investment!

Nobody Cares about Your Money as Much as You Do

This should be obvious. But when the high-pressure broker or adviser is trying hard to sell you something, they do a great job of convincing you that they have your best interests at heart. They might be truly caring, empathetic, and highly professional, but just like you, they work first to enrich themselves. Furthermore, few investment professionals are willing to dedicate much time to small or novice investors. They simply don't make enough money from this group to justify the time. So they either charge excessive fees or quickly talk you into something and move on to another customer. Since you have everything to gain and everything to lose, why entrust the responsibility of your finances to someone else?

Managing Your Own Money Is Easier than Most People Realize

The financial media do a great job of making successful investing sound ominous and mysterious. They are quick to exalt the results of a new guru and his magic investment touch. If your first step is to find perfect investments, making money is extremely hard. But if you start with the investor, in other words, your objectives and your risk tolerance, you will easily find investments perfect for you.

The Most Successful Investors Are Independent Investors

It has been shown that investors who take the advice of Wall Street brokerage firms usually earn mediocre returns. *The Wall Street Journal* periodically runs a contest pitting investment professionals against a portfolio of stocks selected by throwing darts at a newspaper. The darts often win. So who makes money? Statistics show that the most consistent group of market moneymakers are small, independent investors! Unburdened by the conflicting bias of another adviser, these individuals are free to construct a successful investment plan that is uniquely suited to them.

Managing your own investments does require some effort and some knowledge. However, you'd be surprised how little effort and knowledge it takes. Everybody, regardless of perceived lack of experience, money, or time has the ability to become a successful, independent investor. Desire is the ONLY requirement.

Some Additional Steps

Another way of demonstrating wisdom in your investments is to invest only in things you understand. Most bad investments can be eliminated by following two simple rules: (1) You must know what it will take to make your investment go up in price, and (2) you should be able to explain your investment in five minutes to an eleven-year-old. If you cannot apply these rules to every investment, the likelihood of your making money is very small.

Whenever you make any kind of investment, it is crucial that you have a complete understanding of what events you feel must occur for that investment to increase in value. Because something's "at a good price," "everybody else is doing this," or your adviser says, "this can't miss" is not justification for a change in price. You must know what things must occur for other investors to pay increasingly higher prices to own this investment. Likewise, you should have an understanding of what things could go wrong with your "can't miss" decision. If you're investing to receive regular payments of interest, then you must know who is paying the interest, when and how much interest you are getting, and how much risk there is in the payer's ability to maintain regular payments.

The test of this understanding is to explain your purchase decision in such simple terms that a child could easily understand your decision. One of the most successful money managers ever, Peter Lynch, from whom this rule comes, used to give his analysts fifteen minutes to convince him to buy the stocks they were following. After they'd performed hundreds of hours of analysis for each stock, if he couldn't understand in fifteen minutes why he should buy it, he wasn't interested.

If you truly understand what you're buying, using these rules as a standard, chances are you've made the correct decision.

The final way to apply wisdom in your daily financial stewardship is not to think about the money. The great paradox of investing is that while you invest to make money, once you've made the decision to invest, you shouldn't think about the money. Thinking about the money will cause you to stay with winning investments too long as the tendency is to think they can go up forever and allow you to make even more money. It also causes you to stay with losing investments too long, in the hope that you can recover some or all of your original investment.

What you should think about at all times is your investment plan and what objectives each investment is designed to accomplish. Your plan must contain the reasons why you are buying and under what circumstances, good and bad, that you will sell. Thinking about the money will make you modify your plan to fit your view of the current circumstances. Unfortunately, your desire for a particular outcome will always cloud your view of the current circumstances. Not following this basic rule has always cost me money. You cannot control the outcomes of your financial decisions. "In his heart a man plans his course, but the Lord determines his steps" (Prov. 16:9). You can control only your response to current events, and this is best done with an objective plan of action.

You Must Give Your Family More than Money
"A good man leaves an inheritance for his children's children, but a sinner's wealth is stored up for the righteous" (Prov. 13:22).

You will need to take financial stewardship seriously if you're going to provide for your children and grandchildren. We have an obligation to give them knowledge as well as financial support. The story of the prodigal son teaches us that wealth without wisdom is quickly squandered (Luke 15:13). Not only should you give your children sound money management skills, but also you need to teach them well enough to be able to teach their children, that is, your grandchildren. In Genesis we see the sound financial principles of father Abraham (action, tithing), grandson Jacob (tithing, planning), and great-grandson Joseph (planning, saving). We should follow the example of our spiritual father Abraham and pass down a tradition of wise financial stewardship.

Summary
1. More money is never a permanent solution to financial problems.
2. Most financial difficulties have a lack of wisdom at their root.
3. What seems right in the eyes of the majority is often foolishness.

4. You must be wise in dealing with financial professionals.
5. Most people are capable of handling their own finances.

Notes
1. *Luke 16:10*
2. *1 Corinthians 1:25*
3. *Psalm 111:10*
4. *James 1:5*
5. *James 1:6-7*
6. *Mark 11:24*
7. *Job 28:15*

Chapter Three

YOU MUST GIVE
TO RECEIVE

REMEMBER THIS: WHOEVER SOWS SPARINGLY
WILL ALSO REAP SPARINGLY, AND WHOEVER SOWS
GENEROUSLY WILL ALSO REAP GENEROUSLY
(2 CORINTHIANS 9:6)

I have this great agent. He takes care of all my financial needs not to mention a lot of physical and emotional ones too. I don't know how he does it. He always seems to be around, and it's uncanny how he knows exactly what I need. It's almost like he can see what I'm going to need before I need it.

He works incredibly cheap. I just pay him a small percentage of each paycheck plus an occasional bonus whenever I feel like it. I've tried managing without him but my money never goes as far unless I've got him involved. It's as if with him I'm blessed and without him I'm cursed.

F or God so loved the world that He gave His one and only Son, that whoever believes in Him shall not perish but have eternal life" (John 3:16). The Gospel is God's divine story of giving. It would seem only natural that giving be central to Christians in general and to good financial stewards in particular. Rather than being a natural outflow of the Christian spirit, financial giving is instead a source of great controversy. Non-Christians believe the church is interested only in their money. Like the early Protestant reformers, they are greatly opposed to feeling as though they have to buy their salvation. Ironically, there are Christians who believe they can secure their salvation simply by giving 10 percent of their income to the church as required in the Old Testament. Others believe this long-standing church tradition is a standard that no longer exists. If it does still exist, then the average American Christian's gift of less than 2 percent of income presents a major problem.

The Tradition of Tithing

In today's demanding and uncertain economic times, giving to God's work is a challenge. It is also a great responsibility and privilege. It is in the Old Testament law that God first commanded the people to give the *tithe. Tithe* is the Hebrew word for tenth.[1] Tithing, or the giving of 10 percent of one's income, has since become a time-honored tradition. God, however, is much deeper than rote tradition. He wants much more than a simple fraction of our resources. He wants our giving to be our first priority.[2] Not only does He want His offering first, He wants the best you have to give.[3] Finally, once you've given your first and your best, you must release any and all claims to it. It belongs to God, and as they say in banking, there are "penalties for early withdrawal."[4]

People in Old Testament times obviously were as stingy as today's Christians. One thousand years after God's direct command to tithe, the Prophet Malachi chastised the people for their willful financial disobedience. Everybody, including the priests, had become contemptuous, arrogant, and self-indulgent. In being so, they had refrained from tithing. In God's view this was outright theft.[5]

Do We Still Have to Tithe?

Throughout His ministry, Christ reminded us that it is our hearts and our attitudes, not our dedication to laws, that are the true measures of our faith. Jesus was searching within men for their compassion and sacrifice, not their legalist traditions. The Apostle Paul wrote, "Know that a man is not justified by observing the law, but by faith in Jesus Christ" (Gal. 2:16). Indeed, the teachers of the law and Pharisees were hypocrites despite their faithfulness in tithing. "Woe to you, teachers of the law and Pharisees, you hypocrites!" exclaimed Jesus. "You give a tenth of your spices—mint, dill and cummin. But you have neglected the more important matters of the law—justice, mercy and faithfulness. You should have practiced the latter, without neglecting the former" (Matt. 23:23). Jesus' rebuke of those who faithfully tithed stands in stark contrast to Malachi's rebuke of the people who withheld their tithes. Paul appeared to be saying that Christians are no longer under the law. Yet Ananias was instantly struck dead by God for holding back money for himself that was intended to be shared among the believers in Jerusalem (Acts 5:3). A Christian operating under God's grace was punished under God's law. So, do we still have to tithe or not?

I believe since Christ has fulfilled the law on our behalf (Matt. 5:17), tithing is no longer required. However, because we are released from the letter of the law, does not free us from the spirit of the law. Look carefully at Matthew 23:23 again. Jesus reprimanded the Pharisees for neglecting the spirit of tithing: justice, mercy, and faithfulness. However, while He directed them to practice the spirit of the law, He also implored them not to neglect the letter of the law either.

The spirit of tithing is best embodied in Abraham. Throughout the Bible, Abraham is held up as a prime example of true faith. His willingness to tithe even before there was such a commandment demonstrated this faith. "Then Melchizedek king of Salem brought out bread and wine. He was priest of God Most High, and he blessed Abram, saying, 'Blessed be Abram by God Most High, Creator of heaven and earth. And blessed be God Most High, who delivered your enemies into your hand.' Then Abram gave him a tenth of everything" (Gen. 14:18-20). Not only did Abraham tithe, but so did his grandson Jacob who declared that a tenth of his future material blessings belonged to God.[6] Jacob no doubt learned to tithe from his father Isaac, who would have learned it from his father Abraham. The biblical record of Abraham's tithes was more than 600 years before the law required it. Apparently, tithing was important to Abraham and to his physical descendants.[7] Therefore, tithing, while no longer specifically required, should be important to us too.

If There Is No Law, Then Why Give?

There are a number of reasons why giving is critical to faithful financial stewardship. None is more important than the fact that giving is the ultimate expression of love. "This is love: not that we loved God, but that He loved us and sent His Son as an atoning sacrifice for our sins" (1 John 4:10). Only a truly self-absorbed person would accept a gift without wanting sometime to return the favor. Only a person looking for another's approval would feel obligated to return the favor. God gave an unmatchable gift to us, one that we had done nothing to deserve and one that He felt no obligation to give. The gift of eternal life is equally available to anybody who wants it. "Freely you have received, freely give" (Matt. 10:8) is our only possible, appropriate response.

The second major reason we need to give is to demonstrate our faith and our reliance upon God to meet our every need. More than anything else in this world, money has the power to separate us from God, because it is through money that most of our needs, wants, and desires are met. For many people, money has become a god, especially when they turn to money first as the solution to their problems. When something is superior to any part of your relationship to God, it is an idol. An idol is not merely something that pagans worship. If you look to something other than God for your security, it is an idol. If you would sooner be disobedient to God before giving up something, you have made that thing an idol. Once we have done this, we have shown a lack of faith in God's promises. Paul clearly said that trusting in money is nothing short of idolatry: "For of this you can be sure: No immoral, impure or greedy person—such a man is an *idolater*—has any inheritance in the kingdom of Christ and of God" (Eph. 5:5, italics added).

It is not God's will that we look to money as the solution to life's problems. "Blessed is the man who makes the Lord his trust, who does not look to the proud, to those who turn aside to false gods" (Ps. 40:4). The difficulty that we have always had is that money is visible. It is tangible. We can make money our servant and through the use of debt, we can make our money work beyond the limits of what we have. This, unfortunately, is not faith.[8] However, while God Himself may not be literally visible or tangible, His Word—the Bible—is. The record of how He has acted throughout history on behalf of humanity should inspire us to greater levels of confidence than any amount of money. Immediately prior to God's commandment against idolatry, He told the Hebrews, "I am the Lord your God, who brought you out of Egypt, out of the land of slavery" (Ex. 20:2). God was reminding His people that it was He who saw their distress, heard their pleas, and met their needs by taking them out of bondage. Today we are often held slaves to our finances just as the Hebrews were slaves to the Egyptian taskmasters. God's plan for us is to place our trust and salvation in Him, not money. We display a lack of faith if our confidence comes only when the checkbook is full. This is like a steward whose confidence is in the provision rather than the provider. God, the ultimate provider, has a checkbook that is never empty.

It is in this light that we are to understand Jesus' teaching, "So do not worry, saying, 'What shall we eat?' or 'What shall we drink?' or 'What shall we wear?' For the pagans run after all these things, and your Heavenly Father knows that you need them. But seek first His kingdom and His righteousness, and all these things will be given to you as well" (Matt. 6:31-33).

The Spirit of Mammon
A third reason to give is to break the "spirit of mammon." As we've seen previously, mammon is derived from a Greek word for the deification of greed. It means making money into an idol. Jesus understood that money has supernatural power. The source of its power is the source of the world's power—Satan himself. When Jesus said, "You cannot serve both God and Money" (v. 24), He referred to worldly wealth as a person rather than a thing. You cannot be a servant to a thing. You can be mastered only by another being. The irony of money is that we think of it as being a tool for our pleasure even while it

actually controls us. Wealth is deceitful (Matt. 13:22; Mark 4:19), and the father of deceit is Satan.

Being from Satan, a mammon spirit is naturally opposed to God. It separates us from God, which is potentially devastating since money touches virtually every aspect of our lives. Many great spiritual lessons are learned through the use or misuse of money. This is why Jesus spoke so much on the subject. Sixteen of the thirty-eight parables refer in some way to money. Giving breaks the power of mammon. This could be why God commanded it in the law. Rather than being burdensome, this commandment—like all the others—was for our benefit. "For the love of money is a root of all kinds of evil," said Paul. "Some people, eager for money, have wandered from the faith and pierced themselves with many griefs" (1 Tim. 6:10). When we give, we break the spirit of mammon by surrendering our undeserved claim to God's money. God has provided an escape from Satan's financial bondage by giving us the means to "resist the devil, and he will flee from you" (James 4:7).

Giving Is a Test of Our Spirituality

Giving defines our level of spirituality. "But just as you excel in everything—in faith, in speech, in knowledge, in complete earnestness and in your love for us—see that you also excel in this grace of giving. *I am not commanding you, but I want to test the sincerity of your love by comparing it with the earnestness of others*" (2 Cor. 8:7-8, italics added). *It is the attitude, not the amount that matters most to God.* "To do what is right and just is more acceptable to the Lord than sacrifice" (Prov. 21:3).

God wants to know who you serve, and He can know this by how you use your money.[9] If you serve mammon, you are a keeper, but if you're serving God, you're a giver. Jesus said the two greatest commandments are: "Love the Lord your God with all your heart and with all your soul and with all your mind" (Matt. 22:37) and "Love your neighbor as yourself" (27:39). When people love themselves more than God or other people, it will be reflected in their desire for things of this world. You cannot simultaneously be acquisitive about money and inquisitive about God.

Faithful financial stewardship demands sharing the financial fruits of our labor. It is a necessity, not an option. A successful life by God's standards is measured by the emphasis that we place upon giving.[10] He measures lives by the quality of their service, not the quantity of accumulated assets. "Whoever wants to become great among you must be your servant, and whoever wants to be first must be your slave—just as the Son of Man did not come to be served, but to serve, and to give His life as a ransom for many" (Matt. 20:26-28).

Giving is the litmus test of our righteousness.[11] While the ungodly desire to hold on to everything they have, "the righteous give without sparing" (Prov. 21:26). God's wish for us is to draw closer to Him by becoming free of the evil power of mammon. He also desires us to draw closer to others by handling our resources in a manner that enhances their well-being.[12]

How Much Do We Have to Give?—The "New" Standard

The New Testament gives us new standards for giving. However, we must not interpret "new" to mean replacement. The new standards for giving were meant to amplify or enhance the tradition of tithing. The New Testament's silence on a specific giving benchmark is not a repudiation of the concept. Evidently Jesus and especially Paul have established a framework that frees us to give as directed by the Holy Spirit. In this way, those with great resources will be free and even obligated to give more than the tithe. "From everyone who has been given much, much will be demanded; and from the one who has been entrusted with much, much more will be asked" (Luke 12:48).

Likewise, those with fewer resources are not bound to give beyond their ability. "For if the willingness is there, the gift is acceptable according to what one has, not according to what he does not have" (2 Cor. 8:12). However, even those of little wealth can feel free to give beyond a tenth should they feel so led.[13]

Therefore, according to the "new" standards we are told to: Give according to our income.[14] Give as we are able and beyond.[15] Excel in our giving.[16] Give according to our prior commitments.[17] Give when we have plenty.[18] Give generously, not grudgingly.[19] Give according to what we have.[20] Sow generously for God loves a cheerful giver.[21] Give if we are rich.[22]

Are these really new standards? All of these principles are just another way of following the Old Testament law, "love your neighbor as yourself" (Lev. 19:18). In fact, Paul's exhortation to give generously, not grudgingly, in order that we may sow as we reap, was also part of the law.[23]

What the new standards give us is freedom. Just as God freely gives from His kingdom, we are free to choose how much we give back to the kingdom. *Equipoise* is a term that refers to an equal readiness to move in any direction. *Equipoise* is a key characteristic of the New Testament guidelines for giving. It is our enhanced freedom to choose that gives us *equipoise*. We see this principle in action when we read Jesus' statement: "For I was hungry and you gave Me something to eat, I was thirsty and you gave Me something to drink, I was a stranger and you invited Me in, I needed clothes and you clothed Me, I was sick and you looked after Me, I was in prison and you came to visit Me" (Matt. 25:35-36).

Another key characteristic of the new standards is sacrifice. God loved us enough to sacrifice His only Son in order to pay for our redemption. For many people, whether affluent or not, tithing is not a financial sacrifice. Whatever amount we choose to give, it should be a level just beyond comfort and convenience. Indeed, David said, "I will not sacrifice to the Lord my God burnt offerings that cost me nothing" (2 Sam. 24:24). With giving at less than 3 percent of income, it is apparent that American Christians, easily the world's most affluent believers, do not feel obliged to follow the letter of the Old Testament law to tithe. Unfortunately, it seems that, like the Pharisees, we are neglecting the spirit of the law as well. Moreover, our paltry giving does not follow David's example of sacrifice.

Studies suggest that if every Christian tithed, hunger would be eliminated in two years and every church and ministry would be fully staffed and equipped without any debt. Still, I believe this to be the minimum that is financially possible. With our affluence, if everybody gave *"as they are able and beyond,"* the result could conservatively be three to five times that amount.

Who Do We Give To?

God has allowed us the freedom to determine our own levels of giving although we will be held accountable for those decisions. A critical aspect of Christian living is that we must use our resources to make a positive contribution to the welfare of others. In this light, God has chosen to dictate to us who we should be giving to.

We Must Give to Our Family

Family relationships are so important in God's eyes that to neglect them is to renounce your faith (1 Tim. 5:8; Matt. 15:5-6). God wants us to provide financially for our children.[24] He even wants us to provide for our grandchildren.[25] Give to the poor and needy.[26] Give to the one who asks.[27] Give to your local church.[28] In Old Testament times, the storehouse was part of the temple where the sacrifices were offered to God. Its equivalent today is your regular place of worship and ministry. The church relies on regular giving to meet its commitments in the areas of community outreach, missionary support, educational programs, and benevolence.

Give to the church leaders and teachers.[29] It is ironic that people will give financial support more readily to the special ministry needs of others yet ignore how important regular church giving is to their own needs. If you receive any form of ministry from your local church, you have an obligation to support it financially. The pastors and other leaders depend upon generous giving just as you depend upon your salary. It's wrong to think that the teaching of God's Word should be performed without compensation.[30]

When Do We Give?

Just as God's Word is specific about who we give to, we have also been given instructions on when to give. Whenever we receive income, God wants His portion first.[31] Not only does He want our first, He wants our best, and He wants it brought to the place where you usually worship.[32]

Giving the first part of our income to God completely answers the frequently asked question, "Should I give based upon my gross earnings or my net?" in other words, before or after taxes? Presumably, it is people who want to tithe or give some other percentage of their income who want to know. As we've seen, the answer really is immaterial since we have no specific standard that we must adhere to. Even so, while it's doubtful that there was payroll withholding in biblical times, Christ still provided us with timeless advice. "Give to Caesar what is Caesar's, and to God what is God's" (Matt. 22:21). What is God's is the *first* part. Therefore, if you insist upon tithing, it should be based on your gross income. Even if we weren't commanded to give to God first, to whom would you rather give? Is the government capable of doing for you what God can?

It is also God's will that we have the discipline to give on a regular schedule.[33] How would you be able to function if you were never sure when your employer was going to pay you? It would be even worse if you didn't know how much money you were going to get.

It isn't fair to assume that the church doesn't need the same financial consistency as we do.[34] The point that the Apostle Paul was making is that we should not allow our giving to adversely impact those doing the church's work on our behalf. When we fail to give regularly, with the first and best part of our income, ultimately we suffer by not receiving the value of the ministry the church provides us. We should not treat the church's finances any differently than we want our employers or customers to treat ours.

The simplest thing to do is to write a check to the church as soon as you get paid. Make it a joyful habit. Think about how pleasing this is to God and what benefits you directly receive from your church in return for your financial gifts. However, guard against making a show of your giving. Don't wait until the most opportune time for others to see your generosity. Your giving is first and foremost an act of obedience, which glorifies God through your humility and concern for others.

God detests acts that glorify the actor. If you desire the acclaim of others for your charity, then this acclaim is your final reward. God, on the other hand, is waiting to give even greater rewards to those whose giving reflects a servant's attitude.[35]

What Do We Get from Giving?

God is probably the only master that actually gives rewards for simply doing as we're told. How often would we actually drive the speed limit if we got bonuses for doing so? Does your boss ever reward you just for following instructions? And do you do the same for your children?

It's amazing how many times God promises that we will receive something from Him in return for giving to Him. He wants us to do what is right so much that He provides us incentives for acting upon His Word. Furthermore, He tells us over and over to make sure that we don't forget:

> "Bring the whole tithe into the storehouse, that there may be food in My house. Test Me in this," says the Lord Almighty, "and see if I will not throw open the floodgates of heaven and *pour out so much blessing* that you will not have room enough for it" (Mal. 3:10, italics added).

> Honor the Lord with your wealth, with the firstfruits of all your crops; then *your barns will be filled* to overflowing, and *your vats will brim over* with new wine (Prov. 3:9-10, italics added).

> He who sows righteousness *reaps a sure reward* (11:18, italics added).

> One man gives freely, yet *gains even more* (v. 24, italics added).

> A generous man will *prosper;* he who refreshes others will himself *be refreshed* (v. 25, italics added).

> A generous man will himself *be blessed*, for he shares his food with the poor (22:9, italics added).

> He who gives to the poor will *lack nothing* (28:27, italics added).

> He who is kind to the poor lends to the Lord, and He will *reward* him for what he has done (19:17, italics added).

Give, and it will be *given to you*. A good measure, pressed down, shaken together and running over, will be poured into your lap. For with the measure you use, it will be measured to you (Luke 6:38, italics added).

Donald Trump wrote a best-selling book called *The Art of the Deal* extolling his business savvy accumulated over years of wheeling and dealing. Unfortunately, "The Donald" missed out on the best deal of all time, although it's still available to him or anybody else. As we've just seen, this deal has been described by numerous practitioners hundreds of years ago in a bigger selling book—the Bible. One of the practitioners, King Solomon, had real estate holdings that Trump can only dream about.

Looking at this incomplete list of promises, it should be apparent that giving is the greatest deal ever. The art of the giving deal, however, is that its intent is to benefit the other party, not ourselves. In fact, our ability to earn the returns that giving offers is dependent upon our not seeking any return at all!

Then Jesus said to His host, "When you give a luncheon or dinner, do not invite your friends, your brothers or relatives, or your rich neighbors; if you do, they may invite you back and so you will be repaid. But when you give a banquet, invite the poor, the crippled, the lame, the blind, and you will be blessed. Although they cannot repay you, you will be repaid at the resurrection of the righteous" (Luke 14:12-14).

For giving to glorify God, our motives must be as right as our actions. The motive of giving is not the rewards but love demonstrated by obedience to God and compassion for our neighbors. Giving is not a duty or a scheme but a response to what Jesus has given us. We cannot intentionally "give to get" nor can we decide what blessings we want bestowed upon us. Making a formula out of giving is contrary to its true spirit. What we can be assured of is that when we *unselfishly* use our finances to alleviate another's burdens, others will lighten our loads.

Is Your Lack of Faith Robbing God?

It is not a credible argument to assume that the best American Christians can give is only 2 to 3 percent of their income. Clearly, we as a religious nation are intentionally withholding our financial resources from God. Even with one of the lowest savings rates among major nations, we still retain over twice this much as personal savings. We are keeping the first part of our income for ourselves and giving a small part of the remainder to God. As we've seen from God's own Word, this is wrong. But from our own perspective, it is stupid unless we have deluded ourselves into thinking that we can do for ourselves all of the things God has *promised* to do for us! We make ourselves out to be gods and regardless of what we may say, our financial actions expose our folly.

The only other possible reason for our marginal giving is that we don't believe the promises that God has made us. This, quite plainly, is lack of faith, and it doesn't make sense. It is inconsistent to place your trust in someone who promises eternal life and not to trust His promise to meet your daily needs. The God who has promised to give us "the riches of His glorious inheritance" (Eph. 1:18) is the same God to whom Jesus prayed, "Give us today our daily bread" (Matt. 6:11). It is misguided to place so much faith in money, and so little faith in God.

You may feel like you can't afford to be a more generous giver. In reality, you can't afford not to be. While the faithful find their dollars stretched to meet their needs, the unfaithful or uncaring see theirs shrink. God will not accept second place to money and will work against our attempts to manage our own lives. If we refuse to make God our first financial priority, then we are robbing Him, and by robbing God we ultimately rob ourselves.[36]

A Giving Plan

As we will see throughout this book, planning is an essential part of financial stewardship. Having a giving strategy can enhance both the quality and quantity of our giving. This is nothing more than deciding in advance how to apply the concepts described in this chapter, particularly those found in the New Testament. We should not become so ritualistic that our giving becomes a mechanical exercise. However, giving is an important responsibility and it therefore requires deliberation. The basics of giving planning is to establish a starting point that addresses three questions: How much? Who? and When? It should be clear from the New Testament that the correct answers to these questions are individually determined based upon your personal leadings from the Holy Spirit. If we answer these three questions without prayer and subsequent direction from the Holy Spirit, then we have completely missed the point of the kind of giving God is looking for.

The starting point is nothing more than a foundation upon which we hope to build an increasing ability to give. Those who have been allowed to prosper financially have an obligation to make increased commitments to the work of the kingdom. If through improved personal financial management (hopefully as a result of reading this book!) you increase your giving capability, you also have an increased responsibility to share your growing resources. Giving, after all, is the point of having financial resources. Our initial giving decisions are not an end but a beginning to a lifelong process of funding God's work.

It is important that we view giving as a continual process and make plans today for future changes in our ability to give. Increased financial resources, whether through additional income or reduced expenses, have a habit of disappearing very quickly.[37] It is too tempting to increase our lifestyle in direct proportion to an increase in our income. What we need to do is be proactive in increasing our giving proportionally to our increased resources.

One way to do that is to predetermine the cost of an adequate and appropriate lifestyle. This would include your cost of savings for future financial goals, which we'll discuss in greater detail in chapter 5. Any income earned above this amount is simply given away. This plan would probably appeal most to families that are already financially secure and well on the way to meeting their financial objectives.

Most people are still building a strong financial foundation

A suggestion for these people is to plan in advance how much to augment giving whenever the ability to give increases. You could do this in one of two ways. If, for example, you earn $40,000 and give 10 percent of that amount or $4,000 per year, you could decide *in advance* to raise your giving percentage by 1 to 2 percent after your next salary increase. Let's say that you get a $2,000 raise. If you remain at a 10 percent giving level, this would raise your giving to $4,200. However, if you raise your giving level to 11 percent of salary, you'd be giving $4,620. If you decided to give 12 percent of your salary, you'd be giving $5,040. In either case, you'd be enhancing both your funding of the kingdom and personal financial goals.

Alternatively, you could decide to give a percentage of your base income and a predetermined higher percentage of any income above the base amount. This is particularly effective for individuals whose income is unpredictable, such as salespeople or others who receive substantial bonus income. In this example, an individual with base earnings of $30,000 may decide to give 8 percent or $2,400. They then may decide to double this percentage on all bonuses or commissions. Therefore, $30,000 of additional income would generate $4,800 (16 percent of $30,000) of extra giving, resulting in total giving of $7,200.

The underlying philosophy in either of these approaches is to establish a base giving amount that will increase as your financial resources increase. Both the base amount and the increased amount are individually determined in accordance with Paul's New Testament guidelines of quality and quantity. They can be percentages of income or fixed dollar amounts, and they may be above or below a tithe, that is, 10 percent. The crucial point is to plan in advance to turn our increased abundance into thankfulness by increased support to God's work.

Giving to Other than the Local Church
In addition to assisting the church's work in advancing the kingdom, we have an obligation to provide support to others who minister to us and our families on an ongoing basis. Typically, this would be radio, television, or print ministries that exist to educate their followers on various aspects of Christian

living. Many of these organizations are maintained solely by private contributions. To freely avail yourself of their services without supporting them in return is wrong. Many people spend more time with these ministries than they do in church! There is certainly nothing wrong with that as long as your financial commitment to them reflects the value of their ministry in your life. We ultimately bear the cost of the loss of a valuable ministry due to lack of funds.

It is wrong to associate a specific amount with your willingness to give. It is your attitude of "loving your neighbor as yourself" that is the real issue. Furthermore, support of these ministries should not replace that which rightfully should go to your regular place of worship. I can't prove it, but I suspect that no organization would have problems if all those not currently giving only gave as little as $5. If you can't afford to give, pray for the ministry and write occasional letters of encouragement until your resources increase to the point where you can make financial commitments. While true servants are willing to give to you without expecting repayment, stewardship is less than faithful when we freely take without a willingness to give in return.

An excellent source of information on the financial practices of religious groups is the Evangelical Council for Financial Accountability (ECFA). The ECFA's mission is to help donors get information on the financial and ethical practices of evangelical Christian organizations. By doing this, they help these groups earn a high degree of public trust.

Membership in the ECFA is tangible evidence that the Christian organizations that you support adhere to the highest standards of Christian ethics and financial accountability. The members must agree to annual audits, follow strict guidelines for fund-raising, provide full financial disclosure, and avoid conflicts of interest. Membership can be suspended or terminated for failure to meet any of the seven standards of responsible stewardship outlined by the ECFA.

Donors benefit by knowing how funds are being used, what accomplishments are being made by a ministry's programs, gaining access to the member organization, and having the knowledge that appeals for funds are valid and honest.

Many well-known groups are among the 700-plus ECFA members which include Focus on the Family, Prison Fellowship Ministries, Billy Graham Evangelistic Association, and Fellowship of Christian Athletes. Unfortunately, many well-known groups are not. As always, you should give to a ministry as you feel led, but it couldn't hurt to call first and ask if they are an ECFA member, and if not, why not. Not having the ECFA stamp of approval does not imply bad stewardship on the part of an organization, but membership in good standing certainly indicates their good stewardship.

You can get more information on the Evangelical Council for Financial Accountability by calling 1-800-3BE-WISE or writing to ECFA, P.O. Box 17456, Washington, D.C. 20041-0456.

Conclusion

It is God's will for you to be free of financial bondage. You can start breaking the chains by demonstrating your faithfulness through a personal program of regular giving. It is God's desire that you "trust in the Lord with all your heart and lean not on your own understanding; in all your ways acknowledge Him, and He will make your paths straight" (Prov. 3:5-6).

Giving to God's work is an important Christian responsibility. We are to manage the resources God has given us wisely so that we may share these resources as He directs us. The Bible equates the failure to tithe with robbing God, resulting in a curse that ultimately robs us. The New Testament principles of giving make it clear that we should be giving generously and sacrificially, although 10 percent is not necessarily a required standard. However, if we give as God directs us, we should find that tithing (10 percent) is probably a minimum commitment. Furthermore, we must be willing to support other financial needs beyond this tithe as situations arise.

As His stewards, God will hold you accountable for your financial commitment to His plan. Our goal as Christians should be to start by giving 10 percent of our income and living off 90 percent. Wouldn't it be an exciting testimony if our joy in giving and faithful stewardship could lead us to where we ultimately give 90 percent and live off 10 percent?

Summary

1. Our attitude toward giving is the ultimate expression of love and defines our level of spirituality.
2. Our motives for giving are just as important as our actions.
3. The quality of our gifts counts more than the quantity.
4. The level of giving of American Christians indicates a lack of faith that the Bible says robs God.
5. Our financial gifts should first be directed to those churches and ministries where we receive the greatest support.

Notes

1. *Leviticus 27:30*
2. *Exodus 22:29-30*
3. *Leviticus 27:32-33*
4. *Leviticus 27:31*
5. *Malachi 3:8-10*
6. *Genesis 28:20-22*
7. *Galatians 3:7*
8. *Hebrews 11:1*
9. *Matthew 6:24*
10. *Ephesians 4:28*
11. *1 John 3:17*
12. *2 Corinthians 9:12*
13. *Luke 21:1-4*
14. *1 Corinthians 16:2; 2 Corinthians 8:12*
15. *2 Corinthians 8:3-5*
16. *2 Corinthians 8:7*
17. *2 Corinthians 8:10-11*
18. *2 Corinthians 8:14; 1 Timothy 6:17-18*
19. *2 Corinthians 9:5-8*
20. *2 Corinthians 8:12*
21. *2 Corinthians 9:6-7*
22. *1 Timothy 6:17-18*
23. *Deuteronomy 15:10*
24. *Psalm 17:14*
25. *Proverbs 13:22*
26. *Deuteronomy 15:11*
27. *Matthew 5:42*
28. *Malachi 3:10*
29. *1 Timothy 5:17-18*
30. *1 Corinthians 9:7, 14*
31. *Proverbs 3:9*
32. *Exodus 23:19*
33. *1 Corinthians 16:2*
34. *1 Corinthians 9:9-10*
35. *Matthew 6:1-4*
36. *Haggai 1:5-6, 9-11*
37. *Ecclesiastes 5:11*

Chapter Four

You Must Take Control of Your Money

Be sure you know the condition of your flocks, give careful attention to your herds; for riches do not endure forever, and a crown is not secure for all generations (Proverbs 27:23-24)

"Easy come, easy go. There's more where that came from!"

"You can't be too careful. You just never know what can happen to you that you'll need to have money saved up for."

"With all that's going on in the world, why do people worry so much about money? People should spend more time thinking about how they can solve the world's problems, not their own."

"The money doesn't really matter. It's just a way of keeping score. Figuring out how to make more money is actually a lot more fun than spending it later."

One of these attitudes probably fits you closer than all the others. Each of these attitudes controls your relationship to money. This chapter will show you that who you are is more important than what you know about money.

59

According to *Webster's Ninth New Collegiate Dictionary*, *control* means "to exercise restraining or directing influence over; regulate; to have power over." Is your money restraining you from doing the things you'd like to do, including giving generously to church, family, and friends? Does your money have direct influence on your attitudes and behaviors? Isn't your decision to buy or not to buy something usually based upon whether you have enough money? Do you have power over your money, or does it have power over you?

Jesus knew that desire for money has the power to control our lives. In the Parable of the Sower He said there would be those who hear the Word, but fail to mature due to life's riches (Luke 8:14). In the Parable of the Great Banquet, an allegory of heaven, Jesus told a story about three invited guests who excused themselves from the banquet. One preferred to go see a field he had just bought. He was more concerned about his investments. Another left to try out his newly purchased oxen. He was more interested in making money. The fact that apparently neither one had previously inspected their property further attests to their foolishness. Finally, one left to tend to his new wife and presumably her substantial dowry (though not necessarily in that order!).

Possession of money is probably the only common ground between Christians and non-Christians. If our money controls us to the same degree that it controls non-Christians, where is the power of the Gospel in our lives? Nonbelievers need to see where your heart is. "For where your treasure is, there your heart will be also" (Matt. 6:21). They also need to see whom you serve and to whom you are solely loyal.[1]

The Bible calls us to be stewards of God's creation. A steward is a manager, and one of the essential functions of management is control. To be a successful manager, we must exercise control of God's resources. Furthermore, as God's servants we must manage our resources in a manner that demonstrates our complete loyalty to Him. Because concern for money can so easily separate us from God, the way we handle our financial resources is a primary indicator of our spiritual condition.

Since we are managing God's assets, every financial decision is a spiritual decision. Therefore, to seek proper guidance we must understand what God has to say on the subject of taking control of our money. There are three biblical principles we can apply that will allow us to take control of our personal finances. These fundamental principles should serve as the basis for all of our financial decisions. Each can be put in the context of a simple question.

Who Am I?

The first question is "Who am I?" All of our financial decisions should be made in accordance with our God-given personalities and skills. It is clear that God intended each of us to have different skills to be used in unique ways. "There are different kinds of gifts, but the same Spirit. There are different kinds of service, but the same Lord. There are different kinds of working, but the same God works all of them in all men" (1 Cor. 12:4-6). See also Romans 12:6; 1 Peter 4:10.

Knowing who we are and what we do best is the first step to good financial stewardship. God intends for us to serve Him in ways consistent with the way in which we are uniquely created. Recall that in the Parable of the Talents, the master gave his servants responsibility "each according to his ability." Acting in accordance with our God-given temperament is the only way to ensure success. To try to serve God in any other fashion would be to usurp God's authority as Creator. Trying to be something that we're not is to attempt to re-create ourselves differently than what God intended. Obviously this is both sinful and futile. Like the wicked servant in the Parable of the Talents, our failure to produce results consistent with the abilities given to us warrants severe punishment. Therefore, the first step in good financial stewardship is to know who we are and what unique traits we have to use in this critical area of Christian service.

It is true that we "can do everything through Him who gives [us] strength" (Phil. 4:13). However, that does not necessarily mean that we will be given new, personal powers to accomplish God's will. Since God prefers dependence to independence, He often provides another person with complementary skills to assist us. In this manner, Moses, a poor public speaker, was aided by Aaron, a more gifted orator. Knowing our strengths and weaknesses allows us to move forward confidently in our areas of strength. Then, using Moses as our model (Ex. 6:28–7:2), we can ask for God's provision in our areas of weakness.

Where Am I?

The second question is "Where am I?" Once you've established who you are, you must next determine where you are currently. Stewardship is a process, meaning that there is constant movement to a particular end. For Christians, these ends are those that God gives to us. Even if you know where you are moving to, you will still get lost if you don't know where you are moving from. To achieve the long-term goals of financial stewardship, you will always need a complete understanding of your current financial condition. "Be sure you know the condition of your flocks, give careful attention to your herds" (Prov. 27:23). To live without consideration for what we have available is to assume that our resources are infinite. As only God is infinite, to live in such a manner is to imply that we are God. A direct application of how this verse was successfully applied is in the story of Jacob and Laban (Gen. 30:32-43). Knowing the condition of his flock, Jacob became "exceedingly prosperous" as a direct result of this biblical principle.

Where Am I Going?

The final question is "Where am I going?" Most people fail in their finances because they don't figure out how they're going to attain their goals and objectives. To be a good steward is to meet the financial objectives given to us by the Lord. Godly uses of our resources cannot be met without planning.

Planning for the future use of our resources is an important biblical financial principle. Jesus taught that to start things we can't finish due to lack of planning is foolish.[2]

King Solomon, possibly the wealthiest man who ever lived, had much to say about planning in the Book of Proverbs. This is interesting given that Solomon's vast wealth was a direct result of his God-given wisdom. Planning was apparently a key component of this wisdom and a major contributor to his accumulation of wealth.[3]

While thoughtful planning is a critical aspect of good stewardship, we must recognize that it is the Lord, and not our efforts, who decides the outcome. "Many are the plans in a man's heart, but it is the Lord's purpose that prevails" (Prov. 19:21).

Man proposes, but God disposes. Remember, the act of stewardship recognizes that what we have really belongs to God, not for our purposes but for His. It is not just the act but the intent that matters to God. Therefore, in planning our financial objectives, we should heed Solomon's advice: "Commit to the Lord whatever you do, and your plans will succeed" (Prov. 16:3).

Should We Delegate Control to Others?

As stewards we will ultimately be held accountable for the use of God's resources. We cannot excuse ourselves from this accountability by giving up control of our resources to others. Most people feel that because they lack the expertise to handle their money properly, it is best to turn their personal finances over to someone else. This is usually a financial professional such as a stock broker or financial planner. My contention is that this happens far too often. Most people's finances are easily handled alone with a minimal amount of expert advice. Few individuals have an amount of money that makes their financial situation complex enough to hire a professional. However, people must decide for themselves what is best for them.

A wise financial steward guards against too much self-reliance. Since we are not expected to be expert in all matters, we are encouraged to make plans by seeking advice.[4] We must be careful not to rely stubbornly on our own opinions and expertise. Only God can succeed by being totally independent. More importantly, the wisdom of others provides us with the means of success in spite of our own lack of skill. Solomon was not wise because he knew everything. He was wise because he knew himself — the first principle of control — and recognized when he needed to rely on the skills of others. Therefore, our lack of knowledge does not excuse us from achieving God's objectives for our personal stewardship.

However, we must be discerning enough to make sure that the advice we are getting is of high quality.[5] I do not believe this means only Christian counselors are acceptable. Their hearts may be in the right place, but Christians can be just as inexperienced and incompetent as non-Christians. Truth is truth, and the source of truth is God, not people. As creations of God, everyone has an innate access to truth. Therefore, it is more important to have a good adviser than a Christian adviser. Our advantage as Christians is that we have the Holy Spirit in us to guide and assist us in discerning what is truth. We need to rely on the Spirit, rather than blind faith in other people, to know whether we are receiving advice that will benefit us.

If you are using outside assistance, do not forget that *you* are solely responsible for whether or not God's objectives are being fulfilled. You must know enough to be able to tell your adviser what specific goals you intend to accomplish. This will require planning on your part. You will have to know enough to measure the progress being made toward your goals. You'll also have to know whether your adviser is handling your finances within the levels of risk that you are comfortable with and are appropriate for your current financial situation. The bottom line is that you will have to make the time and effort to take control of your finances, even if someone else does much of the actual work. Delegating activity does not mean delegating control or authority. If you are working to meet God's objectives, then you are responsible for making sure that your adviser is reaching those goals on your behalf.

Controlling our money is a lifelong process with serious spiritual ramifications, for money has power. Indeed, Jesus referred to money as "the mammon of unrighteousness" (Luke 16:9, KJV). *Mammon* is an ancient term for personified, deified confidence in wealth. Jesus is therefore implying that money can have a demonic nature. Our relationship with money continually reflects the daily struggle with our sinful nature. It is through money that our covetous nature is exposed. We can win this struggle by the application of God's principles. Knowing who we are gives our stewardship a chance to succeed by using our God-given skills while praying for our shortcomings. Knowing where we are means that we will act in accordance with what we have now, doing no more or no less. Knowing where we wish to go means planning and preparing to meet God's objectives in the future. All three principles work together to put our financial assets under divine direction and influence rather than the world's.

How to Take Control of Your Money — Part I

Who Are You?
The perfect investor is:

- bold enough to take the big risks that come with high-payoff investments
- analytical enough to have a consistent, systematic approach to choosing among a wide spectrum of investment alternatives
- conservative enough to preserve capital by patiently waiting for the best opportunities, and taking cautious but decisive action when those opportunities arise, and
- altruistic enough to understand that devotion to others is more satisfying than the selfish accumulation of wealth.

While everybody has at least one of these qualities, nobody possesses more than one in equal measure.

In 1920, Swiss psychologist Karl Jung wrote that each of us has a preference for how we function, a view introduced by Hippocrates nearly 2,500 years earlier. These preferences emanate early in life and become the foundation of our personalities. All of the issues we face in life are interpreted by our basic personality preferences, which determines our affinities and aversions to people, places, and things.

In the 1950s, Isabel Myers and Kathryn Briggs identified sixteen distinct personality types, which have since become widely used and universally accepted patterns of human behavior. The sixteen personality types can be categorized by four basic temperaments: SP (Sensory-Perceiver), NT (Intuitive-Thinker), NF (Intuitive-Feeler), and SJ (Sensory-Judging).

Temperament is the innate manner in which we consistently approach our environment. It is our preferred, though not exclusive, attitudes and behaviors toward all aspects of our lives, such as choice of career, choice of mate, style of learning, style of managing, and so on.

To become a successful investor, it is critical that we understand our temperament with the goal of maximizing its strengths and minimizing its weaknesses. Furthermore, since each temperament possesses major characteristics of the ideal investor, we must learn something of the other personalities so that we can incorporate their positive aspects into our investment strategies.

You are on the threshold of an exciting self-discovery process that will make you into a more knowledgeable and successful investor. The Investor Profile is a unique system of finding your investment temperament, or preferred style of investment strategy.

Traditional wisdom holds that your investments should be based upon such factors as your age, level of income, and cash flow. While important, these are secondary to personality considerations. Your individual temperament will determine the level of stress and discomfort your investments create for you. Since anxiety in investing causes bad decisions, minimizing stress, rather than maximizing profits, will become one's primary objective.

You will find an Investor Profile Questionnaire at the end of this chapter. Your answers to the thirty-three simple questions will determine your Investor Profile. More importantly, it will help you establish the level of risk that you feel most comfortable with.

As you read through the questions, you may be skeptical that your answers can really provide insight into your investment process. Believe it! This Investor Profile is as powerful as it is simple. It is based upon widely accepted psychological techniques of determining your natural preferences.

There are no good or bad profiles. What is bad is when you steer into investments that suit another's personality. This creates anxiety. Therefore, answer the questions honestly, not as you think they should be. Usually, your response will be immediate. This will occur with personality traits that are very strong.

In questions that refer to your less dominant characteristics, you may have to think about your answers. Try to make a response, but if you're not sure, skip the question. Once you complete the test and determine your Investor Profile, you will find the results to be an encouraging and invaluable aid to assist you in creating investment strategies that suit you best.

When you complete the test, match the two-letter result against the following descriptions of your investment personality.

Temperament: **SP** (Sensory-Perceiver)
Percentage of U.S. Population: 38%
Investor Profile: The Bold Investor

The Bold Investor is the ultimate risk taker and thrill seeker. To the Bold Investor, the thrill of investing, more so than the outcome, is its own end and its own reward. He seeks immediate, tangible results in a bold, adventurous manner, often leaping before looking. Trivial outcomes are not the style of the Bold Investor. He will either win big or lose big.

The Bold Investor is grounded in reality and the here and now. As such, he has an aversion to theory and planning and would much rather get immediate hands-on experience. He also has a need for spontaneity and flexibility. Therefore, he has a disdain for long-range plans and strategies, rules, regulations, and procedures. Any investment process that is tedious or restrictive is too confining to the Bold Investor.

Strengths
The Bold Investor survives setbacks quite well. He can easily cut his losses and move on to another opportunity. Also, since the Bold Investor is comfortable with high risk-high potential investments, he is capable of making money quickly.

Weaknesses
By nature the Bold Investor hates to have any kind of plan. He is not goal-oriented, as the pursuit of thrills exceeds the

attainment of any particular objective. Impetuous and impulsive, the Bold Investor does not understand that in investing, discretion is the better part of valor. It doesn't matter whether it's a bull market or a bear market. The Bold Investor cares only that there is a market. The Bold Investor needs to guard against breaking rules, which they do, not to gain any advantage, but to see if they can get away with it.

Recommendation

The ideal portfolio for the Bold Investor is one that is divided into a high-risk portion to provide the necessary excitement and a low-risk portion to provide stability and prevent self-destruction. Since he is not a planner or a goal seeker, he will need to find someone, a mate, friend, or adviser, who will help develop and enforce a long-term investment plan.

Temperament: **SJ** (Sensory-Judging)
Percentage of U.S. Population: 38%
Investor Profile: The Conservative Investor

The Conservative Investor seeks comfort and security through traditional, long-term investments. Keeping what she has is more important than getting more, and having something set aside for a rainy day is crucial to the Conservative Investor. This person is the original pessimist; the SJ temperament must have created Chicken Little, Murphy's Law, and the Boy Scout Motto.

The Conservative Investor's investment process is methodical, based on facts, history, and experience. The resulting portfolio will tend to be a traditional mix of investments: high quality bonds, blue-chip stocks, and well-known mutual funds with established track records. Avoidance of risk, both financial and fear of the unknown, is more important than the potential for gain. The Conservative Investor is decisive and prefers structure. Therefore, once the portfolio is created, she will make few changes.

Strengths

The Conservative Investor's greatest strength is decisiveness. She is also structured and will use a highly organized and methodical process in making investments. Because of their risk-averse nature, the Conservative Investors generally do not lose money investing.

Weaknesses

Since change frightens the Conservative Investor, she seeks structure and organization. The stock market with its daily fluctuations is a scary environment for the Conservative Investor. Therefore, she will choose overly conservative investments that, after taxes and inflation, will result in the accumulation of little capital. This will leave her poorly equipped to meet long-range financial objectives, such as retirement or college tuition expenses.

Recommendation

The Conservative Investor's temperament will require a low-risk portfolio. However, she should consider diversifying with some assets devoted to investments of average risk in order to accumulate a meaningful amount of money.

Temperament: **NT** (Intuitive-Thinker)
Percentage of U.S. Population: 12%
Investor Profile: The Analytical Investor

The Analytical Investor seeks mental challenges and desires to profit through intellectual mastery of his investments. He delights in demonstrating his competence. He is extremely objective, both in his selections and subsequent assessment of their performance. The Analytical Investor is creative and enjoys building models to make market forecasts. He needs to understand his investment alternatives, rationalize their selection, and predict their outcome.

This temperament is also innovative, always looking for different and better ways of investing. They are the contrarians, those who challenge existing authorities and practices. They are also the critics, quick to point out the flaws of another's investment approach. The harshest criticism, though, is usually reserved for themselves. One way to understand this Investor Profile is by comparison to the Bold and Conservative Profiles. Like the Bold Investor, the Analytical Investor has an affinity to risk. However, he manages his risks through practice, planning, and prediction. Where the Conservative Investor focuses on the past and sees danger, the Analytical Investor looks to the future and sees possibilities. In fact, he uses his understanding of the past in determining events in the future.

Strengths

The Analytical Investor's greatest strength is his imagination, which allows him to develop innovative, logical, and consistent criteria for all investment decisions. He will rarely invest in anything whose risks and rewards haven't been thoroughly studied and understood. He is also contrarian in nature, less likely to follow the crowds and make errors because of emotion. A self-critic, the Analytical Investor continually monitors his performance in an effort to constantly improve his investment results.

Weaknesses

The Analytical Investor's penchant for knowledge can at times lead to indecisiveness through "paralysis by analysis." Also in his desire to master many kinds of investments, the Analytical Investor can become a "Jack-of-all-trades, master of none." Finally, there is also a tendency to create new strategies or models and never implement them.

Recommendation

Because of his ability to assess risk and develop contingency plans, the Analytical Investor is well suited to an above-average to high-risk portfolio. He needs more diversity than the other temperaments, but must be careful not to overdiversify into too many investment areas.

Temperament: **NF** (Intuitive-Feeler)
Percentage of U.S. Population: 12%
Investor Profile: The Altruistic Investor

In the competitive world of investing, the Altruistic Investor is a rare breed, seeking harmony with others and inner fulfillment rather than profits. The quest for an identity in life is her primary pursuit and investing is just a way of answering the question, "Who am I?"

The Altruistic Investor is an idealist, and money is a tool for the expression of those ideals. To her, making money should never come at another's expense, and it's best if the money can be used for another's welfare. Because of the temperament of these people, they lack concern for their own necessities and usually place the welfare of others above their own. The popular children's story "The Little Engine that Could" is a wonderful analogy of the Altruistic Investor. Struggling up the mountain to deliver toys to the children on the other side, the Little Engine must have been an NF temperament.

Strengths
This temperament group provides social benefits for the rest of us self-centered capitalists. The status of the Altruistic Investor's investments will never cause anxiety. Accumulation of wealth for personal concerns is not an overriding factor in their investment program.

Weaknesses
Does the Altruistic Investor even care about money? She shows little interest in buying and selling things with the objective of making a profit. To the other Investor Profiles, the Altruistic Investor's strengths are viewed as weaknesses. Like the Conservative Investor, investment choices that provide psychological benefits may not yield a sufficient return to accomplish long-range financial objectives.

Recommendation
An average to low-risk portfolio of investments that have personal meaning or accomplish interpersonal objectives are best for the Altruistic Investor. Employee Stock Plans or stocks and mutual funds of socially conscious companies should be a major part of her investments. Consideration should be given to some investments of above-average risk to ensure attainment of future financial goals.

INVESTOR PROFILE SUMMARY				
	Bold	**Analytical**	**Altruistic**	**Conservative**
Outlook	Realist	Optimist	Idealist	Pessimist
Seeks	Action	Knowledge	Harmony	Security
	Excitement	Challenge	Fulfillment	Comfort
Key words	Impulsive	Contrarian	Integrity	Traditional
Strengths	Adaptable	Logical	Benevolent	Decisive
Weakness	Not goal-	Over-	Financial	Frightened by
	oriented	analytical	apathy	change
Risk				
Tolerance	**High**	**Moderate**	**Low**	**Very Low**

Chart 4.1

How to Take Control of Your Money—Part II

Where Are You Now?

The next step after determining your risk profile is to plan your financial objectives. I recommend that investors answer three simple questions:

(1) Where are you now? Investors need to analyze their current financial situation to assess their financial fitness.

(2) Where are you going? Investors should list specific financial goals (that is, retirement, college expenses, debt repayment, and so on) and in how many years money will be needed to fund those goals.

(3) How will you get there? Investors must compare the goals in step 2 to their present situation in step 1 and determine what changes need to be made to achieve their goals. This is the essence of establishing an investment portfolio.

It will be difficult to achieve any long-term financial goals without a complete understanding of where you are today. You must know conclusively where you are now before you can even consider making plans for the future. There are two traditional financial summaries that will provide you with the information you need to begin planning your financial future:

- Statement of Net Worth
- Statement of Income and Expense

A statement of net worth is a snapshot of your present financial condition. It summarizes every financial decision that you've ever made. Basically, this statement lists each asset owned and each liability owned. Subtract liabilities from assets and you have your net worth. The objective is to have your net worth growing at a rate consistent with your future objectives. To begin your analysis, complete the Statement of Net Worth form at the end of the chapter.

The statement of net worth contains three critical pieces of information:

- Liquid Assets
- Productive Assets
- Propensity to Borrow

Liquid assets are those assets that can be converted into cash without any penalty or loss of principal. Most advisers recommend that individuals hold liquid assets worth three to six months of living expenses (see Statement of Income and Expenses). However, each investor should hold an amount that makes them feel comfortable. From an investment perspective, substantial liquid assets allow the flexibility to take advantage of investment opportunities as they arise.

Productive assets are those that have the potential to generate income or appreciation. It is the sum of your liquid, nonliquid, and real estate assets and could possibly include some collectibles such as art or coins. Productive assets are the key to investment planning. Investors need to ensure that their productive assets are doing two things. First, they must match the investor's financial objectives. If an investor desires growth, then growth-oriented investments, such as stocks and long-term bond mutual funds, must make up a high proportion of productive assets. Too many investors have excess funds tied up in low yielding investments like money market funds and CDs. However, these type of fixed income investments, as well as bonds and dividend-paying equity mutual funds, would be appropriate productive assets for investors desiring income and stability of principal.

Second, your productive assets must be growing faster than your liabilities. If this is not the case, your net worth will actually decline, and you will be losing rather than gaining wealth. Credit card debt and high-interest bank loans are the worst liabilities to have since (1) they are often used to buy nonproductive, personal assets that will not contribute to long-term growth in net worth and (2) few investment portfolios can be constructed to earn a rate of return higher than the typical rate of interest on credit cards and other consumer loans. To increase your net worth and reach your financial objectives, liabilities should be taken only if they are used to finance productive assets and if they have an interest rate lower than the expected rate of return on your productive assets. If your net worth analysis shows substantial high cost debt, your best investment decision is to eliminate that debt before making other investments.

A final, useful analysis is the **DE**bt for **A**sset **D**emand (D.E.A.D.). This is calculated by dividing assets by liabilities. This ratio will show you how likely you are to borrow to accumulate assets. For instance, a D.E.A.D. of .65 means that 65 percent of your assets were accumulated by borrowing rather than by cash. All things being equal, it is better to have a low D.E.A.D., as this indicates minimal interest-bearing liabilities and faster growth in net worth. That being the case, it should be an investment-planning objective to reduce your D.E.A.D. This can be accomplished by reducing high cost debt and by accumulating productive assets.

The second valuable financial summary is a Statement of Income and Expense. This is simply your monthly expenses subtracted from your monthly income. This statement will help you determine the surplus funds you have available for investment purposes. Careful scrutiny of your expenses will often uncover unnecessary uses of funds that can be used for investing. In investing, little things can mean a lot. Because of the compounding earning power of money, even small amounts of surplus cash can grow to a substantial amount. An investment of an extra $100 per month can become $100,000 in twenty years in a portfolio set up to earn just under 11 percent per year.

Where Are You Going?

The two summary statements—Statement of Net Worth and Statement of Income and Expense—will show you where you are now. The next step in portfolio planning is to assess where you desire to go. This is simply a matter of listing your specific financial objectives—retirement, education expenses, housing, and so on. Estimating how much money you will need to fund your goals is obviously crucial to good planning. However, a critical aspect of your wish list is that you estimate when you will need money for these objectives. How much time you have until you need the money will determine how much risk you can afford to take in investing for these goals. This risk, modified by your Investor Profile, will guide you to the appropriate type of portfolio you should construct.

If your financial goals are less than one year away, they are *immediate*. Your portfolio should have virtually no risk, even if you are a higher risk personality. You need to have absolute certainty as to how much money you will have to fund your goals and have no time to recover from any loss of principal. Therefore, stability of principal, rather than growth of principal should be your only portfolio consideration.

If your financial goals are one to five years away, they are *short-term*. Your portfolio should have low to moderate risk, depending upon your personality. While some level of certainty is needed, with up to five years to fund your goals there is time to recover from investment losses as long as they are not too large. While stability of principal is still a primary concern, growth can be an important secondary consideration. A short-term portfolio should be weighted toward bond and money market funds, and low risk equity funds. The level of equity funds in your portfolio will depend on time and your risk profile.

If your financial goals are more than five years away, they are *long-term.* Your portfolio should have as much risk as your personality will allow. Because your goals are more than five years away, appreciation of principal is usually the method by which you will achieve your objectives. This will generally weight your portfolio more heavily to stock mutual funds for a greater rate of return. For holding periods of greater than five years, most of the volatility and uncertainty associated with the stock market is minimized. Since 1940, the stock market has not lost money in any five-year period, and stocks have outperformed bonds nearly 80 percent of the time. For longer investment periods, the advantages of the equity market are even more dramatic. For thirty-year periods since 1929, stocks have outperformed bonds 95 percent of the time, while providing investors with five times the return. For long-term investors the message is clear: Take as much risk as your personality will allow. In chapter 6, we will explore why this is true and how to use the stock market to enlarge your net worth easily and successfully. However, regardless of your needs and time horizon, you will only be able to successfully implement a plan that is consistent with your individual temperament and current financial fitness.

STATEMENT OF NET WORTH

ASSETS	LIABILITIES
LIQUID (Nonretirement accounts)	**HOUSING LOANS**
Checking Account_____	Primary Residence Mortgage_____
Savings Account_____	Second Mortgage_____
Money Market_____	Vacation Home Mortgage _____
CDs _____	Investment Property Loan_____
Stocks_____	
Bonds _____	**INSTALLMENT LOANS**
Mutual Funds_____	Bank Loans_____
Life Insurance (Cash Value) _____	Car Loans_____
Other _____	Student Loans_____
NONLIQUID	**CREDIT CARDS** _____
Retirement Accounts	
IRAs_____	**OTHER LOANS**_____
401K _____	
Annuities_____	
Other _____	
Real Estate (Resale Value)	
Primary Residence _____	
Vacation Property_____	
Investment Property _____	
Personal Assets (Resale Value)	
Car_____	
Collectibles _____	
Jewelry_____	
Furniture _____	
Clothing_____	
Other _____	

TOTAL ASSETS _____   **TOTAL DEBTS** _____

NET WORTH _____   **LIQUID ASSETS** _____
(Assets minus Liabilities)

PRODUCTIVE ASSETS_____
(Total Assets minus Personal Assets)

DEbt for Asset Demand (D.E.A.D.) ___%
(Liabilities divided by Assets)

EXPECTED RATE OF RETURN   INTEREST RATE ON
ON PRODUCTIVE ASSETS ___%   INSTALLMENT LOANS ___%

Chart 4.2

STATEMENT OF INCOME AND EXPENSE "BUDGET"

INCOME (after-tax)

Salary———————————

Rental Income ———————

Interest Income ———————

Dividend Income—————————

Other Income ———————

EXPENSES

1. Housing
   - Mortgage/Rent——————
   - Maintenance ———————
2. Food ———————
3. Auto
   - Loan ———————
   - Maintenance ———————
4. Utilities———————
5. Insurance———————
6. Loans
   - Major———————
   - Installment ———————
   - Credit Card———————
   - Other———————
7. Entertainment———————
8. Clothing———————
9. Medical ———————
10. Miscellaneous ———————

NET MONTHLY INCOME——— **NET MONTHLY EXPENSE**———

NET MONTHLY SURPLUS

(Income minus Expense) ———————

NEED/WANT RATIO—————

(Mandatory expenses divided by discretionary expenses)

Chart 4.3

He who knows others is learned. He who knows himself is wise.

LAO TSE, *The Art of Worldly Wisdom* (1647)

Learn what you are and be such.

PINDAR, *Odes* (5th B.C.)

Full wise is he that himselven knowe.

CHAUCER, "The Monk's Tale,"
The Canterbury Tales (1387–1400)

It is not enough to understand what we ought to be, unless we know what we are; and we do not understand what we are, unless we know what we ought to be.

T.S. ELIOT, "Religion and Literature" (1935)

INVESTOR PROFILE QUESTIONNAIRE

Instructions: Circle the answers that best describe you.

SECTION 1
INTUITION vs. SENSATION

1. I get more excited
   (a) thinking about the future.
   (b) thinking about what's happening right now.

2. In a group project I would choose
   (a) researching and designing.
   (b) making and delivering the product.

3. When I become excited about something new, I
   (a) want to hurry up or drop what I'm doing.
   (b) am content to finish what I am doing, especially if I'm eating.

4. I like
   (a) reading over doing.
   (b) doing over reading.

5. When I come across a new situation, I am more interested in
   (a) hearing more about it.
   (b) getting involved to see if I like it.

6. The mistake I am most inclined to make is
   (a) to symbolize realistic things.
   (b) to be too realistic about things.

7. People would say that I am more
   (a) imaginative and creative.
   (b) a "get-it-done" person.

8. I am more apt to enjoy
   (a) meditating by the ocean.
   (b) going sightseeing.

9. People would call me more
   (a) up-in-the-clouds.
   (b) down-to-earth.

SECTION 2
THINKING vs. FEELING

1. I am more persuaded by
   (a) facts.
   (b) meaning.

2. People would more often consider me
   (a) too hardhearted.
   (b) too kindhearted.

3. When arguing, I would rather end up being
   (a) right.
   (b) friends.

4. I am more pleased by
   (a) an enemy getting what he deserves.
   (b) the praise of an enemy.

5. Emotional situations
   (a) make me uncomfortable.
   (b) make me want to help.

6. Debate
   (a) excites me.
   (b) upsets me.

7. If a friend is hurt, I want to
   (a) help them.
   (b) hug them.

8. I care a lot more about
   (a) people learning.
   (b) people's feelings.

9. I prefer the quality of
   (a) justice.
   (b) mercy.

Chart 4.4

SECTION 3
JUDGER vs. PERCEIVER

1. I prefer to have things
   (a) settled.
   (b) open for change.

2. I really like
   (a) reminder lists.
   (b) spontaneous ideas.

3. I would prefer
   (a) to be told what someone likes to have done.
   (b) to be able to choose the way to do it.

4. I like more
   (a) traditional things.
   (b) changing things.

5. I can be counted on to
   (a) faithfully "carry on."
   (b) "fight" organization.

6. I prefer
   (a) schedules.
   (b) free time.

7. Imposed order
   (a) helps me.
   (b) makes me "antsy."

8. Time is something that
   (a) I am always aware of.
   (b) I seem to lose track of.

9. Decision-making
   (a) is natural for me.
   (b) is not too easy for me.

10. Being the "boss" is fun if I
    (a) can efficiently carry out the decided mission.
    (b) can "do my own thing."

11. I am more apt to get stuck
    (a) by thinking "either/or."
    (b) waiting for too much information.

SCORING

For each section, count and record the number of occurrences for each response.

SECTION 1: A____   B____

SECTION 2: A____   B____

SECTION 3: A____   B____

Look at your SECTION 1 score. If you have more A's than B's, write "N" on the **first** line below. If you have more B's than A's, write "S."

If your first letter below is "N," go to SECTION 2. If you have more A's than B's, write "T" on the **second** line below. If you have more B's than A's, write "F."

If your first letter below is "S," go to Section 3. If you have more A's than B's, write "J" on the **second** line below. If you have more B's than A's write "P."

_____   _____

(N or S)

Chart 4.5

Notes

1. *Luke 16:13*
2. *Luke 14:28-30*
3. *Proverbs 21:5*
4. *Proverbs 20:8*
5. *Proverbs 12:5*

Chapter Five

YOU MUST SAVE YOUR MONEY

DISHONEST MONEY DWINDLES AWAY, BUT
HE WHO GATHERS MONEY LITTLE
BY LITTLE MAKES IT GROW
(PROVERBS 13:11)

> Bonnie is fifty-five. She's never really saved money. She's always had enough to get her what she wants, but there never seems to be any left over. There's some money in the bank but it's just earned interest and hasn't really grown over the years. Now she's thinking about retiring in ten years but is concerned about having enough money to do so. She knows she needs more money but doesn't know how to go about getting it with so little time left. She tried budgeting but couldn't keep up with tracking her expenses, so she gave up.

Saving money is the cornerstone of personal finance. Until one learns how to spend less than their income, they will never have the funds to achieve any long-term personal financial objectives. Not saving, of course, puts the quality of their financial stewardship in extreme jeopardy. The inability to save money may result in the inability to complete much of God's will for one's finances. A dollar saved can be put to many uses, but a dollar spent is gone forever.

The Bible addresses the issue of saving money in a direct manner: "In the house of the wise are stores of choice food and oil, but a foolish man devours all he has" (Prov. 21:20). In a

81

prior chapter we addressed the issue of wisdom being reflected in one's actions. One such wise action is the storing up of food and oil, which obviously would be available in times of need. On the other hand, the foolish person consumes all that he has. Living completely in the present, he seeks to maximize his current welfare potentially at the risk of his future well-being.

Foolishness—The Opposite of Wisdom

To assist our understanding of wisdom, we should momentarily digress and explore the opposite of wisdom, foolishness. Since wisdom is known by its actions, we can assume that foolishness can be determined in the same way. This will allow us to see into which category our financial decisions best fit. Knowing the difference between wisdom and foolishness will add considerably to our ability to be faithful financial stewards.

The implication throughout Scripture is that a fool acts out of conceit, arrogance, or pride. In the world's eyes, foolishness is equated with stupidity and lack of intelligence. However, in God's eyes a fool is a person deficient in judgment rather than someone of inferior intellect. Foolishness is equated to moral deficiency or lack of character. It is interesting, and no coincidence, that the Scripture's greatest use of the word "fool" is in the Proverbs of Solomon, the wisest and wealthiest man who ever lived. Obviously he believed part of the blueprint for successful living was in our discernment between wise and foolish actions. In his writings, both in Proverbs and Ecclesiastes, Solomon described foolishness as a way of life that is alluring to the immature but leading to eventual ruin. There are ten characteristics of foolishness, each of which has implications to our financial stewardship.

A fool does not concentrate on what is right.[1] Loss of focus undermines our financial stewardship. When we are unclear as to what we should be about, we are less likely to achieve God's will for our finances. Wise people concentrate on aligning their goals with God's.

A fool takes no delight in understanding.[2] Predictions are useless. Anyone who believes wholeheartedly in them fails to understand that nobody can predict the future.

A fool delights in his corrupt behavior[3], hates knowledge[4], and does not fear God.[5] The fool's lack of direction and complacency will be his downfall.[6] This is the natural consequence of a life not directed by God. Fools walk to their own destruction by not planning for the future and allowing their self-satisfaction to lull them into unawareness of life's pitfalls.

A fool can cause the downfall of others.[7] Again, recall from chapter 3 the wisdom of contrary thinking. The company of the financially wise will be smaller in number but greater in power and results. Fools are uninformed.[8] Not only is a fool uninformed, his views are often quarrelsome.[9] A fool has no regard for family.[10] Supporting one's family is arguably the highest godly use of money.

Saving as Preparation for Hardship

Given that Solomon spent so much energy in defining foolishness, it is imperative that we see the importance of saving money with regard to financial stewardship. One of the differences between the financial ways of the wise and the foolish is that the wise steward saves money. It is in vogue among Christians to blame liberal politicians and social activists for the moral and economic decline of our country. What is interesting is that typical Americans have by far the lowest personal savings rate among their peers in other industrialized countries. While we periodically vote for morality at the ballot box, we continuously undermine the impact of our votes at the money box. If we cannot avoid the temptation to devour all that we have, how can we expect elected officials to avoid doing the same? We are merely reaping what we have sown. If we are not saving money, we need to evaluate our lifestyle and financial decisions to clearly understand why this is so. We then need to further demonstrate wisdom by seeking God's direction for how to increase our ability to save money.

If saving is wise, then it must have some benefits to those who practice this principle. We know that God in His omniscience asks of us only those things that promote our welfare, even if we can't see that at the time (one of the many reasons why He's God and we're not!). The reason we save is to be able to meet unexpected needs. Often these needs come as a result of a particular hardship. Christians, even those who practice the highest level of fiscal responsibility, are not immune to financial hardship. In fact, we should expect it.[11] Good stewardship therefore requires an expectation of periods of financial stress. We, like the fool, can neither complacently ignore the possibilities of the future nor assume that our God-fearing attitudes will preclude us from danger. If we wisely expect difficulty, then we should wisely prepare ourselves to minimize their impact. To rely on God to bail us out without first taking the proper precautions is to tempt God. "Jesus answered [Satan], 'It is also written: "Do not put the Lord your God to the test" ' " (Matt. 4:7). We must act before God reacts.

The principle of saving as preparation for financial hardship is best seen in the story of Joseph (Gen. 41:41-57). In fact, there are a number of financial principles demonstrated in this story. Given a vision by God of an impending disastrous famine, Joseph, acting as Pharaoh's steward, set about preparing for seven years of hardship. His wisdom was God-given as is the source of all wisdom (chap. 2). The only way to prevent starvation and the complete devastation of Egypt's prosperity was through careful planning (chap. 4). However, his plan would have been worthless if it had not been turned into action (chap. 1). The essence of the plan was to *save* enough food during seven years of abundance to sustain them through the coming seven years of hardship.

Clearly, divine intervention was ultimately responsible for the survival of Egypt and the surrounding lands during this time. However, it is no accident that Joseph was the man chosen for the job. While we saw that Joseph was given the problem in advance, his solution was a model of wise financial decision-making according to biblical principles. Should we be surprised? After all, Joseph's father was Jacob and his great-grandfather was Abraham. Both of these men had great wealth along with a tradition of generous giving to the Lord prior to the law, which required it. Isaac, Joseph's grandfather, surely learned good financial management skills from his father Abraham and passed them on to his son Jacob. This is a family of faithful financial stewards.

However, we don't need to have prophetic visions to mobilize us to save. What Pharaoh saw in Joseph was not just skill in interpreting dreams, but a man "in whom is the spirit of God" (v. 38). We may not be stewards for a king, but we are servants of *the* King, and our lives need to reflect the life of the King within us. Frugality for the purpose of future provision is one such way the Spirit of God can be seen within us.

The Wise Use of Abundance

Solomon gave us a wonderful model of fiscal responsibility: "Go to the ant, you sluggard; consider its ways and be wise! It has no commander, no overseer or ruler, yet it stores its provisions in summer and gathers its food at the harvest" (Prov. 6:6-8). "Ants are creatures of little strength, yet they store up their food in the summer" (30:25). The lowly ant, one of God's smallest creations, has no master to be accountable to. Yet it knows enough to save during the abundance of harvesttime so that it will have food to eat in the winter. The ant lives in constant preparedness, not complacency. If it were like the fool of Proverbs 21:20, it would devour all that it has and then starve. Every year the little ant lives out the wisdom and experience of Joseph through its energetic and economical applications of God's principles.

The use of creating abundance through savings is God's principle for managing unexpected financial needs. This is true whether the need is as substantial as a costly medical procedure or as ordinary as a car repair. God expects those needs to be met through the use of savings. We may not be able to meet every unexpected financial burden ourselves, but to meet none is to be living beyond our means.

Recall from chapter 3 that God's "Economic Platform" is a form of financial equality (2 Cor. 8:13-15). It has always been God's intention for needs to be met through shared abundance. When we have the ability to meet the needs of others through the sharing of our resources, we have a responsibility to do so. Likewise, the resources of others should meet our extraordinary needs. However, this can occur only when first, resources are saved, and second, resources are shared or given. Your savings ability will limit your sowing capability.

The Danger of Excess Savings

While saving money is a fundamental and necessary stewardship principle, it is possible to save and still be a poor steward. Just as spending all of our money is foolish, so too is hoarding it. Hoarding is the accumulation of wealth as an end to itself. Like excess spending, at the root of hoarding are selfish motives. Money is being used primarily to satisfy the needs of one individual. Any uses outside of oneself are regarded as secondary.

A stern warning against hoarding can be found in the Parable of the Rich Fool (Luke 12:13-21). The rich fool's only concern was how to store his increasing wealth. At no time did he think of who could be helped by his wealth. In fact, in just three verses (vv. 17-19) he referred to himself with the word "I" six times. God, however, was not impressed with his selfish plans and rebuked him for being rich in money but poor toward Him.

Saving money can be wise, but we must be on our guard against financial foolishness. Saving will provide the foundation of a solid financial future. Our savings will provide security, comfort, and the funds to meet long-term financial objectives. However, we must keep these things in their proper perspective. Ultimately, it is God who is our safety net, not our money. Furthermore, accumulating money as an end to itself not only is idolatry—for the love of God is the only real end—but also it is a trap that separates us from God and others. The clear message of Scripture is that we must have heavenly goals for the funds that God has entrusted us with. Richness toward God means that our money will always be available for His purposes before ours. The key to saving money wisely is to always remember that all that we have belongs to God, not us. If saving money either replaces our faith or hinders us from giving generously or showing compassion to others, then we must reorganize our priorities to put our life into its proper perspective.

Saving Requires Discipline Not Money

Faithful stewardship in saving money requires us to strike a balance between spending it all and saving it all. Given a choice, most people would love to struggle with having too much savings. In reality overspending and saving no money is what most people face. For Christians, this is especially unfortunate given that we can so easily pray for wisdom when faced with spending decisions.

Because of God's Spirit, *we already have discipline* (2 Tim. 1:7). By following God's leading each day, particularly in the area of money, we can more naturally exhibit this gift of self-discipline. Unfortunately, we let too many other self-imposed barriers stand in the way, like our spirit of timidity or fear. Paul said that God did *not* give us that spirit.[12]

One of the ways that this spirit of timidity adversely affects us is our unwillingness to save because we believe we can't accumulate a meaningful amount. "It takes money to make money" is the old saying. However, the old saying doesn't say how *much money* it takes to make money. Fortunately, the Bible gives us the answer: "He who gathers money little by little makes it grow" (Prov. 13:11). God is in the habit of making little things into big things. David killed Goliath with one stone. A widow's jar became an oil well. Jesus fed 5,000 with five loaves of bread and two fishes. In these cases, as well as many others, the people involved acted on faith that God could accomplish miraculous results. It would be wrong to demand or expect certain financial rewards for obediently saving money. However, it is even more wrong not to save based upon self-generated limitations of what we think our small sums can accomplish. Demanding from God may hurt only ourselves but limiting God may affect countless others. Nearly 5,000 people would have gone hungry if Jesus had decided that the food the disciples gathered was a meaningless amount. Good stewards worry about their actions, not the imagined impact.

Ray's Ways to Save More Money

Make Saving Money a Priority
with the "Non-budget" Budget

Let's be honest. Spirit of self-discipline or not, the idea of living on a monthly budget is revolting. I realize that there are numerous excellent financial advisers who strongly recommend managing your expenses through a monthly spending plan. The argument is that budgets are freeing rather than enslaving because they give you peace of mind knowing that your expenses are under control. However, budgets are like diets in that they are started with a great deal of enthusiasm and energy which eventually wanes and dies. Tracking your expenses on a consistent basis is more effort than most people care to expend. Furthermore, the guilt that usually accompanies the occasional (or frequent) breaking of the budget guidelines is itself enslaving. There is a way to achieve all of the same goals as a detailed budget, yet requires less effort and is a lot more fun. I call it the "Non-budget" Budget.

The non-budget budget has three simple steps:

(1) *Pay* God first by determining an appropriate regular giving level.

(2) *Pay* yourself next by determining an appropriate savings level.

(3) *Spend* the rest on bills and yourself.

It really is that simple. However, the real beauty of the non-budget budget is not its simplicity but its effortlessness. Once you set up this plan it runs virtually on autopilot. Let's look at each of the steps in further detail.

"Pay" God First by Determining an Appropriate Regular Giving Level

"Honor the Lord with your wealth, with the firstfruits of your crops; then your barns will be filled to overflowing" (Prov. 3:9-10). Unlike the government, God does not impose taxes on us. Even though our money is His, we are free to make our own decisions in using it. However, He would prefer that we honor Him with a portion of our money before we use it anywhere else. Our willingness to give to God moves Him to give back to us. Look at the promise associated with Proverb 3:10. In exchange for the first part of what goes into the barn, God gives back so much that "your barns will be filled to overflowing"! Review the promises associated with giving in chapter 3. It should be no wonder to anyone why the non-budget budget starts with giving. While it would seem to be a paradox that saving money starts with giving, we must always remember that "one man gives freely, yet gains even more; another withholds unduly, but comes to poverty" (Prov. 11:24).

"Pay" Yourself Next by Determining an Appropriate Savings Level

Your willingness to pay God first is recognition on your part that God is more important than you. After your regular giving, you should immediately set aside whatever you've determined to be the right amount of savings. This of course raises the question: What is the right amount of savings? You will have to do some work to figure out what is the right amount for you. It will vary from person to person depending on your unique personal and financial circumstances. We all may desire to be faithful stewards, but we differ in income, cost of living, family size, and financial objectives. Still, there are some general guidelines and benchmarks that will point you in the right direction.

First, you should have specific financial objectives that your savings will be used for. This was discussed in chapter 4. Then set as a goal to save 10 to 15 percent of your income. That may be difficult or even impossible in the beginning. That's OK, but you won't know what is possible until you do the spending analysis in chapter 4. One of the goals of this analysis is to find where the nonessential expenditures are. Your starting point is the elimination of unnecessary spending plus the amount that your income exceeds your expenses. Don't be disappointed if this is significantly below 10 percent. The point is to get started. Something is better than nothing, and don't forget that God is in the habit of making mountains out of molehills. In a moment, we'll look at ways of increasing this amount.

The next guideline is to accumulate savings until you can establish an emergency fund. An emergency fund is just what the name implies. It is a reserve fund that will be used to handle unanticipated expenses, typically home and auto repairs and health expenses. This fund will be used only for emergencies, so this part of the non-budget budget will require some discipline. The size of this fund will vary depending on your personal situation. Financial planners generally advise having three to six months of income in an emergency fund. Unfortunately, financial planners have primarily higher income clients who can afford to pay one month of the average person's salary just to get a basic financial plan. The average person needs more of their income to meet basic living expenses than the affluent. Therefore, they will have a lower capability to achieve the three- to six-month guideline.

This is not to suggest that the guideline is inappropriate. On the contrary, since it is prudent, we should make a strong effort to get there. The idea behind having as much as six months of income in reserve is that this amount will handle virtually every conceivable emergency. On the other hand, having less does not make you a poor steward. In reality, many emergencies can probably be managed with one month's income in reserve. Any additional money in reserve increases your security, but not necessarily by a meaningful amount. As with giving, the size of the emergency savings fund is not the issue. The real issue is recognizing the need for a reserve fund. "A prudent man sees danger"[13] and prepares for it out of knowledge."[14] Each person will have to decide what is best based on his or her temperament and circumstances.

In your analysis of your spending patterns, you may find that some unexpected expenses occur with such regularity that they should be categorized as regular expenses. Perhaps you have an older car or house that is constantly in need of repair. Your family may have ongoing medical problems. If they are frequent but their occurrence cannot be anticipated, they should also become part of your emergency fund. While the timing of the need may be in doubt, the source of funds for those needs should not be. Naturally, whenever emergency funds are used, the next priority is to continue to direct savings into the fund to replenish it.

Spend the Rest on Bills and Yourself

Finally, we get to the good part! Before you go off writing checks, reflect for a moment on how you got to this point. Instead of paying bills, having some fun, and then worrying about how to come up with the cash to put in the collection plate, much less in the bank, we've done the exact opposite. We've first taken care of the most important things—at least, they should be the most important things—instead of last. "First things first" is not a Bible verse, but it still represents wisdom in action. If you agree that taking care of your giving and your saving are high priorities, then the non-budget budget is a great financial strategy.

Before you go off like the prodigal son and blow what's left, let's remember that the whole point of this strategy is good financial stewardship. Therefore, you are still accountable for how you spend the rest. We need to find a middle ground between enjoying what we have and meeting godly objectives other than giving and saving. Enjoyment of life is a gift from God.[15] However, we must at all times be ready to meet the needs of others, especially family. Therefore, I advise periodically examining your spending habits. Go through your checkbook, look at each expense, and honestly assess whether they are justifiable in the light of faithful stewardship. D.L. Moody once said, "I can tell more about a man by looking through his checkbook than I can by going through his prayerbook." Do this exercise as often as you feel it is necessary. If you have a computer, this process can be greatly simplified by any one of a variety of checkbook software programs such as Quicken, Microsoft Money, or Managing Your Money. (This is not meant to be an endorsement of any of these programs. There are many other similar programs available.) These programs are relatively inexpensive and make a mundane, time-consuming task quick and fun. However, even if you must track your expenses manually, it needs to be done regardless of whether or not you use the non-budget budget.

It is important that you approach this assessment with an instructive rather than destructive attitude. The point is to learn something about the way that you are handling your resources, not to induce guilt feelings. If you feel that certain spending habits are nonproductive, then simply stop them and redirect that money somewhere else. Focus on what you are about to do with your money rather than what you didn't do. God has forgiven and forgotten your mistakes and is waiting to bless you once you get on the right track.

That's the non-budget budget. It's just three simple steps: give some, save some, spend the rest, and have some fun doing it. God wants you to.

Reduce Expenses without Reducing Lifestyle.

A second way to save more money is to try to live the life you're living now only cheaper. One of the biggest and most common financial mistakes is to focus all our attention on getting another dollar more rather than using a dollar less. While it is probably more appealing to have more money rather than use less, it is far less productive. Unfortunately, it is not true that a penny saved is a penny earned. The penny saved earns interest while the penny earned gets taxed! Furthermore, there are constraints on our ability to get more money. On the other hand, our ability to use less and achieve the same results is limited only by our own efforts, creativity, and imagination. Ultimately, reducing expenses is far more productive than making more money. For example, it may take an extra half-hour of grocery shopping to save $10 by using coupons and shopping at a discount store. But at today's interest and tax rates, it would take $500 one year to earn that same $10! Do I hear the sounds of grocery store coupons being clipped?

Reducing expenses without reducing lifestyle is the most effective way to create savings. The following list of suggestions is far from complete. Most of the strategies here I've personally used with extremely positive results. However, the results came not from expense reduction itself but by actually *saving* the money created by the lower expenses.

Reduce Credit Card Expense

As we'll see in chapter 8, the goal is really to eliminate credit card expense. But if you have them, they may as well cost you as little as possible. Get or switch to credit cards with the lowest interest you can find. We'll discuss credit cards in greater detail later, but the basic debt strategy is to minimize then eliminate. Take the money you save and put it into the storehouse.

Consolidate Loans into One Low-interest Loan

Taking out a new loan to pay off several loans can lower your total monthly payments, lower your interest expense, and pay off all the loans faster. What's not to like? Well, this takes discipline. We all may have a spirit of self-discipline, but for some of us the spirit is willing but the flesh is weak. The danger of this is that you may create a bigger problem than you had before if you are not able to stay out of debt. Loan consolidation is most appropriate for people who have fiscal restraint and a solid cushion of emergency funds. In reality, these people are the least likely to have enough debt to consolidate. They probably are also already saving enough money. Therefore, if you consider this strategy, take it as a warning that you need greater spending restraint, a greater emergency reserve, or both. Once you lower your payments, take the money you save and put it into the storehouse.

Lower Your Interest Expense with a Home Equity Loan

A home equity loan is probably the lowest-cost way to borrow money. A further advantage of this is that the interest payments are usually tax-deductible. Finally, since the payments are likely to be stretched out over fifteen years, the monthly payments will be substantially lower than the debts this loan replaced. Still, borrower beware! This is only for the disciplined for the same reasons as above with the added concern of having your house as collateral for the loan. From a purely financial standpoint, home equity loans make sense, but as Paul said, " 'Everything is permissible'—but not everything is beneficial. 'Everything is permissible'—but not everything is constructive" (1 Cor. 10:23). Take the money you save and put it into the storehouse.

Keep Your Car after It's Paid Off

Resist the temptation to get another car—and another car loan—right after the loan payments end. Don't use its age and maintenance costs as an excuse. Studies have shown that the cheapest car you can own is the one you already have. Take the money you save and put it into the storehouse, but also put some into the reserve fund to keep up with repairs.

Save Your Overtime and Premium Pay

Hopefully this money isn't needed to make ends meet. The temptation is to reward ourselves for our hard work with a spending spree. There's nothing wrong with this on occasion. Just make sure you give yourself some long-term rewards, not just immediate ones. Take the extra money you've earned and put it into the storehouse.

Save Your Extra Paychecks

If you're on a monthly budget, you'll get two extra paychecks per year when you get paid biweekly and four when paid weekly. Take the extra money and put it into the storehouse.

Trim Your Spending by 2 to 3 Percent

It's a small enough amount that you might not even notice the difference.

Adjust Your Income Tax Withholding to Raise Your Take-home Pay and Lower Your Tax Refund

This, of course, assumes that you will have a tax refund. Take the extra money and put it into the storehouse.

Adjust Your Income Tax Withholding to Lower Your Take-home Pay and Raise Your Tax Refund

If you are going to adjust your withholding, it is better financially to trim your spending by 2 to 3 percent and earn the interest all year than wait for a big refund check. Some people are philosophically opposed to letting the government borrow their money interest free. However, I have to admit that I like the feeling of getting a big check in the mail one day. It's also a method of forced savings for people with low self-discipline (that's not why I like it!). If you have a computer, there are a number of inexpensive tax software programs to help you fiddle with your withholding.

Save a Portion of Each Raise

Try to maintain your existing lifestyle even though you have higher income. Solomon knew the dangers of an escalating lifestyle. "Whoever loves money never has money enough; whoever loves wealth is never satisfied with his income. This too is meaningless" (Ecc. 5:10). Better yet, increase your giving and your saving whenever you get a raise.

Take the Maximum Possible Advantage of Employer-sponsored "Forced Savings" Plans

Many employers have retirement and company stock purchase plans that include matching funds from the employer. The plans may also include discounts for buying company stock. This is free money! There *is* such a thing as a free lunch! In particular, tax-deferred savings plans (401K, 403B) are the greatest financial invention of all time. Not only does your employer give you money, but also the government gives you money through lower taxes, and you get all this for doing something that you should be doing anyway—saving money. Even if what you can save in such plans is small, the employer matching and discounts are likely to be the greatest and most certain return on your money that you'll ever get. In later chapters we'll learn how to get even a greater return in these plans, but for right now just get in. It's financial foolishness not to.

By the way, I admit it—I am addicted to forced savings plans. Forced savings is essentially money that gets saved without action on your part. You don't see the money, so you don't spend it, at least right away. I love forced savings in conjunction with the non-budget budget since what you spend will be a function of what's left in your paycheck after giving and saving. Your spending will tend to adjust itself to whatever is in the paycheck.

Set up Your Own Forced Saving Plan with Automatic Withdrawal

Most employers will allow you to have deductions made from your paycheck to be deposited in the financial institution of your choice. If not, have money automatically withdrawn at regular intervals from your bank account to be deposited in another account. The idea is to have these deposits made automatically so that you are forced to adjust either to the money in your checking account or the money in your regular account. Ask your employer and your bank how to go about setting this up.

Use Christmas Clubs or Vacation Clubs to Save for Large Annual Expenses

This is another forced savings concept, typically available in credit unions. These accounts pay higher rates of interest although they do have penalties for early withdrawal. Money is deducted from your paycheck or bank account each pay period for a year. The money becomes available in time for Christmas or vacation. I have used Christmas Clubs to pay for Christmas gifts, year-end property taxes, *and* after-Christmas sales. Good stewardship not only is wise, but also can be a lot of fun!

Pay Cash as Often as Possible

Studies have shown that people who pay primarily with cash spend less money. It's harder to part with cash than to pull out a credit card.

Give Yourself an Allowance

Rather than spend everything that's left after giving, saving, and bill paying, limit yourself and your spouse to a weekly allowance that's enough to have fun while still being financially responsible.

Start an Empty-wallet Policy

If you have allowance money left at the end of the week, put it into the storehouse. Saving addict that I am, I go a step further. Every night I empty my spare change into a piggy bank. (OK, it's a big coffee jar, but you get the idea.) Every now and then I roll it up and off to the storehouse it goes. My wife thinks it's silly and childish. You probably do too. What isn't silly is the nearly $1,000 of exercise equipment that my childish habit paid for. I also bought a laptop computer. I've also caught my wife now secretly squirreling away money!

Don't Window-shop

If you do, don't take any money with you, especially a credit card. Even without money, window-shopping is dangerous because it creates desire.[16] Perhaps nobody has actually died from window-shopping (of course the verse is referring to spiritual rather than physical death), but there is no point in exposing yourself to desires that you can't afford to have. You won't want what you don't know exists.

Read How-to Books on Cutting Expenses

It goes without saying that you should: (1) borrow one from a library; (2) borrow one from a friend; and as a last resort, (3) buy your own copies but only in paperback from a discount bookstore. There are several good ones that are actually worth the small investment. *Cut Your Bills in Half* (Rodale Press) is one such book. Another is *The Tightwad Gazette* (Villiard Books) by penny-pinching legend Amy Dacyczyn.

The All-time Greatest Place to Save Money

"Leaving money on the table" is a business expression that means someone has not gotten the best deal possible when just a little more effort would have had a major effect on the outcome. Americans leave more money on the table at the grocery store than anywhere else. The books mentioned above have hundreds of creative food shopping ideas. However, you don't need the secrets of penny-pinching masters to cut your grocery bill. The basics will save you hundreds of dollars per year, and you already know what they are:

(1) Buy heavily used items in bulk.
(2) Check the ads for the best prices.
(3) Stock up on sale items, but only those that you normally use.
(4) The conveniently located stores are usually the most expensive. Take the time to go to the stores in less trafficked areas.
(5) Clip coupons. What a great country we live in! It is truly the land of opportunity when they give away money for cutting paper with scissors. Especially look for stores that offer double and triple value for the coupons.
(6) Buy only what you need. Make a list that focuses on

sale items and stick to it.
(7) Learn how to use unit prices.
(8) Prepare lower cost meals.

The problem isn't that people don't know how to do these things. The problem is that people don't want to take the time to do these things. That's a shame because the amount of money you save in relation to the time and effort necessary to reap those savings is huge. Despite adding another child to the family, we've cut $150 per month out of our grocery budget with no decrease in food quality or enjoyment. My wife says we actually eat better now than before. We spend perhaps an extra four hours per month checking ads, cutting coupons, making meal plans, and driving to different stores. At today's interest and tax rates it would take *$65,000* in the bank *one year* to earn the $1,800 per year we're saving. Alternatively, we'd have to find a part-time job that pays over $40 an hour. My belief is that no matter how hard you find it to save money, even for legitimate reasons, everyone can find savings at the grocery store — and stop leaving money on the table.

Reduce Lifestyle, Especially Those Areas that May Represent Poor Stewardship for You

It is far too judgmental for me to make a universal case for a reduced standard of living. I do think, however, that good stewardship requires us to make wise choices as to what an appropriate standard of living is. Since there is no uniform standard, we each have to make our own choices in that regard. God will hold us accountable for those choices. For some, a reduced lifestyle simply means giving up a third car, a summer beach house, or the annual ski trip. Others may face more difficult choices such as owning one car when two are needed, buying a smaller home, or relocating to a lower cost of living. Two excellent books that deal with the issue of lifestyle are *Freedom of Simplicity* by Richard J. Foster and *Descending into Greatness* by Bill Hybels. From personal experience at both ends of the spectrum I will say that fervent prayer and seeking God's will makes those decisions much easier to make.

Saving Your Money in the Right Places

Not to save money is a huge mistake. Putting your savings in the wrong place can be just as big. Don't automatically assume that you'll be using your bank as your storehouse. In fact, your bank is probably the *worst* place to store your money. Yes, it's convenient. Yes, it's safe because the principal is insured. The problem is that money in the bank is at risk of losing its purchasing power. Because of inflation, it will cost more to live in the future than it does now. If your earnings do not keep pace with inflation, your money is losing value. It will purchase less than it will now. Historically, bank accounts have paid a rate of interest that has rarely kept pace with inflation. In fact, if you deduct from your interest earnings the taxes you'll pay, you almost always lose money. Before you decide to use your friendly, neighborhood bank as your storehouse, look at chart 5.1. The column on the left shows various rates of inflation. Find the current rate of inflation—at this writing it's about 3 percent. Then look across to the column that shows your federal income tax bracket. The result is the interest you'll have to earn to maintain your purchasing power after inflation and taxes. Actually, you'll have to raise that slightly to account for

At this rate of inflation:	You need this rate of interest in these tax brackets to avoid losing money:		
	15%	28%	31%
2%	2.35%	2.78%	2.90%
3%	3.53%	4.17%	4.35%
4%	4.71%	5.56%	5.80%
5%	5.88%	6.94%	7.25%
6%	7.065%	8.33%	8.70%
7%	8.24%	9.72%	10.14%
8%	9.41%	11.11%	11.59%
9%	10.59%	12.50%	13.04%
10%	11.76%	13.89%	14.49%

Chart 5.1

state and local taxes. Remember, you're not actually losing money. In fact, you're making money by earning interest. Unfortunately, you are losing the value of your money since it will buy less than it did before you earned the interest. This is a financial tragedy, but one that most Americans experience every year of their lives.

Where you should keep your savings is a function of two things: (1) an acceptable rate of interest, one that will keep pace with inflation and taxes; and (2) how soon you need access to the money. This needs more explanation. Funds that you need instant access to should be handled differently than funds that you don't expect to use right away. Technically any form of savings is an investment. However, I like to refer to funds that won't be used for at least a year as investments and funds that will be used in less than a year as savings. The key difference between savings and investments is the rate of return that can be expected from each. The shorter the time frame, the lower the return. Likewise, the longer the money can be tied up, the higher the expected return. This is highly simplified but basically true. In chapter 6 we'll go into great detail on investing.

Because short-term savings earn such a low rate of interest, try to keep this amount to a minimum. Have enough on hand to pay bills, for an occasional splurge (so you won't have to charge it), and a portion of your emergency money. One or two month's salary should be enough, but your plan must account for your individual circumstances and comfort level. The rest of your emergency money can be invested at higher rates of interest. Here are some storehouses for your short-term money:

Bank Money Market Deposit Accounts (MMDA's)

They are insured, convenient, and pay a rate of interest that moves up or down depending on general interest rate levels. However, they often have restrictive conditions on minimum account size and may not pay any interest if your account drops below a certain level. More importantly, they rarely pay an acceptable rate of interest after taxes and inflation. If you can find one that pays decent interest and you can maintain the minimum account size, an MMDA is fine.

Passbook Savings Accounts

Everybody has one, but almost nobody needs one. The interest rates are far too low to make sense. Even if you need one to open a checking account, they're still borderline. It's probably better to find another bank.

Money Market Mutual Funds

This is the best choice. A money market fund is a pool of money provided by a large number of individuals. The pooled funds are used to buy top-quality short-term investments usually available only to large institutional investors like banks or pension funds. The pooling of money allows small individual investors to participate in instruments such as commercial paper—loans to major corporations—and large Certificates of Deposit of major banks. A professional with expertise in money markets manages the portfolio. Even after a small fee is paid to the manager, money market funds typically earn 1 to 1.5 percent more than MMDA's, and the rates float up and down based upon market conditions.

Money market funds do not carry federal deposit insurance like a bank account, but they are virtually risk free. There are hundreds of money market funds, but only one has ever lost investors money, and that was in 1979. If the need for additional safety is necessary, there are money market funds that invest only in securities of the U.S. government. The safety, however, will cost you. The rate on U.S. government money market funds is about .5 percent lower than regular money funds. That's $25 less per year in a $5,000 account. The insignificant difference in safety is not worth giving up interest for. If the other money market funds fail, the government probably has too.

For individuals in the highest tax brackets, there are tax-exempt money market funds. The interest earned is free from federal and in some cases state and local taxes. Before you rush out to get into one, the rates of interest are considerably lower than taxable money funds. They make sense only if you are in the highest tax bracket or in a lower bracket but in a state with high taxes. The formula for determining whether a tax-exempt fund is appropriate is: **interest rate ÷ (1 − your tax bracket)**. Compare the answer to the rates on taxable money market funds. If the tax-free formula is higher, buy it. If not, buy the taxable fund and pay the taxes on the interest. For example, if you're in the 28% federal tax bracket and are considering a tax-exempt fund paying 2.1%, the computation is: 2.1 ÷ (1 − .28) = 2.92. If you can find a taxable money market fund paying higher than 2.92%, you should invest in it.

Be on the lookout for "junk" money market funds. These funds invest in securities of lower quality than the better money funds. This will typically add a few percentage points of interest, but for the additional risk it's not worth it. An extra .2% on $5,000 is only $10 per year.

There are hundreds of money market funds to choose from. Don't necessarily go for the highest interest rate. Here are some simple guidelines for choosing:

Pick a Fund That's User-friendly

Look for money funds that have check-writing and minimum balance rules that fit your situation.

Pick a Fund That's Part of a Large Financial Organization

The strength of the company is the equivalent of deposit insurance.

Pick a Fund That's Part of a Family of Investments

Eventually you may want to move some of your money into other investments.

Pick a Fund That Invests in the Highest Quality Securities

If the fund invests in corporate commercial paper, it should be rated "P1" or "A," depending on the rating service the fund uses.

Pick a Fund with Low Expenses

Before the fund pays out the interest earned on its investments, it pays the fund manager and covers its operating expenses. Since most of the funds have similar investment styles, it's the fund's expenses that account for the difference in your return. All things being equal, it's better to choose a fund with the lowest expenses. However, all things are never equal. Expect to pay higher expenses for funds with extra convenience features and low minimum balance requirements. Some funds waive the expenses for a limited period of time to attract investors. Make sure you understand what they expect the expenses to be after this period ends. If they are too high, move on.

Where do you find out about the fund's expenses, investment quality, convenience features, and company background? In an incomprehensible document called the prospectus. The fund is required to send you its prospectus before you invest. In fact, you'll get one when you inquire about the fund. Wade your way carefully through it, looking especially for the items noted above. Just be prepared for an exercise in pain.

Almost every investment company, stockbroker, or insurance company has money market funds. If you're working with an investment professional, they'll have a money market fund available for you to buy. Here are three that meet the criteria above:

● Gradison Cash Reserves Trust (1-800-869-5999)
$1,000 minimum investment; $50 for additional purchases; free unlimited checkwriting.

● The Boston Company Cash Management Fund (1-800-343-0573)
$1,000 minimum investment; no minimum for additional purchases; free unlimited checkwriting.

● Invesco Cash Reserves Fund (1-800-525-8085)
$1,000 minimum investment; $50 for additional purchases; some restrictions on minimum balances and checkwriting; but easy access to the excellent Invesco family of investments.

Certificates of Deposit (CDs)
A CD is simply a bank deposit you make for a specified period of time, usually a month to five years. At the end of the period, called maturity, you get your money back plus interest. The rates are slightly better than many other savings vehicles. Most

people use these as their savings storehouse. Unfortunately, they are about as valuable as a savings outhouse. They are the most safe and secure way to lose money. Short-term CD rates usually don't beat inflation and taxes. Long-term CDs are easily outperformed by other investments. Unlike money market funds and MMDAs, the rates are fixed. That's great when you lock in a high rate when rates are dropping, but not so great if you lock in a low rate when rates are rising. If you're good enough to know when rate changes will occur, why are you reading this book? They don't give you instant access to your money unless you're willing to pay a penalty. However, they're great for banks that are all too happy to borrow money from you for a fixed time period and loan it back out at rates three to five times higher.

CDs are appropriate only if you have a known financial need that will occur when the CD matures and you want to be absolutely certain that the money will be there. In fact, if the need is less than five years away, this is the best way to fund them. Because the rates don't fluctuate, they may or may not provide the best return. Only time will tell. The biggest mistake people make with CDs is that they use them as long-term investments. This is absolutely the worst possible and unfortunately most common use of CDs.

Start Saving Now!

Don't think of saving money as an end in itself, for that is hoarding and the act of a financial fool. Know what you are saving for. Have clear goals and objectives for what you want your money to do for yourself and others. Whatever it is you decide to do, budget or non-budget, reduce expenses or reduce lifestyle, you need to do it NOW![17]

Don't assume that you can't save enough to make a difference. We make the choices, but God controls the outcome. What God blesses is the intent, not the amount. If you are not satisfied with the way you save money now, set some modest goals for yourself to start and continually pray that God will increase both your saving ability and capability as you show yourself faithful.[18]

Notes

1. Proverbs 17:24
2. Proverbs 18:2
3. Proverbs 10:23
4. Proverbs 1:22
5. Proverbs 1:29
6. Proverbs 1:32
7. Proverbs 13:20
8. Proverbs 14:7
9. Proverbs 18:6
10. Proverbs 17:25
11. James 1:2
12. Romans 8:15; 2 Timothy 1:7
13. Proverbs 22:3
14. Proverbs 13:16
15. Ecclesiastes 5:19
16. James 1:15
17. Proverbs 24:30-34
18. Luke 19:26

Chapter Six

You Must Multiply Your Money

THE MAN WHO HAD RECEIVED THE FIVE
TALENTS WENT AT ONCE AND PUT HIS MONEY
TO WORK AND GAINED FIVE MORE
(MATTHEW 25:16)

Frequently heard comments by people not making the most of their money:

I don't have enough money to invest.

I don't know anything about the stock market or the economy. I wouldn't even know how to figure out whether a company is a good or bad investment.

I don't have the time to invest my money. Who has time to read *The Wall Street Journal* and *Business Week?* Besides, I work. How can I keep track of what's going on in the stock market?

Investing seems too risky. I keep hearing that our economy is going to crash and we're going to have a depression.

The stock market is just gambling.

None of these excuses are viable reasons for not being an investor. Not only can anybody be an investor, anybody can be a successful investor, regardless of time, talent, or money. It's all right here . . .

Christians have traditionally had an aversion to investing. Many liken the financial markets to a form of legalized gambling. Scripture, however, does not support this view. Instead, the Bible directs us to multiply our resources.

Therefore, today's Christians are called to learn how to use the financial markets to further godly works. To not earn a reasonable rate of return on our financial resources is to ignore economic reality. As we saw in chapter 5, money saved in bank accounts earns interest below the rate of inflation. This means our money will buy less and less the longer we wait to spend it. As a result, our savings are being consumed rather than multiplied, even before we spend it. Before discussing the biblical injunctions on multiplying our money, I'd like to use Scripture to differentiate between gambling and investing.

The nature of gambling is inherently ungodly. It is gambling when you buy something of which you know nothing about.[1] It is an attempt to buy something of no tangible value in the hope of making a quick, substantial return.[2] Since the outcome is based upon random luck, no amount of effort can affect the results. "He who works his land will have abundant food, but the one who chases fantasies will have his fill of poverty" (Prov. 28:19). Finally, one who gambles does not bother to assess the risks involved.[3]

By contrast, investing involves an exchange of money for a tangible piece of property, like shares of stock, bonds, or real estate. Rather than pure luck, it is by our own efforts that we can make our investments increase in value. Wise investing requires *knowledge, caution, thoughtfulness,* and *a thorough understanding of the risks.*[4] Risk, of course, is the common element to both gambling and investing. *It is our response to risk, not the risk itself, that distinguishes gambling and investing.*

In the Parable of the Shrewd Manager, Jesus said, "The people of this world are more shrewd in dealing with their own kind than are the people of the light" (Luke 16:8). Christian hostility to investing proves this statement. That people can and do lose money investing does not make financial dealings evil. In fact, it is by our sinfulness that we place the blame for our lack of godly skills elsewhere.

I firmly believe that after giving, the next most important thing we can do with our money is multiply it to the fullest extent possible according to biblical principles. Why? Naturally, to increase our ability to give.

The Parable of the Sower tells us about "the man who hears the word and understands it. He produces a crop, yielding a hundred, sixty or thirty times what was sown" (Matt. 13:23). What is sown is the Gospel of salvation planted in our hearts. What is produced is the Gospel planted in the hearts of others as a result of our good works. Money allows the Gospel to be spread wider than any other human means. Not all of us are called to vocations of discipleship, ministry, or missions. Yet our generous giving allows churches to reach out to their local communities, establish ministries to feed and shelter the hungry and homeless, and support missionaries to share the Word in foreign lands. The more we give, the more others get. The more we can get, the more we can give.

The Parable of the Talents (Matt. 25:14-30) introduces accountability into the concept of multiplication. Like the sun and rain that make crops grow, it is our wisdom, skill, and faith that make our resources grow. Although we often blame the elements, God will still hold us accountable for our lack of production. As with the crops, God has provided the necessary tools for us to multiply our financial assets. He therefore expects results commensurate with the tools He has provided.

Accountability is critical because not only are we caretakers, but also we are consumers. We are required to spend money just to meet the minimal needs of food, shelter, clothing, and transportation. What good is our stewardship if we consume more than we produce? Since God expects a return of His assets, we must earn a return on our assets. In other words, we must multiply them.

Three parables — the Parable of the Sower (Matt. 13:1-23), the Parable of the Talents (25:14-30), and the Parable of the Ten Minas (Luke 19:11:27) — work together to deal with the issue of attitude with respect to financial stewardship. In the Parable of the Talents, the obedient servants who doubled their master's assets were praised for being "good and faithful." The servant who failed was found to be "wicked and lazy." He was given the least to manage due to his inferior skills relative to the other two servants. In spite of his lack of ability, he was still severely punished. Apparently his lack of skill was not an allowable excuse for his failure to add to his master's wealth.

In the Parable of the Ten Minas, we see that three servants were given ten minas (a mina was about three month's wages) to manage. One servant earned ten minas, another five, the last none. The first two servants were rewarded in proportion to their earnings. This seems to support the idea in the Parable of the Sower that even good soil will produce different amounts: thirty-, sixty-, or a hundredfold. The important point is that our hearing and understanding of the Word produces something meaningful. However, like the wicked servant in the Parable of the Talents, the third servant in the Parable of the Ten Minas was punished for producing nothing.

The wicked servant failed because he thought that his job was too hard and was afraid to put his money to work. He implied that his master was owed only the original sum and not more. He is a specific example of what was referred to in the Parable of the Sower as "the man who hears the word, but the worries of this life" make him unfruitful (Matt. 13:22). The point is that our fears do not justify inaction. The wicked servant was more concerned with avoiding his master's punishment than receiving his praise. Aside from fear, our lack of action implies a lack of faith. Faith "comes from hearing the message, and the message is heard through the word of Christ" (Rom. 10:17). According to the Parable of the Sower, this word, if understood, results in a thirty-, sixty-, or hundredfold yield. (Matt. 13:23)

The clear message of the three parables is that poor skills on our part do not justify merely maintaining what has been given us to produce abundance. He has already given us the ability to learn. Furthermore, He has given us a spirit of sonship, which entitles us to divine guidance from the Holy Spirit. With these tools, some will multiply a hundredfold, some thirtyfold. But all of us must produce something.

It is also clear that lack of funds, like lack of skill, is not an acceptable excuse. The servant with only two talents went about his task just as sincerely as the one with five talents. Each was given what he could handle and each was required to earn some-thing, even if they had just "put [the] money on deposit with the bankers" so that the master "would have received it back with interest" (25:27). However, we must recognize the reality that in today's economy interest isn't enough. After inflation, money in a bank account or other conservative investment will not multiply itself. However, what is also a reality is that even a small amount of money, if invested properly, can become a large amount of money given enough time. We see that in Matthew 25:19, in which the necessary time was allowed, "After a long time, the master of those servants returned and settled accounts with them." In any case, God has a habit of taking small things and making them large things, for His own behalf and on behalf of those with faith. David struck down Goliath with one small stone. Simon Peter, after not catching anything all night, let down his net on Jesus' suggestion and caught so many fish that the net began to break. We cannot forget that Jesus fed 5,000 with just two fish and a loaf of bread. After multiplying the widow's oil, Elisha fed 100 with twenty loaves of bread and some heads of grain (2 Kings 4:42-44).

While we should be satisfied with doing our best, our best will be achieved only if we desire and strive for, figuratively speaking, a hundredfold multiplication. Our goal should not be merely to produce but to produce abundantly. Ambition is both praiseworthy and noble when its goal is to serve others rather than self and when it is subordinate to the will of God. The final lesson in the Parable of the Talents and the Parable of the Ten Minas is that God's gifts are transferable. Blessings are bestowed upon those who are worthy in heart and in deed.[5] God will deal with us according to the fruits of our financial stewardship. Therefore, we must learn to multiply our resources according to godly principles.

A Real Worldview of the Economy

I am of the opinion that Christians are unrealistically pessimistic on economic matters. I find that far too many have a "Chicken Little" ("the sky is falling, the sky is falling") mentality when it comes to the economy. This concerns me because belief in an economic apocalypse as it relates to end times usually results in poor financial stewardship.

End time interest has been around for a long time, probably

even before the Prophet Joel wrote nearly 3,000 years ago, "Let all who live in the land tremble, for the day of the Lord is coming. It is close at hand—a day of darkness and gloom" (Joel 2:1-2). It particularly took hold in the 1970s when *The Late, Great Planet Earth* became a best-seller. The notion of a looming economic apocalypse gained further credence with *The Coming Economic Earthquake,* another best-selling book. Both of these books are credible works, written by well-known Christian authors. While it is not my intent to be a literary critic, I can say as a student of market history that books on imminent financial disaster flourish during poor economic times. The forecasts of the end have always been—let's be charitable—premature. For example:

● *The Late, Great Planet Earth* was widely read in the 1970s, a period that contained two severe bouts of double-digit inflation and two recessions.

● *Crisis Investing* was a #1 bestseller in 1980 during an economic recession year. This book predicted a depression in 1983 and that the first half of the 1980s would be the worst period in investment history. The good news is that the depression never came. The bad news is that the author and his followers missed out on the greatest stock market boom in history!

● *How to Prosper during the Coming Bad Years* was once the biggest bestseller in financial history. It too was written during the inflationary '70s. The fact that the bad years never came didn't stop the author from trying again with *Survive and Win in the Inflationary Eighties,* no doubt inspired by the 1980 recession. We all managed to survive, no thanks to the writer's predictions, but the fact is that inflation was virtually nonexistent throughout the 1980s.

● The 1987 stock market crash made a *New York Times* #1 best-seller out of *The Great Depression of 1990,* whose author admitted he had previously predicted a depression

111

would occur in 1980. If at first you don't succeed, try, try again.

• Most recently, the 1990 recession brought us books such as *The Coming Economic Earthquake* and *Bankruptcy, 1995*. In Canada, economic hard times gave birth to *The Great Reckoning*. (Incredibly, on the same day as I wrote this section of my book, I received a direct mail solicitation from one of the authors along with his booklet *The Plague of the Black Debt — How to Survive the Coming Depression*.)

My problem with these prediction books is not that their economic forecasts are wrong 99 percent of the time. The issue is that they prey upon our innate fear of an unknown future. Our fears make it easy for us to succumb to the kind of negative thinking these books perpetuate and given credibility by the bad economic surroundings that inspired them. This fear paralyzes people into behaving inappropriately with their money. For Christians this is especially dangerous since we are called to use our assets for the benefit of others, not self-preservation. Remember, Jesus said, "Therefore do not worry about tomorrow, for tomorrow will worry about itself. Each day has enough trouble of its own" (Matt. 6:34). Planning for tomorrow is prudent but worrying about tomorrow is to lack trust in God. We cannot let our concern with presumed catastrophes tomorrow affect our stewardship today.

In any case, there is no known investment strategy for a complete financial meltdown. Forget gold, cash, being debt-free, or whatever the experts passionately exhort you to protect yourself with. The social chaos that would accompany a major economic upheaval would render financial concerns meaningless. Anybody who has visited the old USSR or Eastern Europe after the breakup of the Soviet Union will testify that basic day-to-day survival is all that anyone is worried about. If you had anything of financial value, it wouldn't last very long, and the fact that you had money (or gold bullion, silver coins, and so on) would just put your life in severe danger.

Even if someone uses Scripture to support their view of a coming financial upheaval "do not forget this one thing, dear friends: With the Lord a day is like a thousand years, and a thousand years are like a day" (2 Peter 3:8). We cannot use our lifetimes to prepare for something that may occur outside of our lifetimes, even if these dire forecasts turn out to be true. Jesus said to be prepared for His return not by protecting ourselves but by continually using our resources to care for others and work for the kingdom. "Who then is the faithful and wise servant, whom the master has put in charge of the servants in his household to give them their food at the proper time? It will be good for that servant whose master finds him doing so when he returns" (Matt. 24:45-46).

If I accept that, the fact remains that "No one knows about that day or hour, not even the angels in heaven, nor the Son, but only the Father" (Matt. 24:36). From the standpoint of being a good and faithful servant found doing the master's work until He comes, your end time philosophy should not affect your investment strategy!

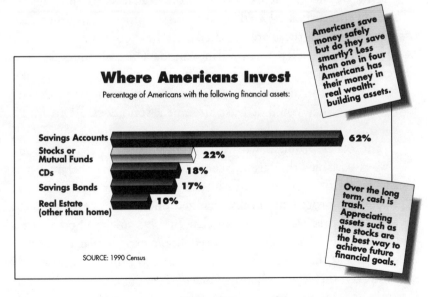

Chart 6.1

113

Why Be Negative?

Optimism Is Realism

While it is true that "You will hear of wars and rumors of wars" (Matt. 24:6) that will precede the end times, the fact remains that we're still here and for the most part in this country, we've prospered. In spite of the well-intentioned efforts of a minority to call attention to the negative aspects of God's sovereign judgment, a realistic view of economic history would call for optimism, not pessimism.

Problems Are Finite, Solutions Are Infinite

While mankind's problems are finite — and I acknowledge the issues of massive government debt, declining morality, loss of traditional values, and so on — man's imagination is infinite. We constantly overestimate the size of our obstacles and underestimate our capacity to overcome them. This is particularly a bad attitude for Christians to have since we "can do everything through Him who gives [us] strength" (Phil. 4:13).

One of the problems with economic analysis is that the resulting forecasts are based on static assumptions. All other variables, of which there are hundreds, are held constant so that the effect of one or two can be measured. This, of course, is not realistic. If I see you and your car hurtling toward a cliff, I could forecast that you're in severe danger, but it might be more safe to assume that you'll at least attempt a serious effort to find a solution to the problem.

The other problem with economic analysis is that there are always variables that are unaccounted for because the analyst is not aware of their existence in the past, present, or the future. Economic progress radically changed once someone figured out that the world was round, not flat. In 1798, Malthus predicted a "gigantic, inevitable famine" based upon exponential population growth and the finite "power of the earth to provide subsistence." However, the view of George Gilder was more correct in that it is "man, not earth, that produces food." In spite of realizing Malthus' population explosion, food as a percentage of household budgets in America is at its lowest level ever. In 100 years, biotechnology may make today's levels seem shockingly high.

Neil Armstrong's giant leap for mankind started with the small steps of Icarus in ancient Greek mythology, the dreams of da Vinci in the 1500s, the flight of the Wright Brothers in 1903, *Friendship 7* in 1961, and finally a man on the moon in 1969. It took eighteen months to print the first 200 Bibles on Gutenberg's printing press in 1455, but by 1500 there were over 10 million books and 35,000 titles printed on 1,000 presses in Europe. It is progress, not problems, that is exponential in growth.

Progress Is Just Beginning

Today's $30 hand calculator has more computing power than the mammoth, first computer made in 1947. Many entertainment devices such as video games, videorecorders, and compact disk players are vastly superior to the first generation computers. Technology is moving at an incredible pace, especially in microchips, the heart of computers. Incredibly, the microchip was only invented in 1971. Unbounded by resource constraints — the microchip is made of the three most common elements in the earth's crust, silicon, aluminum, and oxygen — and man's limitless imagination, the future of this invention cannot be conceived. With the birth of multimedia, the merger of computer, communications, and video technologies, we are in the dawn of a new Information Age. The current administration's dream of a data superhighway network equivalent to our Interstate road system will dramatically speed the transfer of information and even further accelerate our rate of economic progress.

Sir John Templeton, considered by some to be the greatest investor of the twentieth century, projects that the standard of living that took 1,000 years to double may take only 20 years to do the same. Why? Technology provides only half of the answer. The other half is the embrace of free market principles in previously communist/socialist countries. Given what we've accomplished in 200 years in the U.S., without the benefit of today's technology and financial capabilities, the potential that lies within the former Soviet Union, Eastern Europe, and China is staggering. The Lord's return may be the only thing that can prevent an unprecedented worldwide economic revolution!

How to Multiply Your Money

The thought of investing money frightens most people. The daily newspaper listings of thousands of stocks, bonds, and mutual funds can be overwhelming. Fear and intimidation no doubt explain why four out of five Americans have money in savings accounts or Certificates of Deposit (CDs), while only one in four has money in the stock or bond markets (Chart 6.1). In spite of the American dream to increase wealth, people are clearly content to merely protect what they have.

This is unfortunate because the actual process of investing can be quite simple. Everybody already knows 90 percent of what they need to know to be successful. In chapter 4, we laid the foundation of a sound investment plan by analyzing our personality, our financial fitness, and our financial objectives. While there are thousands of different choices one can invest in, not every vehicle is appropriate for everybody. The fact is that any particular investment is suitable only for a small number of people. Each step of analyzing who you are, where you are, and where you are going narrows down the list of possible choices. Rather than trying to include every possible choice in your list of potential investments, your investment plan will exclude those choices that are not appropriate for you.

For instance, if you have a personality that is naturally conservative, all high-risk investments would immediately be ruled out. If you are on a tight budget, then only investments that can be purchased with small amounts of money will be considered. Finally, if you are saving for retirement, you will turn your attention to long-term investments that will provide a substantial increase in wealth. What remains is a manageable number of potential investment vehicles that are perfectly suited to your unique situation. The next step is to actually make the choices to where to invest your money. However, it is important that you realize that the process of understanding who you are, where you are, and where you are going is the key to success. The fear that most people have about investing is that they will make a poor decision. By focusing on those things that you already know and that are under your control, you give yourself a range of choices that are all good.

The Basic Investment Problem

What we need to learn is how to invest in the best alternatives. This requires an understanding of basic investment principles, which are surprisingly easy to master. The basic investment problem is how to maximize return while minimizing risk. Each investor will solve this problem differently, according to their unique set of criteria. However, regardless of the choices one makes, two facts will always remain. First, the greater the return one desires, the greater the risk one must take. Likewise, the lower the risk one wishes to take, the less return they must be willing to accept. The second fact is that risk can never be eliminated. All investment choices, including not making any investments, have risk.

What Is Return?

To master the basic investment problem, known as the risk/return trade-off, we must fully understand what is meant by risk and return. An investor's return is simply what is earned above and beyond their original investment. This return can come in three different ways. The return most people are familiar with is interest. Interest is paid on investments that involve the use of your money by somebody else. When you invest in bank accounts or CDs, you are really lending your money to a bank, which will then earn a profit by lending your money to someone else at higher interest. The bank will pay you a lower interest for the use of your money.

The second type of return is a capital gain. A capital gain occurs when you sell your investment for more than you originally paid for it. This occurs most often in the stock market where you might, for example, buy stock in XYZ Corp. for $20 and sell it later for $30. Your return is a capital gain of $10.

The final type of return is a dividend. When you invest in a company, you become a shareholder and part owner. When the company you own makes a profit, it often pays a portion of the profits back to its owners in the form of a dividend. The rest of the profits are used to expand or improve the company's business in the hope of increasing its value and creating a capital gain for the owners.

117

Preserve or Grow?

The type of return—interest, capital gain, or dividend—that is appropriate depends on what your financial objectives are. Regardless of what your specific goals are, there are only two courses of action that you can take with your money. You can either choose to *preserve* your money or choose to *grow* your money. Recall from chapter 4 that your financial objectives are either immediate, short-term, or long-term. Immediate or short-term goals primarily call for investments that preserve money. Long-term investments, those intended to be held for more than five years, require investments that will grow your money.

Should You Be an Owner or a Loaner?

The choice to preserve or grow will determine whether you become a "loaner" or an "owner." A loaner is an investor who lends his or her money to others in return for interest. Loans are usually made to banks in the form of savings accounts or CDs. However, they are also made to the U.S. government in the form of Savings Bonds, to corporations in the form of Corporate Bonds, or to state and local governments as Municipal Bonds. In addition to receiving regular payments of interest, the lender receives a promise from the borrower to pay back the original amount invested. This promise preserves the wealth of the lender as it protects him or her from the loss of any part of the investment.

An owner seeks to grow his or her wealth by participating in the growth of a business. This is done by buying shares of a company and becoming a part owner of it. If the investor is correct and the company is successful, its profits will grow and with it the value of the shareholder's original investment. This will eventually give the owner a capital gain when the shares are sold. Depending on how successful the company is, the capital gains can be large, small, or even negative. The company may also use some of its profits to pay its shareholders dividends, another way in which the owner can receive a return. Unlike the loaner, the owner does not have a promise of receiving back the original value of the investment. In fact, owners can often lose some or all of their original investment due to the company's business not performing as expected. Furthermore, if the company does not pay a dividend, the owner will not receive regular earnings on the investment. On the surface, it would seem that loaning is a better investment approach to owning regardless of one's objectives. Unfortunately for most Americans, that is not the case. Beyond any reasonable doubt, the best way to multiply money and increase wealth is to be an owner. This means you must learn how to invest in the stock market.

What Is the Stock Market?

The U.S. stock market is a giant auction house where private individuals and public institutions gather to buy and sell shares in over 34,000 companies. In most cases, the gathering is done electronically by telephones and computers. Often the transactions are done through a middleman—a stockbroker—who provides the electronic means to bring two parties together.

The shares of stock represent ownership of a company. When you own stock, you literally own a portion of everything the company owns: the buildings, the inventory, the plant and equipment, and most importantly, a share of the company's profits. As an owner, you're technically the boss, although you exercise management authority by voting for a Board of Directors who will oversee the company on your behalf. Shares trade in a style similar to an auction. Potential buyers tell their broker what price they would like to pay to buy a particular stock. Potential sellers tell their broker at what price they would be willing to sell their shares of stock. When the prices match, a sale is made. Often, buyers and sellers just trade "at the market," which means that they will accept whatever the current price is.

The price of a share of stock represents the firm's market value, or what investors are willing to pay to own part of the company, based upon its past business record, its profit expectations, general industry conditions, the state of the economy, and the popularity of the company. A stock is considered undervalued if its stock is selling for less than its perceived worth. It is considered overvalued if it is selling for more than its perceived worth. Of course, value is in the eye of the beholder, and no shares would ever trade if people did not have differing opinions about company values.

Contrary to the belief of those who see the stock market as a legalized gambling casino, the stock market is truly one of the great economic mechanisms. The high standard of living that we enjoy in the United States we owe largely to the stock market. It is through the stock market that entrepreneurs can raise the money needed to bring products into homes and businesses. By selling shares of stock, they can raise money without going into debt. In exchange for cash, they give up a portion of ownership.

Investors, on the other hand, are willing to provide money because they have some control over the way their money is being used. They also have a quick way of selling their shares and getting their money back when they desire. If their foresight is correct, they can get their money back at a handsome profit. Entrepreneurs win by getting the necessary funding for their business. Investors win by sharing in the success of the company. Consumers win first by getting jobs in these new companies, then by buying the products these companies bring to market.

It's a shame that more people don't own stock. They actually participate in the stock market by buying products, which provide profits to owners of the companies they buy things from. By not owning stock, they literally give their wealth away to someone else.

What Is the Economy?
Buyers of stocks essentially own pieces of the economy. It stands to reason that if you're going to be a shareholder in stocks, you should know basically what the economy is.

Our economy is simply the sum of its business activity. When we speak of the economy, we are in a sense talking about Gross Domestic Product (GDP), which is the value of all goods and services produced in the United States in a given period of time. The GDP statistics are prepared and reported on every three months.

Businesses, households, and the government all contribute to the economy through both their production and consumption.

All the factors of the economy are interrelated. For example, a business makes something for sale. In producing their goods, they pay salaries. The salaries buy goods and pay taxes. The government uses the taxes to pay for public works, which creates another source of demand and salaries and consumption and so on and so on.

The economy grows when GDP grows. There can be no argument that the United States economic system has been incredibly successful at generating economic growth. The economy is 6.5 times bigger now than it was in 1929, even after many regular periods of economic disruption. When economists say the economy is strong, they mean that GDP is growing. On the other hand, a flat or even declining GDP from quarter to quarter is an indication of economic weakness.

Four Basic Terms

A *recession* is a broad decline of economic activity. Technically, the government defines it as two consecutive quarters of declining GDP. There have been thirty-one recessions since 1854. Thus you can see that they are normal, although discomforting, events.

Inflation is commonly understood to mean a rise in prices. Inflation is even more normal than recessions. Since 1926, inflation in the United States has averaged about 3 percent per year. However, there are two distinct periods in inflation's history. Prior to 1965, inflation averaged only 2.9 percent per year. Since 1966, it has averaged 5.7 percent annually, although recent years have seen a marked slowdown. Inflation is closely tied to the strength in the economy. Ironically, strong economies are inflationary as the demand for goods generally increases faster than the supply. This forces prices higher. Slow economies are good for inflation. Weak demand for products causes businesses to lower prices and cut production. Less production often means lower salaries, further reducing demand and continuing the trend toward lower prices. The one exception to this textbook scenario was in the 1970s when skyrocketing oil prices accompanied a recession. The exception was not that prices were rising during a recession, but that they rose at such a significant rate. While some sectors of business activity may see lower price levels, the economy as a whole will still trend toward moderately lower inflation during a recession.

A *depression* occurs when the overall economy experiences a prolonged contraction. As production is reduced substantially, there is significant unemployment and many business failures. For example, the failure of financial institutions and then many businesses followed an unexpected crash in stock prices, which accompanied both the depression of 1873 and the Great Depression of 1930.

There you have it! You now know everything you need to know about the economy. While it's not enough to make you an economist—I wouldn't wish that on anybody—it's the start of making you a successful investor. The next section on the business cycle will complete your education. After you read it, you will possess more than enough knowledge to understand how money is made in the financial markets.

How Does the Economic Cycle Work?

The average investor totally misunderstands the economy's relationship to the market. The single most misinterpreted notion is the belief that a good economy translates into a good stock market and alternatively that a bad economy translates into a bad stock market.

The second misunderstanding about the economy is that it has a major defect due to the continued presence of recessions even after periods of prosperity. These boom-bust cycles, called the *business cycle*, are a normal aspect of our free market economy. The key to being a knowledgeable investor lies in understanding how the market typically reacts to these cycles.

The U.S. capitalist system is based upon the principle that consumers are completely free to demand the goods they desire and that businesses, that is, *capitalists*, will supply the goods at a price and quality necessary to meet that demand. This system, contrary to the naysayers predicting its extinction, has produced the most successful record of economic growth and prosperity in the history of the world. By contrast, the Soviet Union's socialist economy lasted less than eighty years. No wonder most of the world's previously communist and socialist economies are converting to capitalism.

However, because of human nature, freedom of choice carries the seeds of both poverty and prosperity. Greed and lack of omniscience cause the busts that inevitably follow the booms.

The normal business cycle goes through four phases:

(1) expansion
(2) peak
(3) recession
(4) recovery

Over the long term of many completed cycles, the stock market follows the economy. The fact that the stock market as measured by the Dow Jones Industrial Average has risen from 307 in 1929 to nearly 4,000 today is due to a GDP which has grown from 800 billion dollars to over 6 trillion dollars during that same period. The growth of the stock market is a direct reflection of the growth and prosperity of the U.S. economy. It is those who have invested in the economy through owning stocks who have truly reaped the benefits of our capitalist system. Nevertheless, in the short run the business cycle causes the temporary dislocations in the investment markets.

Expansion

To explain the cycle, let's start first with an economy that is expanding, one that is growing at an increasing rate. Business and trade are good, and employment is high. Consumers are confident and are increasing their spending. In response, businesses increase supply by building new factories, hiring new workers, and increasing inventories. Ironically, the seeds of the downfall are now planted.

Consumer spending unfortunately refuses to be limited by income and budgets. Increased confidence of a rosy future and ease of credit allows consumers to spend above their current incomes, especially for high-cost items, like cars, boats, and furniture. An increased demand for borrowed money forces

123

interest rates to go up as lenders raise rates to slow down the demand for a fixed supply of loanable funds. In addition, as long as demand is strong, they'd rather lend money at 10 percent interest, for example, than 7 percent.

To meet the consumer's demand for goods, businesses need to expand plant and equipment. Therefore, they also have to borrow money, further pressuring interest rates. Since it will take time before the new plants come on line, the demand for goods will outstrip supply for some time. To slow down the depletion of inventory and to take advantage of demand, businesses raise prices, causing inflation.

Inflation forces interest rates even higher because lenders want to protect the value of their loaned money. If inflation runs 5 percent the next year, it doesn't make sense to loan $100 when the value of what gets paid back is only $95. To maintain parity, they must raise rates. In addition, using the same example, if they were willing to make loans at 7 percent when inflation was running 3 percent per year, they will loan money at 9 percent if inflation rises to 5 percent per year to maintain a 4 percent differential.

Peak

Despite being at its fastest growth rate, the economy's peak precedes a slowing down in economic activity. Higher interest rates and inflation created in the expansion phase makes consumers spend more money to maintain their standard of living. Eventually they have to slow down their spending. Unfortunately, businesses have expanded their plants, inventories, and work force in anticipation of continued demand. Everybody's lack of foresight has created a major problem! Companies respond by closing plants, cutting the work force, and reducing prices to clear inventory. All of these actions obviously retard economic growth, killing consumer confidence and spending, which sets up an economic tailspin.

Recession

If this tailspin is severe enough, which depends upon the level of miscalculation during expansion, the economy may actually contract. If the national GDP declines in two consecutive quarters, it will technically be a recession, although certain geographic areas and business sectors may have their own contractions independent of the overall economy. We saw this throughout the early 1990s even as the overall economy was beginning to recover and expand.

The lack of demand for goods creates a lack of demand for money, which causes lower interest rates and lower inflation. Now the soft economy plants its own seeds of recovery. Eventually the low interest rates and inflation attract those consumers and businesses that were strong enough to weather the storm. The length and depth of the recession is related to how many businesses and individuals come through unscathed. Favorable economic conditions will spark some activity as there is real incentive to borrow money at low rates. This starts the recovery phase.

Recovery

At this point the economy is limping forward but actually growing again. The economy will increasingly respond to new business activity, higher consumer confidence, and improved business outlooks. The growth will continue until the economy is healthy and expands. In contrast to the sharp, short-lived nature of recessions, the economy spends four times as much time expanding as contracting.

Investing according to the Cycle

If you are truly a long-term investor, you really need to do nothing throughout the business cycle. Over the course of many cycles, which on average are four to five years in length, the economy will grow significantly and so will the stock market. This can be seen in Charts 6.2 and 6.3. Since the length of the cycle is not consistent, this should be used merely as a benchmark. However, if you are somewhat short-term oriented or just looking for the emotional warm fuzzy that comes from knowing what's going on with your money, it's important to understand the normal relationship of stocks, interest rates, and inflation to the economic cycle.

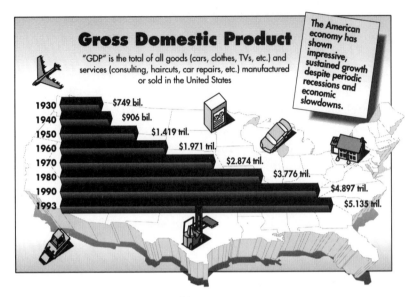

Chart 6.2

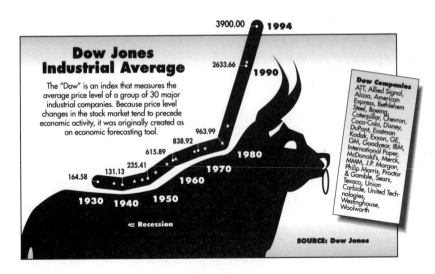

Chart 6.3

The single most important truth about investing is that stocks lead the economy, not follow it! In spite of all their fancy computer models and mathematical analysis, economists will begrudgingly admit that the single best indicator of economic activity six to twelve months into the future is the stock market. This is because investors, who ultimately are the financial markets, make money by predicting the future, not by reacting to the present. Believing otherwise is one of the biggest mistakes individual (and many professional) investors make!

To illustrate, if you were the first to realize that someday a Picasso would be worth hundreds of thousands of dollars, would you buy it today or wait until everybody agreed with you a year later? Obviously if you want to make money, you'll buy it today. The stock market works in a similar fashion, putting a price on tomorrow's economic events today.

With this analogy in mind, here are two important facts. The best time to buy stocks is during a recession! The worst time to buy stocks is near the economy's peak! Why? In a recession, the economy's next move is to eventually improve and grow again at a fast rate. Businesses will once again make huge profits, profits owned by their investors. On the other hand, at the economy's peak, the next move is a contraction in business. Corporate profits will be cut and many companies will even lose money as they lose expected sales and restructure their businesses to keep afloat. Anticipating this, the stock market will have already turned down.

To prove this point I did a study based upon two hypothetical investment strategies using the economy as buy and sell signals. Strategy A bought stocks at each peak of the economy's activity since 1929 and sold them at the lowest point of each following recession. Strategy B bought stocks at the lowest point of each recession (or depression) since 1929 and sold them at the following peak of each economic recovery. Therefore, Strategy B is the exact opposite of Strategy A. Both strategies were started with a hypothetical $10,000 investment.

The results were startling. A $10,000 investment in Strategy A shrunk to $1,743 by December 1993. The worst time to buy stocks is near the economy's peak! Sad to say, this is close to what the typical investors do. Persuaded by glowing reports of economic prosperity, they jump in hoping to benefit financially from the growth of the economy. Unfortunately, they are too late. The next move in the economy is downward, which the stock market has already begun to reflect. This too is seductive as the market's "temporary" weakness is seen as a buying opportunity. After a year of waiting for the economy and the stock market to recover, they give up much poorer than when they started, vowing to never invest in the market again.

Strategy B, on the other hand, is an unqualified success. The original $10,000 grew to $881,770 by following a plan of investing at the worst point in each recession and selling at each following economic peak. This is a strategy most closely followed by shrewd investors who realize that the economy's next big move is up, that recoveries last an average of four years, and that stocks are at bargain prices. The best time to buy stocks is during a recession!

Not satisfied to leave this point alone, I ran another test. This time I wanted to check the theory that the stock market leads the economy by six to nine months. To check this, I did the same study as above but with one difference. I adjusted the buy and sell signals to occur six months prior to each peak and each trough in economic activity. Again, the results are enlightening, startling, and hopefully profitable. Strategy A2, buying stocks six months before the economy's peak and selling six months before its trough saw a $10,000 investment in 1929 shrivel up to $1,177. Strategy B2, investing six months before each economic low point and selling out six months before each subsequent high point, saw $10,000 grow to an incredible $1.5 million! These results clearly show that the stock market forecasts the direction of the economy. The market has already begun to turn down before an economic peak and has begun to turn up before the economy's bottom. That's why the results differ the way they do in the two tests.

Unfortunately, these are hypothetical strategies designed only to prove a point. Since no one really knows until after the fact when the inflection points in the economy occur, there is really no way to duplicate these results. However, the key is to use these tests as a guideline to successful investing. You cannot wait until the economy is booming to make money in the market, at least in the short run. This is a prescription to disaster. It doesn't really matter when you commit money, since you're bound to be successful. But in a short term of five years or less, the best time to buy stocks is during periods of economic weakness. Chart 6.3 of stock market prices has recessionary periods starred so you can see the wisdom of this rule of thumb.

In a normal cycle, interest rates, stocks, and inflation follow a regular pattern. The pattern is as follows:

(1) low interest rates stir economic activity;
(2) increased economic activity and no competition from low interest rate, fixed-income investments boosts the stock market;
(3) eventually strong economic activity leads to inflation;
(4) inflation leads to higher interest rates;
(5) higher interest rates adversely affect the stock market with competition from fixed-income investments that are now providing higher yields;
(6) high interest rates and high inflation retard economic activity leading to recession;
(7) slow economic activity leads to low interest rates and low inflation;
(8) the process starts over.

Each major variable—stocks, interest rates, and inflation—performs differently depending on where you are in the cycle.

Economy	Recession	Recovery	Expansion	Peak
Stocks	Bottom/Increasing	Increasing	Peaking/Top	Declining
Interest Rates	Declining	Bottom	Increasing	Peaking/Top
Inflation	Declining/Bottom	Increasing	Increasing/Peaking	Top/Declining

Chart 6.4

Why Invest in the Stock Market?

There are three basic areas in which to invest money: stocks, bonds, and savings accounts. Stocks represent ownership while bonds and savings represent "loanership." Since 1926, stocks have earned investors an average of 11 percent per year. During this time, every $1 invested would have grown to $1,100. Bonds earned 5 percent per year, making each $1 become $29, while savings earned less than 4 percent, turning each investment $1 into less than $11. Right away we see a huge difference between owning and loaning. The American economic system is the most successful in the history of the world. It has produced more than 200 years of virtually continuous growth. It is the owners of this economy, the business shareholders, who reap the financial benefits of our economic way of life. When you own, you directly participate in our nation's prosperity. When you loan, your money is borrowed by owners who are using your money to create wealth for themselves. To own is to create wealth for yourself. To loan is to create wealth for someone else.

What Is Risk?

To most people, risk in investing means the likelihood of losing money. (This view probably accounts for the reason why four out of five Americans are loaners while only one out of four are owners.) However, this is an incomplete definition. There are two risks one must be concerned with. The first is the risk of losing money. The second is the risk of not having enough money. It is this second risk that is the most dangerous, yet is also the least understood by most investors. Failure to account for the risk of not having enough money will cause most investors to miss achieving their financial goals.

The critical fact that all investors must understand is that all investments have some form of risk. Eliminating one type of risk leads only to another. In my experience, most investors simply seek out the investments with the least risk and accept the low returns. *This is the biggest mistake that you can possibly make* as we'll now see. Most people don't feel that they have the expertise to carefully select investments or predict the economy.

Therefore, they prefer the certainty and security of having money in investments that protect their wealth. With no effort on their part they safely multiply their money at a slow, but sure rate of interest. Unfortunately for most, this is a guaranteed losing strategy! This is because any investor can take simple steps to eliminate most investment risks. However, barring a complete economic collapse, inflation risk is a virtual certainty. *The only investors who make money in an inflationary economy are owners, not loaners.*

The decision to be only a loaner, the investment of choice for most Americans, leaves one exposed to the most dangerous risk of all, *inflation risk*. Inflation means that anything you buy, whether a good or a service, costs more than it used to. Inflation causes you to lose money because it robs you of purchasing power. When it costs $110 to buy what used to cost $100, you've lost $10 even though you still have your original $100. Inflation is subtle because you don't see yourself losing money. A person who earns 5 percent on a CD feels good because their $100 is now $105. They rightfully feel as though they have more money than they did before. But if the inflation rate is greater than 5 percent, they have less purchasing power than they did before. If what used to cost $100 now costs $106 — 6 percent inflation — they actually can buy less even though they have more money. Inflation occurs when people have more money to spend than there are things to spend it on. Inflation is the natural result of economic growth. It doesn't have to be, but in a democracy where the government does not control prices, inflation almost always occurs. This is because people will continually vote into office politicians who promise to give them more rather than less. This makes the government a huge buyer of goods and services.

This government spending, combined with consumer spending, almost always occurs at a faster pace than what businesses can produce. Hence, there is more demand for things to buy than supply, which results in inflation. With just a few exceptions, the United States has always had inflation. As we shall see later, investors who loan almost always lose money due to inflation risk.

Recall that since 1926, the average yearly returns for stocks, bonds, and savings are 11 percent, 5 percent, and 3.7 percent respectively. Inflation over this period has averaged 3 percent. What this means is that over the last sixty-seven years, savers have barely made money after accounting for the effects of inflation. In other words, prices have risen nearly as fast as the interest paid on bank accounts and CDs. Even though the saver's original $1 is now worth $11, not exactly a staggering sum after sixty-seven years, what used to cost $1 now costs nearly $8!

The loaner's apparent $10 gain is actually only a $3 gain. This paltry "gain" actually becomes a loss if you include the taxes paid every year on the interest earned. So much for safety and security, not to mention the multiplication of God's assets. Since 1926, the rate of return on savings has exceeded the inflation rate by only .6 percent per year. At this rate it would take 116 years to double your purchasing power. I don't think the master in the Parable of the Talents was gone quite that long. It should be obvious that you cannot protect yourself against loss by keeping your money in the bank. As you can also see, the 4.5 percent annual return on bonds isn't much better. Only the stock market offers investors protection against the real, guaranteed risk of inflation.

"Stock Market Double Play"
1929–1993

1. Stocks rise more than twice as often as they fall.
   - 47 Advancing Years vs. 18 Declining Years

2. Stocks gain more in advancing years than they lose in declining years.
   - +20.1% average gain in advancing years
   - −13.5% average loss in declining years

Chart 6.5

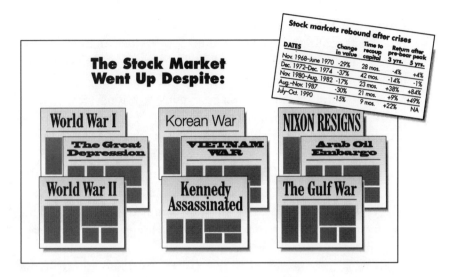

Chart 6.6

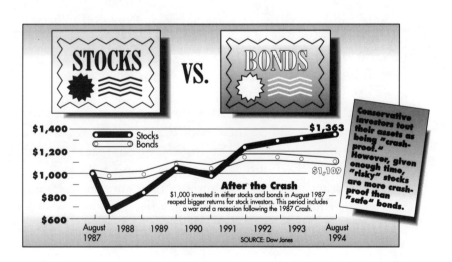

Chart 6.7

How to Minimize Risk

But what about the risk of making poor stock market investments? The best way to virtually eliminate all of this risk is to invest long term. Since most people are investing for either retirement and/or future college expenses, a long-term investment horizon is appropriate. Because of largely unpredictable economic factors, in the short run the stock market is hard to predict. However, for periods longer than five years, the direction of the market is fairly certain—up. Since World War II, the stock market has not been down over any period longer than five years. This means investors can eliminate market risk simply by holding their stock investments longer than five years and riding out the short-term fluctuations.

There is no question that the day-to-day fluctuations in the stock market can be quite unnerving. On some occasions, such as October 19, 1987, when the stock market crashed 25 percent in one day, it can be downright scary. However, most investors need not concern themselves with the market's direction tomorrow, next week, next month, or even next year. In spite of wars and rumors of wars, economic and political upheaval, the stock market has always worked itself higher over time (chart 6.5).

Now it's the '90s, and the stock market is still going up—not every day or even every month, but it doesn't take a prophet to see that it's likely to be higher five, ten, and twenty years from now. The owners will be there with it, reaping the rewards of their investment fortitude. The loaners will not have enough money to meet the future cost of their financial needs.

On the other hand, investors whose time horizons are short because their financial goals are less than five years away should be concerned with protecting rather than growing their assets. With little time remaining to fund your objectives, you will need to be certain that the money will be there. Therefore, loaning rather than owning is the correct strategy. The stock market may provide a higher return than the interest on savings or bonds, but the risk of loss in such a short time frame is too high. Inflation will still eat up a portion of the gains, but your primary concern is to preserve not grow.

What Is the Best Way to Invest in the Stock Market?
Actually, we let someone else do it for us by investing in mutual funds. A mutual fund is an investment company that pools the money of many individuals and invests this money on behalf of these individuals. When the mutual fund takes in money from investors, it issues them shares. The fund's investment managers then use these funds to invest in securities (stocks, bonds, and so on) that meet the mutual fund's stated objectives. When the value of the fund's investments rise, so does the value of the mutual fund's shares. Likewise, should the mutual fund's investments fall in value, so too will the shares of the fund. When the fund receives dividend or interest payments, they are distributed to the shareholders on the basis of prorated ownership. In other words, if you own 1 percent of a mutual fund, you would receive 1 percent of the dividends and interest generated by the fund's investments. Also, when the fund sells an investment for a profit, that profit is likewise distributed to shareholders on a prorated basis.

Mutual funds have clearly become the investment of choice for the individual investor. The first mutual fund was started in Boston in 1924. By 1940 there were sixty-eight funds with $448 million dollars in assets and nearly 300,000 individual shareholder accounts. Incredibly, by 1990, 60 *million* investors had almost $1.1 *trillion* dollars in over 3,000 mutual funds. There are now more mutual funds available to investors than there are stocks on the New York Stock Exchange!

Why Invest in Mutual Funds?
Considering this amazing growth in mutual fund investing, it is apparent that they must offer investors significant advantages. The biggest advantage of mutual fund investing is that mutual funds can significantly reduce the anxiety of investing. Most individuals have a fear of investing because they perceive themselves to lack some or all of the qualities of successful investors: (1) market knowledge, (2) experience, (3) discipline, (4) a sound investment plan consistent with their personality and financial goals, or (5) time. Mutual funds can minimize the stress created by investing by working on behalf of the investor in these areas.

The appeal of a mutual fund investing can be explained as follows:

Diversification

This is one of the two major attributes of mutual funds. Due to limited funds, the typical individual investor may be able to buy only a small number of stocks and/or bonds. A mutual fund often holds hundreds of securities. Because of your mutual funds share ownership, you now own a portion of this highly diversified portfolio. Diversification reduces risk, as the more securities you hold, the less likely you'll lose money if only a few of them go down in value.

Full-time Professional Management

This is the second primary attribute of mutual funds. Few individual investors have the talent, expertise, and resources (research staff, computers, information network) to match the professional mutual fund money manager. For the most part, the fund managers provide the investor with the market knowledge, experience, discipline, and time necessary to be successful. Not only do they make all the day-to-day investment decisions, but they also handle the record-keeping work for you, generating statements summarizing your purchases and sales, gains and losses, and tax consequences of your activity.

The management of the fund is the primary method by which the fund company earns its income. The fund charges its investors a fee to cover the portfolio manager's salary as well as the expenses associated with overhead and administration. The total cost of managing the fund is deducted from the value of the fund's portfolio. Because of the large size of mutual funds, these expenses represent a small percentage of the fund's value. The average expense level is 1.2 percent. To receive professional portfolio management, plus record keeping, at an average cost of $12 per each $1,000 invested is one of the clear benefits of mutual fund investing.

When you buy a stock that you think is about to go up, you are buying it from someone who thinks it is going down. That someone is most likely a professional investor. You, as an amateur don't have good odds of being successful in such an unlevel playing field. Buy mutual funds and hire a professional manager to do your investment work for you.

Public Performance Records

Unlike brokers, financial planners, newsletters, and other advisory services, mutual funds have fully disclosed performance records that are computed according to federally regulated standards. At your request, any mutual fund will provide this information. In fact, a number of widely available publications report comparative data on large numbers of mutual funds. Often your local library will have this information.

Individual Attention

It is estimated that the average stockbroker needs approximately 400 accounts to generate enough commissions to make a living. With much of his or her day spent making phone calls to add new accounts, this stockbroker has little time to spend servicing existing accounts. It only makes sense that he or she would spend this time with larger accounts. If you're a typical, smaller investor, the person you're paying to manage your money can't do a credible job. However, in a mutual fund, all investors receive equal treatment since they are all members of the same investment pool.

Convenience

Mutual funds are easy to acquire, often as simple as a phone call or an application. You can follow your investments easily as most mutual fund prices are generally quoted in your daily newspaper.

Modest Capital Requirements

Many mutual funds have minimum investment requirements as low as $1,000–$2,000. Some funds allow you to invest small amounts ($50–$100) monthly. Furthermore, once you become a fund shareholder, you can usually purchase additional shares in amounts as little as $50. Mutual funds are ideal for people who don't have a lot to invest, and they represent the best way to get started in the stock market.

Mutual Funds Can Be Used for IRAs and Other Retirement Plans

Most mutual funds offer accounts that can be established for IRAs, Keoughs, 401(k)s, and rollovers from corporate pension plans. As such, they are an excellent vehicle to accumulate long-term, tax-deferred savings.

Mutual Funds Pay Minimum Commissions

Another benefit of diversification is that mutual funds can accomplish this at a very low cost. A typical stock purchase by an investor through a stockbroker may cost 5–10 percent of the purchase price to buy and sell. Many small investors make good investment decisions that lose money because of the high commissions. On the other hand, a mutual fund annually pays only a fraction of 1 percent in commissions due to their extremely high volume of transactions. Lower costs enhance the profitability of the investment pool, which eventually will revert back to each investor.

Mutual Funds Are a Safe Haven for Your Money

All mutual funds employ an outside bank or trust company to hold and account for all the assets of the fund. This independent custodian has fiduciary, legal responsibility to protect the interests of the shareholder. Mutual fund bankruptcies are a rare event, but in each instance, no shareholder lost money.

What Types of Mutual Funds Are There?

We previously mentioned that there are over 3,000 mutual funds. We also said the fund's money managers invest the fund's assets (its pooled dollars) in securities that meet the stated objectives of the mutual fund. It is these objectives that comprise the various categories that broadly describe the types of mutual funds available to investors.

To properly build a mutual fund portfolio, it is important to understand the broad categories that the funds fall into. Many mutual funds have similar investment objectives that result in their having similar risk and return characteristics. While funds within the same category may occasionally differ, generally it is not a good idea to hold more than one fund in any category. There can be exceptions to this guideline, most notably if the funds have completely different investment philosophies despite having similar objectives.

Bond

Bond funds are also known as income funds because their primary objective is to produce income through the payment of interest. There are actually many categories of bond funds depending on the types of bonds they tend to buy: corporate, government, municipal, or others. Income funds as a sole investment are not appropriate for long-term investors as the rate of return will not exceed the inflation rate by enough to accumulate meaningfully. However, as a low-risk place to invest for shorter time periods, they are great as they will pay a much higher return than bank accounts or CDs. They are also appropriate for investors in retirement who need the income to meet regular living expenses.

Balanced

Balanced funds hold a mix of stocks and bonds. They are often required to hold as much as 50 percent of their assets in interest bearing securities. Because of the bonds and other money market assets, Balanced funds are stable and conservative. They traditionally have been good long-term investments because they lose little value during bear markets. However, in inflationary markets, the fixed income portion of the funds tends to suffer quite badly. I prefer Equity-Income (see below) funds over Balanced as they generally will have higher returns for a small increase in risk. Still, a Balanced fund is perfect for a conservative, long-term investor who wants to hold only one mutual fund.

Equity-Income

Equity-Income funds invest primarily in high dividend paying stocks. While most invest heavily in bonds, some will occasionally diversify into growth stocks. Equity-Income funds are desirable for their ability to hold value during market declines while appreciating nicely during market rises. Historically, about half of the stock market's returns come from dividends while the other half comes from price appreciation. Therefore, these funds are perfectly positioned for good performance under a variety of market conditions. I believe a well-diversified mutual fund portfolio should include a significant Equity-Income component.

Growth and Income

Growth and Income funds attempt to profit by investing in stocks whose earnings are expected to grow at an above-average rate. However, pure Growth funds provide more growth while Income funds provide more income. Therefore, one should expect better results by owning a good Growth fund and a good Equity-Income fund. A top Growth and Income fund would be most appropriate for the investor willing to take average risk and wanting to own only one or two funds. I'm not a fan of these funds. In fact, owning a large-stock Index fund may better serve this type of investor (see below).

Index

This is a special category of funds that are designed to track the overall movements of a stock index. An Index is a benchmark of the price movements of a group of stocks. The most widely followed index is the Dow Jones Industrial Average, which tracks thirty of the largest U.S. firms such as General Motors, IBM, and General Electric. Another important index is the Standard and Poor's 500 (S&P500), which consists of the 500 largest firms in the United States. Index funds exist because portfolio managers have a difficult time outperforming the stock market as a whole, especially after commissions and expenses. For instance, the Vanguard Index 500, which tracks the S&P500, has outperformed two thirds of all Growth and Income funds during the past five years. It has also outperformed 87 percent of all mutual funds during the last ten years. Index funds are basically unmanaged. Because they are designed to hold all or most of the stocks in a stock index, no manager is making stock selections, which results in low transaction costs and fees, making Index funds difficult to beat. It is estimated that an actively managed portfolio must return 2 percent more per year to make up the expense difference. Since an actively managed fund will hold many of the same stocks as an Index fund, this 2 percent annual difference is hard to overcome. Index funds are an interesting and recommended area of mutual fund investing.

Growth

Growth funds invest in the stocks of large, well-established companies whose sales and profits are expected to appreciate faster than average. Typical Growth fund stocks are Disney, PepsiCo, McDonald's, Wal-Mart, and Home Depot. Little or no consideration is given to stocks paying dividends. Growth funds typically rise and fall in line with the overall stock market.

They will fall sharply in down (bear) markets but rise significantly in up (bull) markets. Over the long haul, since the stock market has always gone up, Growth funds are the best way to participate in its gains. Every long-term portfolio should have a significant growth fund component.

Small Company Growth

Small company funds are a special category of growth-oriented funds. As the name suggests, they specialize in stocks of small but rapidly growing companies. Small is usually defined as the smallest 20 percent of actively traded companies. The stock market historically has five- to seven-year cycles in which small stocks either underperform or outperform larger companies. However, over the long term it has been shown that small stocks have given their investors better returns than large stocks. This is because new products and services will have a greater impact on the earnings of a small company than a large one; they tend to be more innovative; they are usually closer to their customers and marketplace; and their management often owns much of the company's stock. These funds are volatile, but worth owning. One dollar invested in small companies in 1926 would be worth $1.4 million today, while that same dollar

141

invested in the S&P500 would have grown to only $.5 million. I believe we are in a decade where we will see strong performance by small companies.

Aggressive Growth/Capital Appreciation

These are two other special categories of Growth funds. These funds use a number of high-risk strategies in an effort to attain maximum capital gains. They invest in speculative stocks and often use many high-risk techniques or securities such as options, futures, selling short, and margin. If you don't understand these terms, you definitely don't want to buy these funds. While these funds can be spectacular during rising markets, you don't want to be near them in declining ones. The average aggressive growth fund lost 22 percent in just three months of 1990. One fund, the Prudent Speculator Leveraged Fund, dropped a sickening 50 percent between July and October 1990! This same fund then rose 90 percent over the next seven months. Few aggressive funds have good long-term track records because their gains in rising markets have not offset their losses in declining ones. Many small company growth and growth funds will achieve similar results with less risk. There are some good ones, such as Founders Special or the Kaufmann Fund, but the whole group should be approached cautiously and only by knowledgeable and experienced investors.

Sector/Industry Funds

Sector and industry mutual funds invest in stocks of a specific industry or business group, such as finance, technology, or health. The allure of sector funds is that each year the top performing mutual fund is usually a sector fund. Buying these funds, however, usually doesn't make much sense. If you were smart enough to know which industry's stocks were going to rise, you'd be picking stocks yourself instead of buying mutual funds. The problem with the sector funds is that they buy virtually every stock in an industry, both good and bad. Furthermore, this year's top group is usually next year's bottom group. These funds don't always follow the market, often to their shareholder's detriment. The once high flying Fidelity Select Technology Fund earned 238 percent in 1982–83. Unfortunately, it lost 11 percent from 1985–88 while the stock market was gaining over 200 percent. Sector funds fly directly in the face of the reason to buy mutual funds in the first place: to own a diversified portfolio of stocks selected for their appreciation potential. Even if you have specialized knowledge of an industry, I feel that sector funds should be avoided.

International/Global/Overseas

Like Index funds, this category of mutual funds is growing in size and complexity. Like sector and industry funds, it is growing in specialization. The objective is to either buy stocks of quality companies in foreign countries or to participate in the economic growth of a particular country or area of the world. Some funds buy only the stocks of one country, while some diversify by buying into many countries, including the United States. There are even international index funds. The long-term record of these funds is mixed, mostly due to exchange rate fluctuations. Changes in the value of the local currency relative to the U.S. dollar will affect the investment return of these funds. Therefore, the fund manager must also manage exchange rate risk, perhaps in several countries, in addition to selecting the right stocks. Needless to say, this is a daunting task. However, when the country, the stocks, and the exchange rates all work out, the results can be spectacular. Like sector and industry funds, this category of mutual funds requires great skill and caution to successfully invest in. However, from the standpoint of diversifying one's portfolio, a small position in an international fund may be desirable.

How Do I Buy Shares in a Mutual Fund?

There are essentially three ways to buy a mutual fund: (1) through a full-service stockbroker, financial planner, or insurance agent, (2) directly from the fund itself, or (3) through a limited number of discount stockbrokers. Funds purchased from a full service broker, insurance agent, or financial planner are often referred to as "load" funds because the buyer is expected to pay a fee, or "load," to compensate the salesperson selling the fund. A "load" is a fancy word for commission. More than 60 percent of all mutual funds sold in this way charge some form of sales load. These loads can be as much as 8.5 percent of the purchase—$85 on a $1,000 fund purchase—although the average is 4.5 percent. Fortunately, many mutual fund companies sell their shares directly to the investor, which eliminates the need to compensate a salesperson. These funds are commonly called "no-load" because there are no sales charges associated with them.

There is a tremendous debate in the financial services industry as to whether sales loads are justified given that there are hundreds of funds available without sales charges. Studies consistently show that no-load funds as a group offer equal or better performance as compared to load funds. Certainly the no-load investor gets off to a better start as all his or her money goes to work right away, while the load fund investor has to overcome the immediate loss of dollars associated with a sales charge. That is not to say that there are not load funds with excellent track records. It's just that there are a number of no-load funds also with excellent track records. Why pay a load if you can get the same or better performance at no cost? Before paying any sales charges, make sure that you are receiving truly outstanding performance or service that you feel is not available elsewhere.

An investor can buy shares in any no-load fund with only a phone call or by mail. All funds must send you a prospectus (see Surviving the Prospectus) before they will take your order, although the Securities Exchange Commission has proposed legislation to allow investors, at their option, to receive a prospectus after they buy. Unless you are familiar with a mutual fund, it is advisable to read the fund's prospectus before sending money. Among other information, the prospectus will contain all the necessary information for buying shares of your selected fund.

Finally, a growing number of discount stockbrokers offer load and no-load mutual funds. The nation's leading discount broker, Charles Schwab, has an exciting program that offers many of the best mutual funds for no commissions or fees at all. Besides the lack of cost, this service provides outstanding convenience to an investor who desires to build a portfolio of several mutual funds. The investor will be able to track all the funds with one statement and be able to make changes with one phone call. This type of service would also appeal to aggressive investors who are often switching among different funds.

What Are Hidden Loads?

Another twist to sales loads is deferred or back-end loads. Rather than charge an investor on entry, the fund charges an investor when he or she sells. This charge is based upon a percentage of the assets originally invested. This percentage, usually 4–6 percent to start, is decreased each year for four or five years until it eventually reaches zero. The sliding scale is an incentive to keep your money in the fund, which insures that the fund manager will earn a consistently high fee for having a large sum of money under management.

An exit fee is a fee that is charged to discourage investors from frequent withdrawals. Once again, this can serve to keep the fund manager well-paid. However, it should be noted that frequent withdrawals by large numbers of investors can upset the manager's investment strategy and negatively impact performance.

An increasing practice by mutual fund companies is the charging of marketing expenses to the investor. This fee, called a 12b–1 fee, is to compensate the funds for expenses incurred while advertising and promoting the fund to prospective investors. It is also used to compensate sales professionals. By present law, the 12b–1 fee is limited to 1.25 percent but it can be charged annually. The fee is taken out of the fund's assets each year, which reduces the fund's performance by the amount of the fee. Over half of all funds have 12b–1 fees. I have two problems with them. First, funds that charge it can still call themselves no-load since the fee is not paid upon the fund's purchase. This is deceptive since you are still paying a sales fee. Second, it doesn't seem reasonable to pay a sales fee each year for something you usually buy at one time.

Over time, the accumulated cost of the 12b–1 fee will far exceed any sales loads. Products that are good can stand on their own merits and shouldn't need aggressive marketing tactics to generate sales. Fund groups such as Twentieth Century and Janus, among others, have demonstrated that you can get billions of dollars under management primarily by performance.

Publicly available information, not to mention the free publicity in the financial press received by top managers eliminates the need for high-priced sales people to push a fund.

How to Select Winning Mutual Funds

Choosing among nearly 4,000 mutual funds can be an overwhelming task, much like trying to find a needle in a haystack. My approach to the problem is to first get rid of some hay by eliminating funds that don't meet specific criteria. Then I look for the "needle." When you define what your needs are, based upon your temperament, time frame, and objectives, the needle will actually find you rather than you having to find it. Your objective is not to find the perfect mutual fund but the one that's perfect for you.

The most important universal criteria is the investment objective of the fund. Remember, you're not trying to find the best funds, but the funds that are best for you. It doesn't make sense to buy the number one aggressive growth fund if what you really want is a conservative income fund.

Once you ensure that the fund in question has the right objective for your investment goals, you should then focus on five key variables: fees, minimum required investment, performance, manager tenure, and the size of the largest annual loss.

Fees

Fees are critical to performance since you have to pay for them regardless of how well your fund does. The key question is whether you should buy a load or no-load fund. Load funds are those that are sold with a commission charge to compensate the financial professional. There is absolutely no truth that a load buys a better fund. In fact, for every good load fund—and there are many—there is as good a no-load fund for the same investment objective. The only possible exception is in the area of international mutual funds, a sector dominated by load funds. Still, there are some very fine no-load international funds, Scudder International and Oakmark International being two good examples.

The only legitimate reason to buy a load fund is to pay for a needed service from the sales professional. If you're selecting and buying the funds yourself directly from a no-load company, there's no reason to buy a load fund. You'll be throwing money away on a service you won't use or need. If you're getting a service that's worth the load, and it's a quality fund, then you should buy a load fund. *But* how do you know whether or not you're getting a good fund or one that the salesperson talked you into? To figure that out, you'll have to do some work on your own, in which case you might as well buy a no-load fund.

Some funds eliminate a front-end load at the time of purchase for a back-end load to discourage withdrawals. Based upon when you decide to sell your fund, you will be assessed a fee. The longer you wait, the lower the fee. I feel that this is worse than a front-end load since it restricts your freedom. This can be an issue if the fund changes its investment objective, style, or fund manager or if the performance of the fund is poor.

Marketing fees, or 12b–1 fees, pay for the marketing expenses of the fund. Here the load is hidden in that you don't pay it up front but get a periodic assessment as a deduction against the value of the fund. I have heard the arguments in favor of this, but the idea that I have to pay for someone else to buy my mutual fund makes no sense to me.

Basically, I do not buy the argument that fees provide a larger, more stable pool of money in a fund that can be better managed for good performance. It still does not explain the fact that there are excellent funds that charge no sales commissions or marketing fees. Call me biased, but the bottom line is that I hate fees. I want all of my money going to work for me, not somebody else. However, if you honestly feel that the fees associated with a prospective fund purchase are justified, then you should gladly pay them.

Minimum Investments

If you've got a lot of money to start investing with, forget about this criteria. If you're like the rest of us, however, you'll have to start small. There are a number of quality, no-load mutual fund companies that allow you to start with low minimum investments. I call them Penny Pinchers. The advantage of Penny Pinchers is that they allow you to have a diversified portfolio with little money. We'll be discussing what diversification is and its importance later in this chapter. Here are some great mutual fund families that allow you to invest with very little money:

20th Century
• no money down, $25 per month

T. Rowe Price, Janus, Invesco, Founders, Neuberger/ Berman, American Association of Retired Persons (AARP), Strong
• no money down, $50 per month

Babson, Gabelli
• no money down, $100 per month

USAA
• $100 down, $50 per month

Vanguard Star Fund
• $500 minimum. This interesting fund is actually already a portfolio of mutual funds. This allows small investors access to a group of four mutual funds, each with a different investment objective, from one of the best mutual fund companies.

Many of the Penny Pincher funds have even lower minimum investments to open an Individual Retirement Account (IRA). Twentieth Century actually has no required investment minimum for their IRA accounts.

Performance

Three variables make up a performance record: return, risk, and consistency. You want a fund that, relative to other funds with similar objectives, has better than average returns with lower than average risk for a long period of time. A good fund has at least three- and five-year rates of return that are above average for funds with a similar objective. It's even better, though not absolutely necessary, if the fund has an above average ten-year track record. The reason long track records are important is so that you can see the manager's performance across a wide range of economic and market conditions. Anything less than five years is not enough as the typical economic cycle from boom to bust is about four years in length. There are very few fund managers that are able to provide superior returns over all market conditions. The three-, five-, and ten-year records should be reviewed for consistency. Depending on your time horizon, you will give different emphasis to each time period evaluated. For long-term holdings of ten years or more I emphasize, in order, the five-year, ten-year, and three-year records. If your intent is to hold a fund for three to ten years, I emphasize the three- and five-year records with little weight given to the ten. For short-term investments of less than three to five years, I look at just the one- and three-year performance.

A track record is only meaningful in light of the fund manager's tenure. When you review a fund's performance, make sure that you check to see when the fund last changed its portfolio manager. The time periods you're reviewing should have the same person in charge. It's the performance of the manager that you're buying, although the fund companies would like you to believe that portfolio managers are interchangeable. Nothing could be further from the truth. Buying someone else's track record is like hiring someone based upon another person's résumé. It's safest if a fund manager has at least a five-year track record with the fund or another fund with a similar investment style. It's crucial to see how a manager has responded to a variety of market conditions. Also be cautious when a successful manager takes over another fund with a different investment objective. He may be moving outside his or her area of expertise.

Risk

You also want to consider the fund's risk level in relation to its returns. A fund that earns a high rate of return with very high risk is not as good as a fund that had a similar return with less risk. All things being equal, a relatively low risk fund is more likely to be a consistent performer over time. A high risk is not always bad, however. A well-managed aggressive fund, like 20th Century Ultra, more than makes up for its high volatility with outstanding long-term returns.

An interesting statistic worth looking at is the fund's beta. Beta is a statistical measure of a fund's sensitivity to movements in the overall market. A fund with a beta of 1.1 can be expected to perform 10 percent better than the market when the market is up and 10 percent worse in down markets. In other words, if the stock market is up or down by 10 percent, a fund with a beta of 1.1 will, on average, be up or down 11 percent. A fund with a beta of .8 performs about 80 percent as well in up markets and 80 percent as poorly in down markets. In this case a 10 percent move in the overall stock market will result in an 8 percent move in the fund. The higher the beta, the more volatile the fund. You should not use beta as a way of predicting a fund's performance, even if you are lucky enough to predict how the market is going to do. Betas are not accurate enough to do that, but they can give you a good indication of how risky a fund is. High-risk investors will want to look at funds with betas greater than 1.1. During strong markets, these funds will provide outstanding returns. For example, the 20th Century Ultra fund is a small company growth fund with a beta of 1.58. This fund doubled in value in twelve months from November 1990. On the contrary, lower risk investors will probably prefer funds with betas of .9 or lower. They will provide more security during down markets. For example, the USAA Income Stock fund is an equity-income fund with a beta of .71. While the more aggressive 20th Century Ultra lost 18.3 percent during the stock market's 1990 decline, USAA Income Stock was down a mere 1.3 percent.

Another great way of determining if a fund is too risky for your taste is to check out its largest annual loss or its performance during down markets. *The Individual Investor's Guide to No-Load Mutual Funds* (published by the American Association of Individual Investor's) provides data for bull (up) and bear (down) markets for most no-load mutual funds. Other services provide grades for up and down markets. Long-term performance is far more important, but if the size of a fund's loss during down markets is too scary, buy a different fund. However, it is normal for stock funds to lose 10–20 percent during bear markets. High beta funds can lose even more. Remember, long-term, growth fund investors usually win, since bull market returns for these funds are typically 50 percent or more.

The best source of mutual fund data is available from Morningstar Mutual Funds. It publishes a massive database that can be found in many local libraries. They also have a ranking system that gives funds one (bad) to five (good) stars based on a comparison of the fund's return relative to the riskiness of the fund. On this basis, all funds are compared to one another. Obviously, a fund that earns high returns with low risk is likely to be a five-star fund. While I wouldn't restrict my search to only four- or five-star funds, one can safely eliminate one- and two-star funds from consideration.

The above suggestions should steer you to a small list of potentially excellent investment choices, regardless of your personal risk tolerance or objectives. The following list of don'ts should keep you from buying a clunker.

- Don't buy a fund simply because it has a high rating from a service or newsletter. Check it out on your own using the criteria above to make sure it's right for you.

- Don't buy a fund on the basis of its advertising or a salesperson's pitch. With so much data available, even the worst fund can be made to look great according to some statistic. Check out all claims on your own. The data can be easily found.

- Don't buy a fund on the basis of one chart in a newspaper or magazine. Any fund can look good at one point in time. Consistency is the key. Few funds are consistently good, but those are the ones you want.

- Don't buy a fund with a new manager, even if it has a

great track record. That's like hiring someone on the basis of somebody else's résumé.

● Don't buy a new fund. There are too many established funds of known quality to take the risk of a new fund, even if it's with a reputable fund family.

● Don't buy a fund that is consistently in the bottom half of its peer group, even if its performance is improving. Its investment style may be in vogue for the moment but not for the long haul.

● Don't buy a fund just because it was hot last year. Consistency, consistency, consistency is the key to long-term success.

How to Track Performance

Mutual fund price quotations are available each day in almost every newspaper in America. Additionally, most Sunday papers have tables that summarize the week's activity for mutual funds. For a fund to receive a newspaper listing it must have over 1,000 shareholders or $25 million of assets under management. A typical mutual fund listing looks like the table below:

	Bid[1]	Ask[2]	Chg.[3]
AAL Mutual:			
CaGr p[6]	13.88	14.57	+.02
Inco p	10.19	10.70	...
MuBd p	10.46	10.98	...
AARP Invst:[5]			
CaGr[4]	29.85	NL	-.12
GiniM	15.90	NL	...
GthInc	28.64	NL	+.01
HQ Bd	15.90	NL	...
TxBd	17.45	NL	...

The superscripts are explained as follows:

(1) *Bid.* In some papers this column would be "NAV" or Net Asset Value. This is the per share value of the fund as of the

previous day's close. The Net Asset Value is the value of all the securities held by the fund, minus the fund's expenses and liabilities, divided by the total number of shares held by investors.

(2) *Ask.* In some papers this column would be "Offer Price" or "Offer." This is the price paid that day for new purchases of the fund. The difference between the Bid and Ask price is the sales load charged by the fund. The load percentage can be calculated by subtracting the Bid (NAV) price from the Ask (Offer) and then dividing this amount by the Bid. For instance, the AAL Mutual Capital Growth (CaGr) fund charges a 5 percent sales load (14.57–13.88 = .69/13.88 = 5%). When this column contains the letters "NL," the fund is a no-load fund, although a no-load fund may still charge marketing and redemption fees (see #6).

(3) *Chg.* This is the per share change in price, in dollars and cents, for the mutual fund from the previous day. No change in price is denoted as "...".

(4 & 5) This is the abbreviated name of the mutual fund (#4) and the family or fund group that the fund is a part of (#5).

(6) Many mutual funds will be followed by a code that connotes some special aspect of the fund. The most common codes are: "p"—the fund charges a 12b-1 marketing fee; "r"—the fund, under certain circumstances, charges a fee for redeeming its shares; "t"—the fund charges *both* marketing and redemption fees; "x"—the NAV has been reduced to reflect a dividend that will soon be paid to shareholders; "f"—yesterday's price not available, so the prior day's price is quoted.

At some regular interval, say quarterly or annually, you may wish to calculate how well your fund is doing. To compute the percentage gain for any fund, the formula is as follows:

$$(\text{Ending NAV} + \text{Distributions} - \text{Beginning NAV}) \div \text{Beginning NAV}$$

Beginning and ending NAV refers to the Net Asset Value at the beginning and ending of a given period. Distributions include all capital gains and income distributed to shareholders during the period and is included in the formula above on a per share basis. This amount will be zero if there were no distributions made for the period in question.

> Example: The First Century Growth Fund had a Net Asset Value of 16.11 on December 31. On March 31 of the following year the NAV was 17.28. The fund also made a capital gains distribution of .15¢ and an income distribution of .01¢. The fund's quarterly return was: (17.28 + .15 + .01 − 16.11) ÷ 16.11 = 8.03%.

To compute your personal return, use this formula:

$$\text{(Current Account Value − Initial Investment)} \div \text{Initial Investment}$$

An account statement from your fund will have the value of your investment as of a given date. To calculate it yourself, simply multiply the number of shares you own by the fund's NAV, which you can either get from the newspaper or by calling the fund itself. Your initial investment should include any sales charges or other commissions and fees that you paid to buy shares of the fund.

> Example: You currently own 145,675 shares of the First Century Growth Fund. Yesterday's NAV from the morning paper was 17.28. Your account value is currently 145.675 x 17.28, or $2,517.26. Your original investment was $1,500 to buy shares of the fund at $10.30 per share. First Century Growth is a no-load fund. Your current return is ($2,517.26 − $1,500) ÷ $1,500, or 67.8%.

Many investors buy mutual fund shares through a Regular Investment Program or Dollar-Cost Averaging strategy. Since shares will be purchased on a number of dates at varying prices, computing investment returns is difficult. A good approximation is as follows:

$$\text{(Total Investments + Distributions)} \div \# \text{ of shares = Average Cost per Share}$$

Once you've calculated the average cost of your shares, then compute your approximate return:

$$\text{(Current NAV} - \text{Average Cost)} \div \text{Average Cost}$$

When Should You Sell Your Mutual Fund?

Selling investments is by far the most difficult part of being an investor. This is ironic because the decision to sell should often be based on a single, simple criteria—the investment is no longer meeting our objectives. This, of course, is a rational course of action. However, greed and fear—two irrational criteria—generally affect our investment decisions.

Greed keeps us in investments too long. Even after we've made a substantial amount of money, we want more. Once we've been proven right in our judgment, we want to stay right by seeing our investments continually increase in value.

Fear also keeps us in investments far too long. What we fear the most about investing is losing money and pride. When our stocks or mutual funds go down, we are hurt in the pocketbook and the ego. To sell out and take our loss would be to admit that we made a mistake. Rather than face the facts, we tend to ignore the situation entirely and avoid making a decision altogether.

Fear and greed are the catalysts for hope. Hope is a very expensive emotion. Hope will cause the loss of objectivity and soon your money. All investments have some underlying economic value, but hope will not increase their value one cent. If there are sound reasons why a profitable investment should continue to rise in price, hold it. If there are good reasons why an investment has declined in price, sell it. Actually, the decision to sell is made much easier by having made the right decision to buy. If you understand why you're buying, and what personal objectives are being fulfilled, and if you have a plan for when

155

you expect to sell, then the selling decision becomes easy.

Rather than give a fixed answer to the issue of when to sell a mutual fund, I feel that it is more important to describe fund investing as a process. The decision of how to best implement the process is best left to individual discretion. What's right for one person is not right for another. However, certain guidelines are appropriate for everybody. These are:

(1) make a good buying decision
(2) review performance periodically, every three to six months, against appropriate benchmarks
(3) determine after a year's worth of informal reviews whether the performance trend is acceptable or unacceptable
(4) make a change, that is, sell your fund and buy another after no more than two years of poor performance
(5) consider changing funds if the fund manager leaves the fund
(6) change funds when they no longer make sense for your financial goals

Selling a poor mutual fund investment is difficult. There are both financial and emotional costs involved. However, would you allow your business to continually suffer due to poor performance? As the "supervisor" of a mutual fund manager, the decision will be yours.

How to Survive the Prospectus

A mutual fund's prospectus is a comprehensive document that describes the key facets of a mutual fund. It is required by law to be sent to all fund investors. Reading a prospectus is torture. However, since it is a legal document, it is also a fairly standardized document. There are basically five key sections in each prospectus, usually found in the following sequence: (1) Fee Table, (2) Financial Data, (3) Objective, (4) Management, and (5) Services.

The "Fee Table" is required to be near the front of the prospectus. It contains information on all the fees and expenses that the investor must pay. It also must include an example of how the various fees charged by the fund will affect a $1,000 investment, growing at 5 percent per year.

The "Financial Data" usually consists of a table showing a detailed, year-by-year account of the mutual fund's performance. This is often the same data, as seen in various financial publications. However, some caution must be exercised when comparing data between the prospectus and an outside publication as the fund may use a different reporting period for their prospectus. Since the prospectus is usually published annually, its data may not be as timely as that available elsewhere.

The data table usually contains the following information:

- Investment Income: dividends and interest earned on the fund's investments.
- Expenses: a summary of the expenses detailed in the "Fee Table."
- Net Gains and Losses: the difference between realized gains and losses (securities bought and sold) and unrealized gains and losses (securities that have not yet been sold).
- Distributions: dividends and interest paid to shareholders, plus profits from realized gains passed through to shareholders.
- Beginning and Ending NAV (Net Asset Value) — the per share value of the fund at the beginning and ending of the fund's fiscal period. Because of the fund's accounting conventions, the fiscal period may not start and end based on a conventional calendar year. This may cause performance data to deviate from that published by outside sources.
- Other.

A discussion of the fund's "Objective" and its "Management" generally follows the financial data. This information is usually straightforward. In discussing the fund's objective, the prospectus will provide information on the types of securities and investment strategies the management will employ to provide investors with a return. Some funds may be required to provide information on special risks involved in certain types of transactions. Much of this section can be complex. While you may read something that would cause you not to buy a fund, of greater importance is the stated track record the fund has developed employing their strategies. This is the best way to evaluate whether their investment decisions are good or bad.

Finally, the rest of the prospectus is devoted to the various "Services" the fund offers. Here you will find out how to buy shares, how to redeem (sell) them, automatic reinvestment plans, exchange privileges, IRA plans, and tax aspects of the fund. Despite the regulations, no two mutual fund prospectuses are alike. However, the information above is common to most of them. Before buying a fund, you should try to read the prospectus carefully. This is simply part of the due diligence necessary to understanding your investments, a requirement for success. As difficult as they are to read, don't be so scared of it that you won't invest. If you have a question, just call the fund itself. This is a competitive arena. They will be glad to help you. You should also be careful not to go to the other extreme of picking it apart to find reasons not to invest.

Never make a purchase decision solely on the basis of the prospectus. Using publicly available information, such as magazines, books, and newsletters, or trusted financial advisers, you should be able to narrow down the very wide field to a small list of candidates. The fund's objectives and historical performance data should provide most of the information you need to make an investment decision. The prospectus will then complement the data you should already have, mostly by providing data on the fund's services and unique aspects of the manager's investment policies and strategies.

Mutual Funds and Taxes
A mutual fund is simply a conduit for income taxes. As a corporation, a mutual fund would normally pay taxes on its profits, and shareholders would then pay taxes on any dividends or capital gains they received. To avoid this "double taxation," mutual funds are granted special tax status as long as they meet

certain federal regulations. In essence, this status allows mutual funds to distribute their tax liabilities straight through to the shareholders, eliminating the double tax.

These distributions come in the form of either: (1) capital gains, resulting from the profitable sale of individual securities by the fund manager and (2) income, which is derived from dividends and interest paid by the fund's holdings. Both types of distributions are taxable events, which will be reported to the IRS on a 1099-DIV and must be included in the investor's 1040 tax return, on Schedule D. When you redeem (sell) your fund shares, the capital gain or loss also must be reported on Schedule D of your 1040. The mutual fund will report this to you and the IRS on a 1099-B.

Most mutual funds make their distributions of income and capital gains once a year near the year's end. If you wish to buy a mutual fund near the year's end, you must be careful. You will incur a tax liability even if you buy shares one day before the day the distribution is declared. This is true even though this distribution represents income and profits from securities bought and sold before you were a shareholder. Most funds announce distributions in advance. Contact your fund and inquire as to the scheduled date. It may be advantageous to wait until after the distribution before purchasing. Likewise, if you are selling a fund, you may want to sell before the distribution date to avoid a further tax liability.

Filling out your tax return for your mutual fund investments can be maddeningly complicated. It can be helped by keeping good records. More information regarding mutual funds and taxes can be obtained in IRS publication 564, Mutual Fund Distributions.

Other than being aware of the buying or selling near the distribution date, the best advice regarding taxes is not to make investment decisions simply because of the tax consequences. Invest to make money, not to avoid taxes.

The best way to minimize taxes is to do your long-term investing in an IRA or other tax-deferred vehicle. Not only do your contributions generate tax-savings each year, but also the effect of compounding your earnings without an annual tax bite is significant. If you need the money prior to retirement, you'll pay income tax on your withdrawal plus a 10 percent penalty, but this may be far less than the tax avoided through your years of tax-free investing.

Good Sources of Information

With several thousand mutual funds available, one would expect it to be easy to obtain information to help select funds, and that is the case. The following is a good, if not comprehensive, list of sources of mutual fund information, many of which can be found at a local library:

Newspapers

Compared to your local newspaper, financial newspapers such as *The Wall Street Journal, Investors Business Daily*, or the *New York Times*' Business section have expanded mutual fund coverage. These sources usually provide information rather than specific investment recommendations.

Magazines

Barron's, a weekly journal, *Money*, and *Kiplinger's Personal Finance* carry the most frequent articles on mutual fund investing. *Forbes, Fortune, Business Week*, and *U.S. News and World Report* devote less frequent space although most will publish special mutual fund issues throughout the year. Even *Consumer's Digest* has excellent articles devoted to mutual fund investing.

Be careful not to take the financial publications too seriously. Their primary purpose is to entertain, not to enrich (they enrich themselves by being entertaining), and to appeal to as wide a readership as possible. They are not written at a sophisticated level.

Newsletters

There are a number of fine newsletters (including the author's) offering buy and sell recommendations, fund information, or both. Before using a newsletter's advice as an aid in your own investment program, make sure that you understand how the adviser makes his or her recommendations and that the methods and strategies are consistent with your own goals and personality.

Summary
1. Investors either try to grow or preserve their money.
2. The best and only effective way to grow your money is in the stock market.
3. The economy does not predict the stock market; the stock market predicts the economy.
4. The best time to buy stocks is during a recession; the worst time to buy stocks is during the peak of economic activity.
5. Long-term investors need not worry about when to buy stocks—anytime is the right time since the long-term trend of the stock market is up.
6. Be a successful, independent stock market investor by using mutual funds. Making consistent profits in the stock market is very difficult and requires skills and resources beyond what most individuals have. However, mutual fund shareholders have these necessities available to them, at very low cost, through the fund's management. Rather than trying to compete with professionals as an amateur, level the playing field by hiring a professional. It's much easier to select a good mutual fund than find a good stock.
7. Find reliable, outside sources of information. While mutual fund investing is easy, it's still sufficiently difficult that it pays to have some independent form of advice at your disposal. This can take the form of a broker, adviser, magazine, or newsletter. This advice is best if it (1) is independent, (2) is free from any conflicts of interest, (3) is consistent with your personality and financial goals, and (4) makes you feel more comfortable about your decisions. Advice that meets these criteria is priceless and hard to find. Therefore, cost should not be a factor.
8. Avoid conventional wisdom. If everybody were right, everybody would be rich. Most financial advice is based upon what is easiest to sell to the public. Very little of it can stand the scrutiny of sound scientific testing. Don't assume that everything you hear or read is correct. If it sounds too good to be

true, it probably is. The stock market is the last place you will ever find a free lunch.

9. Think long term. The stock market on average has returned investors 11–15 percent per year. Good mutual funds have averaged several points better than that. This means that you can expect to double your money every five or six years. Over twenty or thirty years, any amount of money, no matter how small, will become a large amount of money. However, the market goes up and it goes down, sometimes at frightening speeds. But it has always gone up more than it has gone down. Patience is a virtue.

Notes
1. *Proverbs 13:16*
2. *Proverbs 13:11*
3. *Luke 14:28*
4. *Proverbs 18:15; 21:5; 14:15; 27:23*
5. *Luke 19:26*

Chapter Seven

YOU MUST GUARD GOD'S POSSESSIONS AGAINST LOSS

A PRUDENT MAN SEES DANGER
AND TAKES REFUGE, BUT THE SIMPLE
KEEP GOING AND SUFFER FOR IT
(PROVERBS 22:3)

Bob just can't seem to get it right. The experts say to "buy low and sell high," but Bob always buys high and sells low. His instincts tell him the best time to buy is when all the news is bad and that the best time to sell is when all the news is good. The problem is his emotions override his instincts and he ends up losing money. He just wishes (and prays) that he could find a way to make better decisions.

Bob, your wishes (and prayers) are answered in this chapter!

God Wants Your Money to Have Value to You

As stewards of God's resources, we should not find ourselves like the shrewd manager "wasting his possessions" (Luke 16:1). This suggests that we must preserve and protect what is under our management. However, as we see in the Parable of the Sower and the Parable of the Talents, we must multiply and grow our resources to further the work of the kingdom. Unfortunately, the reality of multiplying our financial assets is that it dictates an investment game plan that is contradictory to preserve and protect strategies. How can we resolve this apparent dichotomy?

Actually, the dichotomy is an illusion since all investment strategies have risk regardless of the investor's objective and intent. Risk-free investing is inherently impossible. You will eventually lose some money to inflation, taxes, lack of investment demand, a poor overall economic climate, bad industry conditions, and your own mistakes. Every investment strategy is subject to one or several forms of risk. Since we can neither control nor predict future events, the most reasonable assumption about risk is that our investments will never attain the results we anticipated. They will do better or worse than expected. The error most people make is in thinking the difference in doing better or worse lies in their ability to control or predict the events that will determine a particular outcome. The truth is that the number of errors you make rather than the number of correct prophecies determines the difference between good and bad performance.

None of us can be immune from financial difficulties at all times. The truth is that most financial hardships are self-induced by poor choices, not lack of skill. Therefore, we must assume that mistakes will be made.[1]

Not only are external factors like economic, global, and political events in a constant state of flux, but also our own personal circumstances frequently change, all of which may necessitate a change of direction on our financial road map. The only prediction that is guaranteed is that we will make money-losing decisions. I recognize that this thought will make many people uncomfortable, but it must be said. You can avoid losing money by doing nothing, which we'll see later is totally wrong, or by always being right about the future, which only God is capable of.

Since risk and change cannot be avoided, they must be managed. Managing risk means three things. First, it must be defined in personal terms. To some people risk means losing money, to others it means uncertainty, and to others it means lack of knowledge. To you, it may be some combination of all three. Second, risk must be understood. How much money represents a loss, what is uncertain, what is unknown? Finally, risk must be minimized in two ways: minimizing the occurrences of money-losing errors, and minimizing the extent or degree of money lost due to poor decisions.

There are four things we must "Be" if we are to be good risk managers:

(1) Be Safe by taking known and fully understood risks;
(2) Be Comfortable by managing our money according to our personality, financial condition, objectives, and skill;
(3) Be Consistent through discipline and perseverance;
(4) Be Patient by recognizing that it takes time, not money, to make money.

God would not have demanded that we be faithful stewards without providing us with a clear set of directions to accomplish this task. All that we need to know about handling the risks of investing for an unknown future is in the Bible.

Making Money Requires Effort on Your Part

There is an old adage, "You can't get something for nothing." The Bible makes an even stronger statement: "He who works his land will have abundant food, but the one who chases fantasies will have his fill of poverty" (Prov. 28:19).

Money is the most universally desired commodity. There is hardly anybody who can't use more of it, Christian or not. To get money, you have to get it from somebody else. It is simply illogical to wish for someone to give you something that other people want more than anything else. The financial markets are particularly competitive because conflicting opinions regarding value determine the value of all investments. One investor thinks an investment is worth less than its current price. Therefore, the investor sells. Another thinks the same investment is worth more than its current price. Therefore, that investor buys. Only one can be right. The future will determine which one it is, but over the long run, the future favors those relying on effort rather than those depending on luck.

Many people think that investing requires too much effort.

They would much rather have an expert tell them what to do with their money. These people want something for nothing. Life doesn't work that way, and the market is the best way to find that out. The financial markets have never been in the habit of giving away money for free. Successful investing requires some effort. The exciting part, however, is how little effort is really required and how few people make it. This makes the odds of success very high for those who "Just Do It."

How to Know a Good Investment

Another common mistake is thinking that you have to know what professionals know to make money. Often, knowing what the professionals know can cost you a lot of money since the best decisions are usually made contrary to the consensus opinion. You don't have to spend eight hours a day studying the market to find good investments. If you invest according to personality, financial fitness and objectives, 95 percent of all the possible investment alternatives can be ruled out. With the remaining 5 percent, three simple rules will help you avoid most bad investment decisions.

First, *seek* out reliable advice—from *many* advisers and *listen* to it.[2]

In seeking advice, the Bible suggests three principles. First, get the facts. Too many people rely on instinct or gut feeling.[3] Second, be open-minded. Preconceived notions and biases are often expensive to have.[4] Third, make sure to hear both sides of an issue. This is critical in investing, since all investment decisions are a matter of opinion about the risks and rewards.[5]

Where do you get good advice? We touched on this subject somewhat in chapter 2 on wisdom. The best sources of advice generally depend on your needs. Affluent and experienced investors are best served by financial service professionals. Not only are stockbrokers and financial planners more motivated to deal with wealthier clients, but also the costs of their services can be provided more economically to affluent individuals. If you need broad financial advice and coordination of your taxes, insurance, retirement savings, investments, and estate plans, you should seek out a financial planner. If you are looking for specialized investment expertise such as stock selection and portfolio composition and buying and selling advice, you should work with a stock broker. In either case you should want to look for the following:

- An adviser who is easily accessible since you will probably spend a lot of time together, at least in the early stages of the relationship.
- The adviser's educational background, professional training, and continuing education.
- Your adviser should disclose their method of compensation. It is crucial that you know the extent of compensation received through the sale of products. Sales commissions and fees are not necessarily bad, but they can limit objectivity and restrict the number of alternatives made available to you.
- Use the first meeting — usually free — to find out if an easy rapport can be established with your adviser. Ask all pertinent questions.
- Get references and ask about the adviser's typical clientele. You'll probably do best with someone who frequently works with individuals like yourself.
- If you're working with a financial planner, ask if he or she is registered with the Securities and Exchange Commission (SEC), and if so, ask for his or her brochure and/or form ADV. All financial planners are not required to register with the SEC, but if they are, they must submit a form ADV. The ADV, which may be given to clients in the form of a brochure, will contain relevant information on the planner's practice, philosophy, fees, education, and potential conflicts of interest. Ask for both Part I and II of the ADV. Part I is optional and contains information on any regulatory or legal problems involving the planner.

Small and novice investors should rely on professional advice through mutual funds. There has been an explosion of books, magazines, and newsletters devoted to the mutual fund field. Caution must be exercised when looking for advice from these sources. Some books by big-name experts are ghost-written with little or no input from the so-called expert. The advertising claims used to sell financial newsletters can rarely be substantiated. Furthermore, the subscription prices of $200–$400 per year are beyond all but the biggest investors. Reading the popular financial magazines is like eating white bread. You get filled up but not with anything substantial. The Appendix at the end of the book contains some excellent sources of reading material for small and novice investors.

Whether you are a large or small investor, don't automatically assume that you need a Christian adviser. What you need is a competent adviser, one that is going to help you the most. Remember the words of Jesus: "For the people of this world are more shrewd in dealing with [worldly wealth] than are the people of the light" (Luke 16:8). A good Christian adviser is the best of both worlds, but a choice between a good non-Christian adviser and a bad Christian adviser—and sad to say, there are many—really shouldn't be too hard to make.

Second, invest only in things that you understand.[6] Whenever you make any kind of investment, it is crucial that you have a complete understanding of what events you think must occur for that investment to make you a profit, over what time frame you expect to make money, and what types of risks you are bearing. Furthermore, you should be able to explain these issues simply so that a child can understand.

A third great rule is "if it sounds too good to be true, it probably is."[7] An unfortunate fact of money management is that one in five Americans will fall prey to a financial scam. Is it because these scams always sound believable or is it because our innate desire is to turn a health, wealth, and prosperity lie into the "truth"?

Recall that as good stewards and investors we have conflicting goals. We want to make as much money as we can, but we also want to do so without facing the prospect of losing money. The financial con artists know this and take advantage of our emotions to take our money. *Wealth without Risk* is an aptly named best-selling book because the author is now facing fraud and other charges in several states.

Avoiding fraud or just plain inappropriate advice requires discernment on our part.[8] The apostle's admonition against false prophets could just as easily apply to fraudulent financial advisers and teachers. We can test false financial spirits with the wisdom we gain by listening to sound advice.[9]

The con artists try to make their pitch sound safe and comfortable, two of the four important Be's outlined earlier. However, the safety and comfort they promise are counterfeit sensations. What they say sounds good, but it's what they don't tell us that costs us money. In addition, the safety and comfort are according to their standards, not ours, which should be predetermined by our personality, financial fitness, and objectives. Furthermore, their ideal investment strategies are missing two Be's — consistency and patience. Their lies flourish only because we forget that sound investments require perseverance, discipline, and time to succeed. "Dishonest money dwindles away, but he who gathers money little by little makes it grow" (Prov. 13:11). The best investment strategies are those that use time as a key element in their success. The worst schemes are those that hold out the promise of getting rich quickly. It takes time, not money, to make money. We cannot be good and faithful stewards if we allow our emotional desire for easy money, inspired by greed and covetousness, to overcome the logic and correctness of the biblical truth that we *can't* get something for nothing. The financial markets are the last place to look for a free lunch.

Avoid Making Quick Decisions

"The plans of the diligent lead to profit as surely as haste leads to poverty" (Prov. 21:5).

Diligent. "Characterized by steady, earnest, and energetic application and effort" *(Webster's Ninth New Collegiate Dictionary)*.

Any financial act that requires a quick decision or any financial decision made in haste is likely to end up with a poor outcome. It is human nature to want whatever we want right now. However, since it is God's nature to be patient and to instill this quality in His followers, He makes us wait to receive His divine guidance.[10] Furthermore, we need to demonstrate our worthiness to receive God's direction through our willingness to apply ourselves diligently to the problems at hand.[11]

Thinking that there is only one chance to take advantage of a good opportunity causes many financial mistakes. "Once in a lifetime" is a phrase that has cost many investors considerable money. A once-in-a-lifetime attitude also causes people to ignore their own plans, especially their financial condition, in the hope of striking it big on a golden opportunity. Greed causes us to quickly act alone, without thinking and without guidance.

There is no such thing as once in a lifetime. Opportunity knocks many times, not just once. The financial markets are simply too big to present once-in-a-lifetime opportunities. If you miss out on a good opportunity because of lack of information or lack of money, another opportunity will certainly come along when the time is right. However, to know that the time is right and to recognize a real deal from a phony one demands steady, earnest, and energetic effort on your part. In other words, you must be diligent, not hasty. If any opportunity requires a quick decision on your part, don't do it!

Occasionally the quick decision will, in retrospect, turn out to have been a good one. That isn't the point. Being hasty and right once will only tempt us into doing it again. Sooner or later this will have unfortunate consequences. The Bible guarantees it. Don't look for easy answers. The right road is usually not the one that looks best at first inspection. On the other hand, the wrong decisions often look best at first glance without the benefit of facts, advice, and study. "So Abram said to Lot, 'Let's . . . part company. If you go to the left, I'll go to the right; if you go to the right, I'll go to the left.' Lot looked up and saw that the whole plain of the Jordan was well watered, like the garden of the Lord, like the land of Egypt, toward Zoar. (This was before the Lord destroyed Sodom and Gomorrah.) So Lot . . . pitched his tents near Sodom" (Gen. 13:8-12). It's safe to say that Lot's snap judgment was not a good decision in the long run. "Then the Lord rained down burning sulfur on Sodom and Gomorrah—from the Lord out of the heavens" (19:24).

What we can learn from Lot is not to be in such a hurry to make an investment that we fail to take the time to research and understand its potential risks and rewards. Nothing worth buying requires an instant decision.

Avoid No Decision

"A prudent man sees danger and takes refuge, but the simple keep going and suffer for it" (Prov. 22:3). Just as making decisions too quickly can be disastrous, likewise making decisions too slowly. The world is moving even if we don't want to, and we must make every effort to move faster than the circumstances that affect our finances. Recall from chapter 4 that a key quality of good stewardship is control. We know that it is impossible to completely control our environment. However, whether we are proactive or reactive will determine the degree of control we have.

To be proactive we must anticipate how changes in our financial environment may affect us. Then we should take steps to protect ourselves against possible adverse circumstances. Jesus taught this principle, saying, "Or suppose a king is about to go to war against another king. Will he not first sit down and consider whether he is able with ten thousand men to oppose the one coming against him with twenty thousand? If he is not able, he will send a delegation while the other is still a long way off and will ask for terms of peace" (Luke 14:31). It appears that the king in the story is being forced into military conflict. Events outside of his control have forced him to take action. He has three choices. He can fight, but to do this he must assess his chances of succeeding. Loss of life is, of course, very costly. Therefore, if he has some doubts, he can opt for a second choice—that is, make peace before any hostilities begin. He may have to accept concessions that would have been avoided by fighting and winning, but the concessions would certainly be better than losing.

The king's third choice is unspoken but should be apparent. By doing nothing he places himself in a position where events will overcome him. This choice is the worst of all choices. This choice follows the principle of doing nothing. It is better to do something and be wrong than to do nothing. By doing something, you'll at least get somewhere, but by doing nothing you'll get nowhere. The world is moving even if you won't. You can ignore reality by sticking your head in the sand, but in a changing world you'll only fall behind. Furthermore, since you're not moving and not looking, you'll probably get run over.

Inactivity in the area of financial stewardship is not only dangerous but also disobedient. God has given us resources to manage with the understanding that we're going to make something good happen with them. If we're not even going to try, then He will take what was meant for us and give them to somebody else more willing to advance the kingdom.

Our unwillingness to make financial decisions implies a lack of faith inspired by fear.[12] God is not concerned that we might do things that fail. Failure must be temporary since He has given us only what we can handle. We should use our mistakes as learning experiences, rather than as barriers, to correctly managing our finances, and then we should move on.

Ultimately, it is not mistakes that make poor stewards but action that makes good stewards. If we exercise good judgment by applying biblical decision-making principles, our errors will be few and far between. Naturally, there is no excuse for foolishness in our decision-making. However, there is little difference between the decisiveness of the fool and the indecision of the enlightened.[13]

Invest According to a Predetermined Plan

"The wisdom of the prudent is to give thought to their ways" (Prov. 14:8). The first step to making money in investments is good, thorough planning. Investments made on a whim can occasionally make money, but over time investing without objectives or strategy is a losing game. Unfortunately, the typical plan for most investors is to buy stocks or mutual funds and then do nothing. We've already seen that doing nothing by avoiding decisions is a financially terminal disease. The biggest problem most people face is not making bad choices but not having a clear plan for their choices. First of all, if you don't have a plan, how will you know if you did make a bad decision? Without a plan, how will you know

- where you are?
- where you should be?

- where you could be?
- how much further you have to go?
- how and when to make changes?

Three things can happen when you make an investment. It can go up, go down, or go nowhere. To be a successful investor, you should have a clear idea of what you will do in any of those instances and when you will do it. That is a plan. Planning reduces stress and discomfort. It is important because in the heat of the moment, we tend to react based upon our emotions and make decisions that later we see were poor. We need to decide ahead of time what course of action we will take according to what our investments are doing at any moment. The stress goes away because we don't fret about "What should I do now?" We simply act in accordance with what we've already determined is the right thing to do. Since losing a lot of money is devastating both to our confidence and our pocketbook, more time should be spent thinking about what to do if our investments are going down. Getting into a situation is far easier than getting out of it. Thus planning for how to handle potential losses is crucial to our success.

Remember, you're always in uncharted territory. Without a road map, you're sure to get lost. Intellectually, successful investing does not have to be demanding. However, successful investing is very difficult emotionally. Several factors make the psychology of investing demanding even for market professionals.

First, there is the fear of losing money. Certainly we all have this fear to varying degrees. To this is added the uncertainty of the future. When we make big decisions we like to find out quickly whether we are right or wrong. Remember the anxiety we felt in school while waiting to get our exams back from the teacher? The uncertainty of the future is exacerbated by the day-to-day fluctuations in the market, one day confirming your skill, the next exposing your ineptitude.

Finally, successful investing is uncomfortable because it's usually lonely. It is the contrarians who do the best. They are the investors willing to go against the views of the majority. It's hard to think you're right when nobody else agrees with you; yet this is the way money is made in investing. The right road is the one with the fewest travelers.

The emotional demands of investing make investment plans a priority. Your plan is your anchor that holds its place against the storm of uncertainty. You must have a specific plan for each investment you make—why you bought it and when you intend to sell it—or your emotions will frustrate your goals and intentions. Make an emotional commitment to your plan, not the desired outcome, and you'll be well on your way to becoming a successful investor.

How to Create an Investment Plan
In chapter 4 we discussed the elements of taking control of your money: acting in accordance with your innate personality temperament; acting in accordance with your financial condition; and having quantified objectives with respect to money and time. These are known variables that are completely under your control. Ninety-five percent of what you need to know about investing is contained in these initial steps. Proper attention to getting your money under control will help you avoid many potential pitfalls.

Once you complete these preliminary steps, it then comes time to actually construct an investment plan with which to manage your money. A good investment plan addresses four issues:

- buying
- selling
- diversifying
- making revisions

Have a Plan for Buying

Your plan for buying any investment should answer several questions. The most important question and the one that must be asked before committing any funds is "Why am I buying this?" In other words, you need to know what financial need the investment in question is supposed to fill. Some investments are designed to meet long-term goals; others are designed to meet short-term objectives. Some investments are for growing wealth; some are for preserving it. Once you've matched your investment choices to specific needs, then the next step is to ask yourself whether the particular investments are the best possible choices to meet those needs, based on what you know today. Always bear in mind that there are no perfect investments, only investments that are perfect for you.

The final question to answer after "why am I buying" and "what am I buying" is "when do I buy?" "There is a time for everything, and a season for every activity under heaven . . . a time to plant and a time to uproot . . . a time to scatter stones and a time to gather them" (Ecc. 3:1-2, 5). All of the planning and analysis in the world can't beat being in the right place at the right time. Everybody knows the formula for profitable investing: buy low and sell high. The problem is what is low and what is high? Timing your investments by waiting until their price goes down, a common and naive investment strategy, usually doesn't work. The good investments never go down, leaving you empty-handed. The bad investments keep going down, making you poor. Fortunately, mutual fund investing allows a near perfect way of being in the right place at the right time. Later in this chapter we'll talk about a virtually risk-free method of investing.

Have a Plan for Selling

I once heard a great story about selling. A brokerage firm issued a negative opinion on a particular stock and suggested the stock be sold in favor of another that they were recommending. One of its brokers called his client to suggest this transaction, but the client balked because he had a *rule* of never taking a loss. The broker then suggested that they take a look at the client's entire portfolio to see whether there was something else that could be sold instead—perhaps a stock that had gained in price—to supply the funds needed for the new recommendation. The client wouldn't allow that either because he didn't want to pay taxes on the profits. Frustrated, the broker pointed out that the only choice left was to sell a stock that hadn't yet moved in price. Alas, the client rejected this idea too because he couldn't sell anything that hadn't had a chance to go up. It's unclear how this investor ever intended to make any money. However, it's not unusual for people to have self-imposed restrictions that will hamper their investment results.

The following "rules" are commonly used to the detriment of their followers:

- "I don't sell until I get at least a 10 percent (or 20 percent, 30 percent, etc.) profit."
- "I won't sell until I get even."
- "I don't sell my investments until I've held them at least six (or eight, twelve, etc.) months."
- "I'll sell when the price gets to _____ (pick a price)."

It's not what you buy, but when you sell that matters. Selling investments is by far the most complicated part of being an investor. This is ironic because the decision to sell should often be based on a single, simple criteria — the investment is no longer meeting your objectives. This, of course, is a rational course of action. As mentioned in chapter 6, our investment decisions are generally affected by two other *irrational* criteria: fear and greed — both of which cause false hope.

Actually, the decision to sell is made much easier by having made the right decision to buy. If you understand why you're buying, what personal objectives are being fulfilled and have a plan for when you expect to sell, then the selling decision becomes easy.

Have a Plan for Making Plan Revisions

Learn to be a "respondable" investor. Investors who consistently make money have a personality trait that I like to call "respondability," which is a combination of responsibility and adaptability.

They are responsible in that they approach their investments as a serious, thoughtful endeavor. Accordingly, they have a highly disciplined, well-planned strategy for each investment. They know exactly why they are buying, what they expect their investments will do, and when they plan to sell.

However, they are also adaptable. Despite their best laid plans, they understand that either their judgment can be wrong or something not previously accounted for may occur. Therefore, they need to quickly adapt their expectations to the current situation.

Being respondable means that you will change your plans as your personal and financial circumstances, goals, and objectives change. It also means that you will recognize bad or inappropriate investments immediately and sell them at a loss if necessary. Losing a little money and some pride is better than keeping your pride at the expense of all of your money. Being respondable also means that you maintain an open mind to the markets. The economic environment changes every day. To succeed you need to be willing to change also.[14]

Be careful, though, not to be too respondable. Once you make your decisions, give them time to work out. It's amazing how often long-term investors get disappointed if they're not making money the first week after buying a stock or mutual fund. You have to be persistent. Investing would be a breeze if the markets went up every day or we never made a bad decision. But if your plan is good, and you did your homework before investing money, then you need to have the discipline to see the plan through to success. This doesn't mean futilely clinging to poor investments. Persistence means not giving up altogether when things are temporarily not going your way.

Above all, you must believe that you are going to succeed. Without a winning attitude, anything else that you do is meaningless. However, it is attention to the biblical principles of decision-making that builds a winning attitude. These are the elements of successful investing. Money and brains have little to do with making money. In fact, I have always felt that they were the biggest inhibitors to making money. In addition, luck is nice to have, but it is out of your control and also comes in two flavors—good and bad. If you learn how to manage rather than avoid risk, you'll be doing something that a vast majority of investors don't do, and this, rather than dollars and smarts, will be your advantage.

Four Great Ways to Make Money in the Market

Here's what you've been waiting anxiously for. All this investment philosophy is interesting, but it's no good without con-
crete ways of applying it in the real world. The four strategies
presented here will not guarantee that you won't lose money
investing. That's impossible. But if you follow them in a
thoughtful and disciplined manner, it's as close to a lock as
you'll ever get. In investment slang it's a "slam-dunk"!

Near-Lock #1. Regular Investment Plan (RIP)

The Regular Investment Plan (RIP) is a simple but highly effective investment strategy. It is designed to substantially increase
your capital over a long period of time by making market fluctuations work for you rather than against you. Also known as
Dollar Cost Averaging, RIP has the following advantages:

(1) It is ideal for investors with limited amounts of capital to
invest.
(2) It puts market volatility, the thing investors fear most, to
your advantage.
(3) It is easy to implement. In fact, most mutual funds will set
up this program for you, and once implemented, you need do
nothing else except wait for your money to grow.
(4) You need to make no market forecasts or predictions to
make money.

How to Implement RIP

It is very simple to implement the RIP strategy. Quite simply,
all you have to do is to make a consistent, periodic investment
into the mutual fund or funds of your choice. The timing of the
investments can be any interval you consider convenient. But it
is critical that the interval or time between investments be the
same as well as the amount of money. For instance, you may want
to invest $100 at the end of every month. It is crucial then, that
you consistently make your month-ending $100 investment.

Many investors use employer-sponsored savings plans to make
investments with each paycheck. This is a perfect way to implement RIP. However, anybody can set up their own RIP strategy

by writing a regular check to the mutual funds of their choice. But if you want greater convenience, most mutual funds will arrange to have your contributions made directly from your bank account at a time of the month that you specify. This can be shortly after you deposit your paycheck. Many employers will even allow you to specify a financial institution to make regular contributions to, which, of course, can be your selected mutual funds.

How RIP Works

The principle behind RIP is that by making regular contributions to your investments, you make market fluctuations work for you rather than against you. If you invest periodically the same amount each month, for instance, you will be buying more mutual fund shares when the price is low and fewer when the price is high. You no longer have to worry about whether

---

How RIP Works

$	month	price	shares	profit
100	1	10	10.0	$0
200	2	9	11.1	($10)
300	3	8	12.5	($31)
400	4	7	14.3	($65)
500	5	6	16.7	($113)
600	6	5	20.0	($177)
700	7	5	20.0	($177)
800	8	6	16.7	($73)
900	9	7	14.3	$49
1,000	10	8	12.5	$184
1,100	11	9	11.1	$332
1,200	12	10	10.0	$491

Total Shares Purchased: 169.13
Total Amount Invested: $1,200
Final Investment Value: $1,691.27
Profit: $491.27 = 29%

(This hypothetical, but realistic example, makes two interesting points. First, the RIP investor made a 29 percent profit despite the fact that the price in month "12" was the same as the starting price in month "1." A lump-sum investor would have only broken even.)

Chart 7.1

---

any given time is the right time to invest.

Basically, you'll be making the correct decision every month. The effect of buying many shares at low prices and fewer shares at high prices means that you will always have a relatively low-average cost per share. The chart on page 179 is an example of how RIP works, using a hypothetical mutual fund for simplicity.

The RIP investor made a profit even though in seven of the twelve months the portfolio showed a loss. Again, this was done with no change in price after twelve months. This should be heartening to conservative, long-term investors.

The key to these two observations is that more shares are bought when prices are low than shares are bought when prices are high. The profits on the relatively large number of low-priced shares more than offsets the losses on the smaller amount of high-priced shares. Even though this and all the following examples are set up to highlight these points, it is this process of buying many shares at low prices and fewer shares at high prices that makes RIP such a powerful investment strategy.

RIP—A Low Risk Strategy

Since no investment or investment strategy is perfect, RIP must have some risk associated with it. Remember though, that the biggest risk in the stock market, volatility—is put to your advantage. However, the risk in RIP is if your mutual funds never increase in price. If this happens, you will lose money. Buying more shares at lower prices only returns a profit if those shares eventually sell for higher prices. Therefore, the market has to go up at some time for RIP to increase your capital. However, look at the example on page 181.

In this hypothetical example, the fund suffered an immediate 60 percent drop in price to $4 and ended up $2 below the price where it started, and yet it returned a profit. Again, the build-up of shares bought at favorable prices created profits once the fund's price started to recover. That's the tremendous advantage of RIP. The investor who made a one-time, lump-sum investment in the first month had a loss at the end of this example.

It is critical to understand that RIP, like any other investment, will lose money if the investments never increase in value.

$	month	price	shares	profit
		How RIP Works with a Fund That Doesn't Recoup		
100	1	10	10.0	$0
200	2	9	11.1	($10)
300	3	8	12.5	($31)
400	4	7	14.3	($65)
500	5	5	20.0	($161)
600	6	4	25.0	($228)
700	7	4	25.0	($228)
800	8	5	20.0	($111)
900	9	5	20.0	($111)
1,000	10	6	16.7	$47
1,100	11	7	14.3	$222
1,200	12	8	12.5	$411

Total Shares Purchased: 201.35
Total Amount Invested: $1,200
Final Investment Value: $1,611.79
Profit: $411.79 = 26%

Chart 7.2

However, it is more important to realize that, in the entire history of the U.S. stock market, stocks have always gone up if given enough time. The stock market has never failed to increase in any period longer than ten years. In fact, it has been higher in 96 percent of all five-year periods and higher in 76 percent of all one-year periods. Therefore, based on history, which is all we have to go on, RIP is virtually foolproof for long-term investors.

The Best Mutual Funds for RIP

The best way to implement the RIP strategy is with mutual funds. Individual stocks are not appropriate vehicles for RIP. First, you'll have to pay a commission each time you buy stocks, which will add significantly to your costs and reduce your overall profits, perhaps even negating them. Second, since you can't buy fractional shares of stocks as you can with mutual funds, you won't be able to invest the same amount each month. In other words, a mutual fund selling for $9.58 per share will allow you to invest $100 and buy 10.435 shares. If you were buying stock you would have to buy ten shares for $95.80 or eleven shares for $105.38. In either case, the integrity of the RIP strategy is lost.

However, some types of mutual funds are clearly better for RIP than others. Since the key element in the success of RIP is the ability to buy more shares at low prices, ironically you want to have a fund that periodically goes down substantially in price. Typically, this will be some type of growth fund. But caution should be exercised. Since large losses are always difficult to make up, you don't want to choose a fund that is too volatile. Let's look at some examples on page 183.

Chart 7.4 on page 183 is interesting in that it has the lowest profits in spite of the fact that prices rose throughout the example. Once again, this highlights the fact that RIP needs market fluctuations to be completely effective. It is through buying low-priced shares during market drops that the RIP investors make the largest profits. A steadily rising market is the only one in which a lump-sum investors would outperform the RIP investor. This proves the validity of RIP as a long-term investment strategy since there is no such thing as a constantly rising market.

A good methodology to use when choosing a mutual fund for RIP is to choose a quality fund, which has a "beta" greater than one. As mentioned in chapter 6, beta is a statistic that measures the volatility of a given mutual fund or stock. It tells you how sensitive or volatile a mutual fund has been historically, relative to the whole stock market.

Since we've seen that a volatile fund is best for RIP, it makes sense to choose funds with a beta above 1. These funds will provide the volatility necessary to create the low-cost buying opportunities that are critical to the RIP strategy. Nevertheless, since the fund must go up eventually for RIP to succeed, it is critical to choose a top-performing mutual fund regardless of its beta.

RIP Summary

A Regular Investment Program (RIP) is a perfect way for small investors to begin accumulating wealth. It works well because it puts the biggest disadvantage of stock market investing — mar-

How RIP Works with a More Volatile Fund

$	month	price	shares	profit
100	1	10	10.0	$0
200	2	9	11.1	($10)
300	3	8	12.5	($31)
400	4	7	14.3	($65)
500	5	5	20.0	($161)
600	6	3	33.3	($296)
700	7	4	25.0	($195)
800	8	6	16.7	$57
900	9	7	14.3	$200
1,000	10	8	12.5	$357
1,100	11	9	11.1	$527
1,200	12	10	10.0	$708

Total Shares Purchased: 190.79
Total Amount Invested: $1,200
Final Investment Value: $1,907.94
Profit: $708 = 37%

Chart 7.3

How RIP Works in a Rising Market

$	month	price	shares	profit
100	1	10	10.0	$0
200	2	10	10.0	$0
300	3	11	9.1	$20
400	4	11	9.1	$20
500	5	12	8.3	$58
600	6	12	8.3	$58
700	7	13	7.7	$113
800	8	13	7.7	$113
900	9	14	7.1	$183
1,000	10	14	7.1	$183
1,100	11	15	6.7	$268
1,200	12	15	6.7	$268

Total Shares Purchased: 97.85
Total Amount Invested: $1,200
Final Investment Value: $1,467.78
Profit: $267.78 = 18%

Chart 7.4

ket volatility—to work for you. As long as the market rises over time, and history indicates that it always does, RIP is virtually foolproof. The consistent use of RIP, with quality mutual funds of decent volatility, should allow any investor to achieve their long-term financial objectives.

Questions and Answers on RIP

Q: What if I have a lump sum to invest?

Unless your investment timing is perfect, over time the RIP investor will generally have superior performance over the lump sum investor. Therefore, it makes sense for the lump sum investor to use a modified RIP strategy by dividing his lump sum into three or more equal portions and invest each portion at a regular interval until the entire amount is invested. A further modification might include investing half a portion if your fund goes up considerably or a double portion if your fund goes down.

Q: When do I sell?

The RIP strategy is one of capital accumulation. Since there are no set selling guidelines, one should sell whenever their overall investment objectives are met. Even if the market declines, you should maintain your periodic investments to take advantage of lower prices as the market drops.

Q: What if I want to increase my regular investment?

The more you can contribute, the greater will be your capital growth. Therefore, it makes sense to always look to increase your regular contribution. An excellent personal financial strategy would be to create a budget that meets all of your monthly expenses; then allocate all or a portion of every salary increase to your RIP.

Q: What should I do with my capital gains and dividend distributions?

When your mutual fund sells stocks at a profit, it has a capital gain, a share of which you are entitled to in proportion to your ownership stake in the mutual fund. Likewise, you are entitled to a share of its dividends when the fund receives dividends on its holdings. For tax reasons, the fund must distribute this income to its shareholders. You have the option of taking these distributions in cash or having them immediately invested in additional shares of your mutual fund.

To maximize the long-term growth of your capital, you must reinvest all distributions in additional fund shares. Wealth is created by compounding your money, in other words earning profits on your profits. As the fund increases in price over time, your capital will increase dramatically as you earn these profits on a larger number of shares. Therefore, always have your mutual funds automatically reinvest your capital gains and dividends. This feature can be set up when you open your fund account.

Q: How do I figure my average cost and profit or loss?

Your mutual funds will send you periodic statements showing all of your purchases. Your average cost is calculated by taking the total dollar amount of your investments and dividing by the total number of shares you've bought. For example, if you've invested $100 per month for twelve months, you have invested a total of $1,200. If you have bought 235.456 mutual fund shares during this time, your average cost per share is $1,200 divided by 235.456, or $5.10.

To calculate your current profit or loss you first multiply your total number of shares by the current price of your mutual fund. This you can generally find each day in your local newspaper or by calling the fund. The result of this multiplication is the current value of your fund investment. To figure your profit or loss just subtract your total regular investments from this amount. To continue the example above, let's say your fund ended the day at $7.50 per share. Your 235.456 shares have a current market value of $1,765.92 (235.456 x $7.50). Therefore, your profit at the present time is $1,765.92 minus $1,200.00, or $565.92.

Please note that for income tax purposes the calculation of your profit or loss may differ from the procedure just described. The IRS regulations in this area are unnecessarily complicated. This should not scare you from investing according to an RIP strategy. It's just a fact you should be aware of so that you can prepare yourself by knowing the rules and keeping proper records. IRS Publication 564, Mutual Fund Distributions, is a good source of information on this subject.

Near-Lock #2. Diversification

No single investment performs best under all economic and stock market conditions, and it's impossible to invest consistently in the top performers. Therefore, it is wise to implement an investment program capable of weathering a wide variety of investment climates.

Diversification is a strategy that will provide a safe haven during economic storms while still allowing you to make "hay" while the investment sun shines. The idea is to invest in a diverse group of assets that will perform differently during varying economic conditions. Putting all of your investment eggs in one basket is fine if it's the right basket but a real problem if it's the wrong one. It was legendary investor Bernard Baruch who said, "Put all your eggs in one basket and watch that basket!" Unfortunately, investors with Mr. Baruch's ability to pick the right "basket" are extremely rare.

It is safe to assume that with tens of thousands of investment alternatives available, the likelihood of picking a clunker instead of a winner is high if we're restricted to one choice. However, the Bible tells us that if we expand the number of our selections, the odds are much higher that we'll make a great choice.[15] Furthermore, it's better to spread your investments across several areas so that poor performance in one can be offset by strong performance in another.[16]

The reason diversification works is that something different always does well. Therefore, you need to diversify in order to maintain exposure to the best investments. Despite losses in some areas, a diversified portfolio will eventually offset them by being in position to take advantage of prime opportunities in others. Chart 7.5 shows the best-performing investment class each year from 1981–1993. Notice how the best performer changes each year and that any one class rarely dominates.

While diversification is a good thing, too much of it can be bad. Too much diversification results in extra complexity for little additional benefit either in added return or less risk. Usually it ends up lowering return and increasing risk, not too mention the risks and costs of tracking an unnecessarily large portfolio. For most individual investors, no more than four mutual funds with unrelated objectives are all that is needed. Decent diversification can be achieved even with just two, such as a growth mutual fund invested in stocks and an income fund invested in bonds or money market securities. If you are going to invest in a number of funds, take extra care to ensure that they have completely different investment objectives and that the extra complexity can be accommodated.

Best Performing Investments

1981 Treasury Bills	1988 Small Stocks
1982 Corporate Bonds	1989 Common Stocks
1983 Small Stocks	1990 Treasury Bills
1984 Corporate Bonds	1991 Small Stocks
1985 Common Stocks	1992 Small Stocks
1986 Long-term Government Bonds	1993 Small Stocks
1987 Treasury Bills	

Chart 7.5

Diversification Key Points
1. Diversification helps lower risk.
2. No single investment is best under all economic and market conditions.
3. Most of the return to a portfolio is due to mix of investments, not their specific characteristics.
4. Guard against overdiversification. Two to four mutual funds with unrelated investment objectives are sufficient for most investors.

Near-Lock #3. The 3-Stage Strategy
The 3-Stage Strategy is a long-term investment plan that adjusts your portfolio to your changing needs for growth relative to safety. The cornerstone of the 3-Stage Strategy is the use of the stock market to maximize capital growth. However, the strategy is designed to emphasize stocks when the risk is the lowest and to emphasize safety when the risk is much higher.

Essentially, the 3-Stage Strategy is a changing, diversified portfolio of mutual funds that will emphasize growth, income, or safety depending on where you are in terms of your particular investment goals. This could be retirement, college, or any other long-term objective. Let's assume that the specific goal is retirement, which we'll discuss more fully in chapter 9.

The first stage is to be heavily weighted toward stocks when you are more than ten years away from retirement. As we saw earlier in this chapter, for investment holding periods longer than ten years, the risk of losing money in stocks is extremely low but the rewards are potentially very high. Assuming an early start, this portfolio will establish a solid foundation for maximum long-term capital growth.

As the time to retire gets closer, most investors will want to protect themselves against the short-term volatility and uncertainty of the stock market. The 3-Stage Strategy will adjust the risk of the portfolio by emphasizing fixed-income mutual funds that are more appropriate for capital preservation. In Stage 2, usually implemented with five to ten years until retirement, growth has reduced emphasis in favor of increased priority for income and safety. With as many as ten years to go there is still time for substantial growth in your retirement fund. A good portfolio can easily double in this time. However, since the bulk of your money has already been made in Stage 1, now is the time to protect those gains.

Stage 3 begins with less than five years left in the retirement countdown. The object now is to preserve capital near and during retirement. Safety of principal is the primary goal by investing in high-quality, fixed-income securities. However, growth is not completely abandoned, even once retirement starts. Some portfolio growth is still necessary to keep pace with inflation and preserve purchasing power.

The 3-Stage Strategy should be individually customized to account for individual differences in risk tolerance. Higher risk personalities may want to stay in Stages 1 and 2 for as long as possible, while lower risk personalities will desire to move to Stages 2 and 3 more quickly. It will also need to be modified to account for personal financial circumstances and how soon the plan can be implemented. Investors who either start too late, save too little, or both will have to stay in the more aggressive

Stage 1 portfolio for a longer period of time. Investors who have their retirement funding needs met early can spend more time in the less volatile Stages 2 and 3 portfolios, which should be less emotionally taxing.

Chart 7.6 is a matrix that shows guidelines for implementing the 3-Stage Strategy given your tolerance for risk and time remaining until retirement.

3-Stage Plan Portfolio Guidelines
Numbers in the Matrix Represent Stage Portfolios

Risk Profile	0–5 yrs.	5–10 yrs.	10–20 yrs.	20+ yrs.
High	2	2	1	1
Moderate	3	2	1	1
Low	3	2	2	1
Very Low	3	3	2	2

Chart 7.6

Chart 7.7 can be used as a guideline to understanding the different potential performance characteristics of each portfolio.

Annualized Returns (1971–1991)

Portfolio	Risk	Average	Best Year	Worst Year
Stage 3	High	+11.7%	+33.8%	-23.0%
Stage 2	Moderate	+10.7%	+25.8%	-13.2%
Stage 1	Low	+8.9%	+18.8%	+.6%

(Based on actual performance of stocks, bonds, and Treasury Bills from 1971–1991. Past performance does not guarantee future results.)

Chart 7.7

The 1 percent difference between the Stage 3 and Stage 2 portfolios is not as small as it appears. One thousand dollars invested each year for thirty years at 10.7 percent grows to

$188,000. The same amount becomes $228,000 if invested at 11.7 percent. That's $40,000 or 20 percent more money for a small increase in risk.

As you can see from the chart above, a typical Stage 3 portfolio has the potential for wide fluctuations but the long-term difference of 1 percent is important. Stage 2 portfolios have exhibited less volatility while still achieving excellent growth potential. Stage 1 portfolios have historically preserved capital by never losing money but still keeping pace with inflation and also allowing potential for modest growth.

3-Stage Strategy Model Portfolios

The following can be used to implement the 3-Stage Strategy. While these funds meet previously discussed criteria, you should feel free to replace any of the mutual funds with your own choices as long as they pursue similar investment objectives.

The best way to implement the 3-Stage Strategy is through Charles Schwab and Co.'s Mutual Fund OneSource program. You can invest in over 200 well-known mutual funds with no loads, transaction fees, or commissions. The advantages of this program is that all of your investments will be in one account; you can track them all in one statement from the broker; and you have access to your entire portfolio with one phone call. Schwab offers lower minimum investments on many of the funds. Since you can easily switch among your funds, the Mutual Fund OneSource service is great for investing with the Regular Investment Plan and the Constant Ratio Plan (discussed later in this chapter).

Highlighted in italics are funds that are available in the service but with Schwab's normal discounted commission rates. These no-load mutual funds can be bought directly from the fund's parent company at no charge. The advantage of buying them through Schwab is the simplicity of having all your funds at one account. However, the italicized funds cannot be used for the Regular Investment Plan.

Stage 1: Highest Risk
Growth: 85%, Income 15%

Simple
Growth (85%): Janus
Income (15%): Dreyfus A Bonds Plus

Best
Growth (45%): Janus Fund
Small Company Growth (20%): 20th Century Ultra
International Stock (20%): *Scudder International*
Income (15%): Dreyfus A Bonds Plus

For SP/NT temperaments (see chap. 4): lower Janus Fund 10%, increase 20th Century Ultra and *Scudder International* 5% each

Stage 2: Moderate Risk
Growth: 55%, Income 20%, Preserve 25%

Simple
Vanguard STAR (100%)

Best
Growth (35%): Neuberger/Berman Guardian
Small Company Growth (10%): 20th Century Ultra
International Stock (10): *Scudder International*
Income (20%): Dreyfus A Bonds Plus
Preserve (25%): Schwab Money Market

For SP/NT: (1) lower Neuberger/Berman Guardian 5%, increase 20th Century Ultra and *Scudder International* 5% each; (2) replace Schwab Money Market with *Vanguard Fixed Income Short-Term*

Stage 3: Low Risk
Growth: 15%, Income 20%, Preserve 65%

Simple
Growth/Income (35%): *Vanguard Wellesley* (for SP/NT temperaments substitute *Vanguard Wellington*) Preserve (65%): Schwab Money Market

3-Stage Strategy Key Points
1. The 3-Stage Strategy emphasizes growth, income, or safety based upon your changing investment needs.

2. Risk is adjusted over time based upon the portfolio's ability to recover from temporary losses.
3. The 3-Stage Strategy can be modified to account for individual differences in risk tolerance due to personality temperament.
4. A 1 percent difference in long-term annual return matters.

Near-Lock #4. Constant Ratio Plan
This is a variation of the Regular Investment Plan, which also combines risk control with automatic buying decisions. However, it goes one step further than RIP by including predetermined selling decisions that are generally much harder to make than buying decisions. It is one of the best methods for fulfilling every investor's desire to "buy low and sell high." When used over time in conjunction with RIP the results can be dramatic.

The idea behind the Constant Ratio Plan (CRP) is to use the profits on your best performing investments to buy more of your laggards. When these laggards become leaders, you'll sell them and start the process again by buying the new laggards. The reason it's called Constant Ratio is that you will periodically sell and buy within your portfolio to reset the asset allocation to a predetermined target. While this sounds like a mouthful, it's an easy concept as the following example will demonstrate.

Let's assume you are a mutual fund investor starting the year with a $50,000 portfolio diversified as follows: $30,000, or 60 percent of the assets allocated to a stock fund; $10,000 or 20 percent allocated to a bond fund; and $10,000 or 20 percent allocated to a money market fund. At the end of the year, you will buy and sell to reset the portfolio's assets to this constant ratio allocation, that is, 60 percent stocks, 20 percent bonds, 20 percent money market. At the end of the year, the portfolio performance was as follows: the stock fund rose 20 percent, the bond fund dropped 5 percent and the money market fund rose 5 percent. This means the portfolio now has $36,000 or 64 percent of the assets allocated to the stock fund; $9,500 or 17 percent allocated to the bond fund; and $10,500 or 19 percent allocated to the money market fund. Since the allocations have changed, the Constant Ratio Plan needs to be implemented. The idea is to sell some of the leaders and buy some of the laggards in order to restore the original 60%/20%/20% ratios for stock, bonds, and money market funds, respectively.

The portfolio is now valued at $56,000. Therefore, to restore the original asset allocation, you need to do the following:

(1) The stock fund should be 60 percent of $56,000 or $33,600 instead of its current value of $36,000. Sell $2,400 of this fund.

(2) The bond fund should be 20 percent of $56,000 or $11,200 instead of its current value of $9,500. Buy $1,700 of this fund.

(3) The money market fund should be 20 percent of $56,000 or $11,200 instead of its current value of $10,500. Buy $700 of this fund.

As you can see, profits made on the leading investment, in this case the stock fund, were used to purchase more of the lagging investments — the bond and money market funds. Here, the Constant Ratio Plan works similar to RIP in that you will be forced to buy more of the investments that are down in price. It goes one step further in that the plan forces you to realize profits on your winning investments. It also significantly improves performance because without clearly defined buying and selling rules, most investors do the exact opposite. They will wait for assets to drop before selling and wait for assets to go up before buying. The Constant Ratio Plan allows you to "buy low and sell high" without any guesswork. Ironically, this strategy works best after steep market drops. We saw in Chart 7.5 that each year it's highly likely that a different investment class will be the top performer. The Constant Ratio Plan forces you to load up on the investments whose turn it is to explode in price while protecting you from the ones most apt to fall. To get the most out of this strategy, there are several steps you can take to maximize its effectiveness.

First, this strategy takes time to be at its best. The effect of continually selling leaders and buying lagging investments shows up only after the cycle is repeated a number of times. Time is a wise investor's biggest ally. The longer you let this strategy work, the better it gets.

Second, this strategy works best with a diversified portfolio that includes aggressive, growth-oriented investments. These funds typically drop sharply in down markets and can be bought at bargain prices before rising strongly in up markets and generating huge profits. Investing in a group of funds with similar characteristics defeats the purpose of the plan since you'll essentially be buying and selling the same thing.

Third, this strategy is best if you diversify into investments that tend to move in opposite directions or do not follow each other closely. The best example of this is international mutual funds since they buy stocks of foreign countries whose economies ebb and flow in different cycles than the U.S. economy. Another good example is small company mutual funds since they either greatly lead or greatly lag behind the rest of the stock market.

Fourth, decide on a good time period for rebalancing. Too short a time between adjustments fails to take advantage of large price moves before they fully develop. This cuts down both profits and bargain buying opportunities. Too long a time between adjustments may allow prime buying and selling opportunities to pass by. Unfortunately, the best amount of time is impossible to know in advance. Besides, trying to know in advance runs contrary to the philosophy of the strategy. I recommend rebalancing every six to twelve months, with aggressive portfolios tending toward six months and conservative portfolios tending toward a year.

Finally, since you will be selling frequently, this plan works best within tax-favored investment vehicles such as IRAs, 401Ks, or tax-deferred annuities. These vehicles will be discussed more fully in chapter 9. Every time you sell at a profit, the IRS will want its share. Tax-advantaged investing allows you to delay paying Uncle Sam, and more importantly, it makes your money grow much faster.

Constant Ratio Plan Key Points
1. The Constant Ratio Plan is an easy way to buy low and sell high.

2. It automates difficult selling decisions.
3. It needs time to work best.
4. It is powerful when used in conjunction with the Regular Investment Plan.

P.I.ST.O.L. – The Perfect Investment Strategy Of a Lifetime

Need to shoot down your investment fears? Get a P.I.ST.O.L.! P.I.ST.O.L. is a combination of the four basic investment concepts: Regular Investment Plan, Diversification, The 3-Stage Strategy, and Constant Ratio Plan. Besides being incredibly easy, P.I.ST.O.L. requires little knowledge, little money, and little time. Best of all, P.I.ST.O.L. works, providing the potential for tremendous rewards with reduced risk, without regard to market conditions. P.I.ST.O.L. is implemented simply by executing four basic investment concepts.

First, start your Regular Investment Plan by deciding how much you want to periodically invest in mutual funds. The time period (weekly, biweekly, monthly, and so on) should not change, and the amount committed should stay level for an extended period of time. Naturally it is to your advantage to increase your commitment as your budget allows, as long as you can maintain the increase for the foreseeable future.

Next, diversify your regular investment amount among a portfolio of funds designed to provide a combination of growth, income, and safety. The types of mutual funds you buy, not the specific choices, are what matter most to your investment performance. Diversification may be possible even with small amounts of money since a number of fine mutual companies permit investing with low minimum investments. Most employer-sponsored savings plans such as 401Ks/403Bs make it easy to diversify with small amounts of money. If you're investing long term and can't afford to buy two or more funds, choose a growth fund first until you can add other funds.

Third, using the 3-Stage Strategy, set allocation ratios according to the time horizon of your goals and tolerance for risk. These ratios will change as your needs for growth, income, and safety change.

Fourth and last, buy low and sell high through the Constant

Ratio Plan. At predetermined time intervals, nail down profits by selling your leaders and use them to buy laggards at advantageously low prices. This will enhance your performance by automating difficult buy and sell decisions, the bane of individual investors.

That's it! If you stick with P.I.ST.O.L. you'll be on your way to building wealth in a prudent, safe, and comfortable manner. It is not wealth without risk. However, it is wealth within reason. P.I.ST.O.L. will enable you to combine the best financial practices with the values of biblical stewardship. If implemented consistently, it should be a winning combination.

Summary
1. Protecting God's assets requires effort on your part.
2. Good investments can be found by
   (1) seeking and heeding good advice;
   (2) investing only in things you understand well enough to explain in simple language;
   (3) avoiding "get rich quick without risk" propositions.
3. You will eventually lose money by making quick decisions.
4. You will eventually lose money by making no decisions.
5. Have plans for
   (1) buying;
   (2) selling;
   (3) diversifying;
   (4) making plan revisions.
6. Follow the Four Be's:
   (1) Be Safe;
   (2) Be Comfortable;
   (3) Be Consistent;
   (4) Be Patient.
7. Shoot down your investment fears with P.I.ST.O.L—The Perfect Investment Strategy Of a Lifetime.

Notes

1. *Romans 7:15, 19*
2. *Proverbs 18:15; 15:22; 19:20*
3. *Proverbs 18:13*
4. *Proverbs 18:15*
5. *Proverbs 18:17*
6. *Proverbs 14:8*
7. *Proverbs 14:15*
8. *1 John 4:1*
9. *Proverbs 4:7; 2:12-15; Psalm 1:1*
10. *Psalm 37:7*
11. *2 Timothy 2:15*
12. *Matthew 25:24-26, 28-30*
13. *Ecclesiastes 11:4*
14. *Proverbs 27:12*
15. *Ecclesiastes 11:6*
16. *Ecclesiastes 11:2*

Chapter Eight

You Must Learn How to Use Other People's Money

The wicked borrow and do not repay,
but the righteous give generously
(Psalm 37:21)

Dan read Romans 13:8, "Let no debt remain outstanding, except the continuing debt to love one another, for he who loves his fellowman has fulfilled the law," and has decided that he needs to eliminate all his debts, including his mortgage, to be a good financial steward. Not only is he working twenty to thirty hours overtime each week to earn extra money, but money that could be directed to other good uses is being used to become totally debt free. Dan and his family aren't particularly happy but feel bound to "follow the Bible."

Earl and Barb want to buy a house because they've heard that rent is a waste of money and that owning a home is a great tax break. They're saving their money for a small down payment and are eager to make this wise financial move.

Both Dan and Earl may be making big financial mistakes! Why? Read on!

Probably the most misunderstood area of financial stewardship is that of debt. Many Christian financial "experts" believe the Bible preaches against the use of debt.

In their zeal to free people from the bondage of debt, they misapply and take out of context Bible verses they believe teach a debt-free lifestyle as being biblically correct. Unfortunately, in doing so they have created a new bondage—unnecessary guilt about having debt. This bondage creates a fear that often leads to poor financial decisions. However, we must recognize that the use of debt means using someone else's money. God has already given us a portion of His money to manage according to our abilities. If He thought we could handle more, He would have seen to it that we had more. Therefore, we must exercise great caution to ensure that we are not trying to get something through others that was not intended for us. This happened long ago in a garden with disastrous consequences!

Debt Is Not a Sin

One of the verses often used in the anti-debt doctrine is Deuteronomy 28:12—it is actually first seen in Deuteronomy 15:6: "You will lend to many nations but will borrow from none." This verse, however, is not a command. It is a blessing based upon a condition that appears in Deuteronomy 28:1: "If you fully obey the Lord your God and carefully follow all His commands I give you today, the Lord your God will set you up on high above all the nations of the earth. All these blessings will come upon you and accompany you if you obey the Lord your God."

Freedom from debt is a blessing, not a commandment. It would appear that God would prefer that His people not have to borrow money. However, this is not exactly a great spiritual revelation. Obviously, we would all love to be able to never have to borrow money, especially for a house or a car. By the grace of God, some of us may actually go through life without ever incurring a dollar's worth of debt.

If being debt-free is a command, why would God allow us to force others to sin by borrowing from us as Deuteronomy 15:6 says? In fact, we are commanded not to cause others to sin by our actions. "Be careful, however, that the exercise of your freedom does not become a stumbling block to the weak" (1 Cor. 8:9).

At first glance, there would appear to be a number of Old

Testament injunctions against charging interest, at least according to many modern translations. The word "interest" is called "usury" in the King James. The original Hebrew word for either term is *neshek*. Nowadays, we associate usury with loan sharks charging illegal rates of interest on loans, which also occurred in the Old Testament era. Archeological studies of ancient times, however, show that charging interest on loans was a normal occurrence.

The way loans were made was to give a borrower a discounted obligation. In other words, a debtor would receive eighty shekels on a loan of one hundred shekels. The difference between the amount borrowed (eighty shekels) and the amount paid back (one hundred shekels) represented the interest, or *neshek* due on the loan.

When someone failed to pay their obligation, including the interest, it was a common practice to increase the interest rate, take the person as a slave, or both. The increasing of the amount of interest necessary to satisfy the original loan is worded in various Bible translations as "increase" or "unjust gain." Here, the original Hebrew word is *tarbit* which refers to the practice of charging additional interest whenever a debtor failed to make the required payments. The use of the words "interest" or "usury" then refers to the charging of extra interest for late payment, not the normal interest for the use of borrowed funds. While enslavement and usury were common practices in neighboring cultures, it was these specific practices that God disallowed among the Jews.

God recognized that there would be those in financial need.[1] To maintain financial equality among His chosen people, God forbid them to charge extra interest to each other, make slaves out of their own people who were unable to pay their debts, and commanded that they cancel all debts every seven years.[2]

There are many other verses critical to the antidebt doctrine, the two most prominent being "Let no debt remain outstanding, except the continuing debt to love one another, for he who loves his fellow man has fulfilled the law" (Rom. 13:8) and "the rich rule over the poor, and the borrower is servant to the lender" (Prov. 22:7). It is not my intention to debate their misapplication, except to say that

(1) the debt referred to in Romans 13:8 does not refer to financial debt but to the task and responsibility of loving our neighbor as Christ loved us. This is probably the most abused verse in the entire Bible when the issue is financial debt;
(2) slavery as a condition of debt is no longer a reality in our culture. As we'll soon see, Proverbs 22:7, also widely misunderstood, refers to the abusive use of debt in Old Testament times.[3]

It Is My Conviction that the Use of Debt Is Not a Sin

I believe there are legitimate uses for debt, although they are few. However, debt can create financial bondage if the use of credit is indicating sin in other areas of your life. If you are using money that is not your own, it is due to one of two reasons. Either you have failed to save enough money or you have spent too much. Lack of savings violates the principle discussed in chapter 5: You Must Save Your Money. Excess spending is a strong indication of covetousness—a violation of one of the Ten Commandments.

What *is* a sin is the use of money to the detriment of others or ourselves. It is not the use of debt that God is concerned with. It is the use of money as a tool of oppression that the biblical injunctions against debt are referring to. At stake is something far more fundamental than financial stewardship. Any act that allows us to take control of another's life essentially puts us in the position of playing God. This puts us in direct violation of the first of the Ten Commandments, "You shall have no other gods before Me" (Ex. 20:3). Likewise, any act that allows another to enslave us, puts that person between us and God.

In fact, the Prophets Ezekiel and Nehemiah spoke out against this oppressive use of money. In direct opposition to God's commands created to promote financial harmony, the rich were exploiting the needy.[4] And in Nehemiah's time, the wealthy natives were taking advantage of those returning to Jerusalem from exile. The rich would loan out large sums of money, and when the borrower failed to pay, they would be forced to give up their fields. Then, without a source of income, they would have to sell their families into slavery. This corrupt system was established in order for the wealthy to enrich themselves at the expense of their own people.[5]

On the other hand, lending money to help people meet needs they couldn't otherwise meet was not only allowable, but it also was encouraged. Nehemiah himself loaned money at the same time he was being critical of those who were abusing what were intended to be compassionate lending practices. "I and my brothers and my men are also lending the people money and grain" (Neh. 5:10).

Compassionate lending took into account that reasonable interest should be charged. However, the essence of compassionate lending is that the lender, while intending to earn a reasonable profit, is completely willing to receive no payment in return. This includes even the refusal to accept collateral to satisfy an obligation.[6] Sympathetic, sacrificial lending was clearly not the intent of the rich money-lenders referred to in the Old Testament.

It was compassionate lending that Jesus spoke of in Luke 6:35: "But love your enemies, do good to them, and *lend* to them without expecting to get anything back. Then your reward will be great, and you will be sons of the Most High, because He is kind to the ungrateful and wicked" (italics added). The original Greek word for lend in this verse is *daneizo*, which means to loan on interest. Even Jesus encouraged the practice of lending. As always, though, Jesus was looking at the attitude behind the action. The primary motivation for making an interest-bearing loan is not to earn the interest but to demonstrate your love for people through your sacrificial willingness to meet their material needs. It then becomes the responsibility of the borrower to repay the interest rather than the responsibility of the lender to collect. Ezekiel's words tell us how loans should be made. "The word of the Lord came to me: . . . [a righteous man] does not lend at usury or take excessive interest" (Ezek. 18:1, 8).

Three Guidelines for the Use of Debt

I believe there are three guidelines that apply to the decision to borrow money. All three guidelines fall under the biblical principle that money should never be used to the detriment of yourself and especially another person. Therefore, this principle should regulate the behavior and attitudes of both the borrower and the lender. First, there should be a valid economic reason for borrowing money. Second, there should be spiritual comfort when borrowing money. Finally, the borrowed money must be paid back.

Let's deal with the payback issue first. The Bible is clear about paying back loans (Ps. 37:21). The failure to return something belonging to another is obviously stealing, which the Bible is also clear about.[7] Therefore, before making a decision to borrow money, one must thoughtfully consider their ability to pay it back. Since this ability will vary from person to person, you must assess your situation on its own merits. However, as we saw in chapter 4, faithful financial stewards take control of their money by realistically understanding their financial circumstances.

In determining your ability to meet your loan obligations, you must take great care not to depend upon future events to provide the necessary funds.[8] Your ability to meet tomorrow's debt payments should be based upon today's financial situation. To assume that you will be able to pay your debts because of a future pay increase or financial windfall puts you in the position of believing you control your own future. This makes you out to be your own god.

But what if your present financial situation becomes adversely affected? We certainly have no guarantees that we will be able to maintain our present standard of living. That is why we need to approach the issue of debt very carefully and very spiritually. Having adequate savings is one strategy that would help in this type of situation. The other is to try to restrict debt to those assets that have investment merit.

Assets with investment merit are those that have underlying financial value. In times of financial hardship, they can be sold to completely pay off loans against them and eliminate their financial burden. They are also assets that can normally be expected to appreciate in value over a long period of time, like a house. However, as stated above, we must exercise great care not to presume upon the future.

A home loan is the classic case of investment debt. Another example of investment debt is a car loan. I consider this an investment loan in that a car provides transportation to and from your job, which provides you income. Another loan with economic and investment rationale is an education loan. Again, this debt is being used to provide a source of income. Both car and school loans can be viewed as borrowing money to invest in your earnings capability. In theory, you should be able to earn far more than the cost of the loan. This is the essence of an economic purpose for borrowing money. There must be a reasonable expectation that the return on the borrowed money is greater than the cost of the money after taxes and including the interest.

Once again, these decisions need to be passed through an individual spiritual filter. You may not need a car for work if public transportation or car pools are readily available. Likewise, there are a number of ways to fund a college education without borrowing. Your individual situation may allow you to avoid or minimize the amount of debt you need to take on. For instance, while you may need an automobile, buying a $50,000 luxury vehicle may be inappropriate. Any car loan may be inappropriate if a cheaper car or maintaining the one you currently own is a better alternative, as it generally is. Remember, borrowing is not specifically a sin. However, we will be held accountable for how we used the financial resources given to us. Borrowing money for an inappropriate need is a waste of God's resources and represents unfaithful stewardship. Therefore, we need to prayerfully seek spiritual guidance before making any major expense, particularly if it involves debt.

If you're married, one of the best places to receive this guidance is through your spouse. Many times, one or the other spouse is uncomfortable with the idea of assuming a debt to make a particular purchase. This is clearly a sign to reassess the situation and work toward a solution that is mutually agreeable to both partners. The question we need to ask ourselves, or each other, before borrowing money is "Why am I using resources that are not my own?" After realistically considering the use of the money and your financial condition, if you are comfortable with the answer, the debt is probably legitimate.

A final legitimate use of credit is for convenience. For most people, buying by phone with a credit card rather than sending money through the mail is a preferred way to shop. Many people, especially travelers, don't like to carry cash. In many places it is simply unsafe to carry cash. Using a credit card instead of cash or check allows you to earn interest on your money in the bank. The use of credit cards for cash makes sense only under one condition—you must pay the accumulated charges within the time allowed to pay no interest. Unfortunately, most people lack the discipline to consistently do this. This brings me to the Pandora's Box of personal finance—credit card and consumer debt.

The Perils of Consumer Debt

Probably the biggest financial problem facing most people is excess consumer debt. Consumer debt is the use of credit for consumption rather than investment. While investment debt is only occasionally wrong, consumer debt is almost always wrong. The Bible clearly states that we must pay our loans back. The reason consumer debt is such a problem is that it is easy to get, it generally carries very high interest rates and it is revolving—that is, there is no defined schedule of payments that eventually results in the loan being fully paid off.

Consumer debt, quite simply, is spending money you don't have for something you don't need! This is a wasteful use of God's resources to fulfill your own spirit of covetousness. It is clearly sinful. There will of course be times when emergency expenses exceed your ability to pay. God understands that, and you should not feel guilty about borrowing money to meet that need. Your only obligation is to pay that loan back. Unfortunately, most of the trillions of dollars of consumer debt has been used to finance a lifestyle above our given resources. There can be little justification for this use of someone else's money.

You should make every effort to reduce your consumer debt to as close to zero as possible. Furthermore, you should not think about investing until you have virtually no consumer debt. You should probably even consider selling any investments you have to pay off these debts. The rate of return on most investments is well below the interest rates on consumer debt. This means your debts are growing faster than your assets. It is difficult to get ahead financially while being strangled by 15 to 20 percent annual interest charges. For many people, their debts are growing faster than their assets and incomes. This means each day they are moving closer to a financial meltdown.

An excellent source of guidance in the area of better credit card management is the Bankcard Holders of America (BHA). BHA is a nonprofit consumer protection group whose mission is to save consumers money, provide credit management counseling, and protect consumers' rights. Membership in BHA costs only $24 per year and includes applications for one no-fee credit card and one low interest rate card. The low cost of using these cards should help you recoup your annual membership fee.

In addition, you will receive a thirty-two-page Credit Secrets Manual, twenty-two pamphlets on various aspects of credit management (that is, managing Family Debt, Auto Leasing vs. Buying, Getting Out of Debt), and a one-year subscription to their bimonthly consumer advice newsletter. The BHA can be reached by writing them at 524 Branch Drive, Salem, VA 24153.

Debt Warning Signs

The following signs indicate that debt is a major financial burden that needs to be addressed immediately:

- Twenty-percent of your take-home pay is being used for debt payments, not including home mortgage.
- Fifty-percent of your take-home pay is being used for debt payment, including your mortgage.
- Your bills are not being paid on time.
- You make only the minimum payments each month, and that's difficult.

- You never get credit cards completely paid off.
- Your next raise is already committed to paying debts.
- Your debts exceed your assets (see chap. 4 — "How to Take Control of Your Money")
- The total amount of your debts is unknown.
- You've taken out a loan to consolidate your debts, and you've since added new debt.
- You are charging purchases that you used to pay for with cash.
- You are taking out credit card cash advances to make regular purchases.
- You are continually applying for additional credit cards.

Debt Reduction Strategies

- Set aside in your household budget a regular amount to be used for reducing consumer debt.
- Pay off small credit balances first. This will build confidence and personal momentum in reducing your debts. Once you eliminate one balance, move on to the next. As you pay off cards, raise the amount in your budget used for paying debts.
- Given the above, also pay attention to the interest rates being charged on your various loans. Try to pay off your higher interest rate cards first.
- Try to consolidate your loans into one. This has several advantages. First, it will probably reduce your monthly payment. Second, it may reduce your interest rate and save you a lot of money in interest charges. Finally, it will give you a fixed payment schedule and a definite time to finally pay off your loans. The disadvantage is that most people lack the discipline to keep from making new additions to their credit cards.
- Always pay cash. This, of course, will not reduce your debts but is the most effective way of preventing credit difficulties.

What to Do When You're in Trouble

If you are in over your head, don't hesitate to call your creditors and explain your difficulty. They will often be generous in offering you a repayment plan with affordable terms. Many lenders have temporary payment reduction programs for borrowers in financial difficulty. These programs too often go unused. If you have problems making debt payments, take the initiative and explain your situation early to your creditors. It is then that you have the best chance of successfully resolving your problems. It's a bad idea to ignore them and allow adverse information to enter your credit report. This often has devastating long-term consequences.

It would also be wise to seek professional assistance. Many localities have financial assistance programs that provide expert volunteer counselors. If this is not available, try the National Foundation for Consumer Credit. They have Consumer Credit Counseling Service (CCCS) offices across the country. A CCCS is a community service organization dedicated to helping people live within a budget and repay outstanding bills.

CCCS will work on your behalf with your creditors to get you out of debt. If your financial problems are not short term, most creditors would prefer to work with CCCS than directly with the borrower. There is no charge for CCCS services. They offer free professional money management and debt-reduction plans as an alternative to personal bankruptcy and adverse consequences to your credit rating. They also offer educational materials on budgeting and the wise use of credit. You can find the CCCS nearest you by calling 1-800-388-CCCS.

If you are having credit difficulties, you should take advantage of the services offered by organizations such as CCCS and Bankcard Holders of America. They may be able to help you before your credit rating is damaged. Furthermore, this will help you avoid credit assistance firms. Many of these are rip-off artists preying on desperate people by charging a substantial up-front fee and doing no work.

Car Loans

Studies consistently show that the cheapest car is the one you own regardless of the maintenance costs. But let's be honest—it's hard to not get excited about owning a new car, especially if yours is an old clunker. If you "have to have" a new car—and remember, this is God's money you're using—you may as well buy it smart. Try to do the following when buying a car:

- Pay cash if at all possible. A 12 percent loan for five years on a $15,000 car actually costs you over $20,000 or 33 percent more for your car. So much for negotiating 5 percent off the purchase price!
- If you can't pay cash—and few people ever can—try to make as large a down payment as possible. This will lower your monthly payment and reduce your total cost. Try to make a 20 percent down payment and never make less than 10 percent. The value of your trade-in can count in this figure.
- Try to take out as short a loan as possible. The additional interest cost of long loans is significant. A 12 percent, five-year, $15,000 loan has $5,020 of interest. This same loan for three years has only $2,936 of interest, a savings of over $2,000. If you took this loan for seven years, the interest is $7,242. If you can't afford the payments of a five-year loan, you can't afford the car.

There's another reason to try to make a decent down payment and have a shorter loan. Cars depreciate rapidly in value. Most people find themselves "underwater" for the first few years of car ownership. In other words, the amount they owe is greater than the value of the car. When the loan period is short, more money goes to debt reduction and less to interest. A large down payment virtually assures that you'll never go underwater.

One way to achieve all of the above goals is to buy a used car. The original owner has already paid for the rapid depreciation that occurs in the first years of ownership. Naturally, you'll have to consider the costs of maintenance. Also financing rates are usually higher on used cars than new. Shop around for financing. You'd be surprised how much rates vary from bank to bank. Try to avoid dealer financing unless they are offering below market rates.

Mortgages
A discussion of the ins and outs of financing a house is beyond the scope of this book. A good real estate agent should be able

to help you through the maze of financing options. It's worth educating yourself enough to shop around for home financing. This is likely the largest purchase you'll ever make in your lifetime. It's worth the time and effort to make some phone calls to various real estate lenders. Just let your fingers do the walking through the yellow pages. Keep an eye out for lenders who try to trap "rate shoppers" by quoting irresistibly low rates on the phone that don't seem to be available when you get to the office to apply.

An alternative to doing a lot of your shopping is to contact a mortgage broker. This is a firm that acts as a middleperson between borrowers and lenders. Since they usually represent more lenders than you're likely to call yourself, they're in a better position to find you the best loan for your situation. They charge a fee for this service, of course. However, a good mortgage broker is worth the cost.

There are two mortgage issues I want to specifically address. The first is that of reducing your total interest cost and becoming debt-free faster by either

(1) taking out a fifteen-year loan instead of thirty-year loan or
(2) paying extra each month to reduce the principle, which the interest is calculated on.

The second issue is whether it always makes sense to own rather than rent your own home.

Are Mortgage Reduction Strategies Wise?

The issue is whether it is wise to pay off your mortgage faster by either taking out a fifteen-year loan or by taking a thirty-year loan and paying extra each month. Except in certain circumstances, I am opposed to either of these strategies! Most people do either of these to reduce their total interest, which is a laudable goal. A $150,000 house financed at 8 percent for thirty years results in nearly $250,000 of interest, almost twice the cost of the house. If that same house were financed for fifteen years, the rate would probably be around 7.5 percent and the total interest only $100,000. Have I gone crazy? The problem with the above analysis is that it looks at the mortgage in isolation and not as part of one's overall financial picture. The goal of money management is to increase your assets. If you could create assets greater than the difference in interest savings you will be ahead. Let's look at an example using two home buyers.

30-Year versus 15-Year Mortgage
Buyer A
Loan Amount: $150,000
Term: 30 Years
Rate: 8%
Monthly Payment: $1,101 per month
Tax bracket: 28%
Total Interest before Taxes: $246,233
Total Interest after Taxes: $177,288

In evaluating the cost of interest on a home mortgage, only the interest *after* tax is relevant. Since the total interest is tax-deductible, 28% (or other appropriate tax bracket) of the interest is actually paid by the government through a lower tax bill.

Buyer B
Loan Amount: $150,000
Term: 15 Years
Rate: 7.5%
Monthly Payment: $1,391 per month
Tax bracket: 28%
Total Interest before Taxes: $100,293
Total Interest after Taxes: $72,211

So far it looks like Buyer B has a substantial advantage by saving $105,000 in interest. But . . .

Buyer A invests the $291 difference in monthly payments in a stock mutual fund for 30 years and earns an average of 12% per year, the historical return in the stock market. This investment is done in a tax-deferred plan like an IRA or tax-deferred annuity.

211

Investment Return: $1,017,035
Total Return: $1,017,035 − 177,288 (after-tax interest) = $836,252
    The total return is the investment return less the true, after-tax cost of carrying a mortgage.

Buyer B has to wait fifteen years, but then will have $1,391 to invest each month for fifteen years. Unfortunately, A's early start is too much of an advantage.

Investment Return: $694,676
Total Return: $694,676 − $72,211 (after-tax interest) = $622,465

Buyer A wins because of the power of compounding and the advantage of early investing. Furthermore, A's advantage will grow even more through time since A's already so far ahead. Both buyers will own the homes free of debt. But in another ten years, A's million dollars will have grown to over $3.2 million, while B's stake will be worth only $2.2 million. The key to A's successful financial management is to invest to create wealth rather than to avoid interest.

To Pay or Not to Pay Extra Principle?

That is the question. The same analysis applies to the decision to pay extra principal each month. Many homeowners like to pay an extra $100 or so per month. This substantially reduces the total interest paid and shortens the life of the loan. Many advisers state uncategorically that this should be done to have a debt-free home before investing money. Some even say you should do this before investing in a retirement fund. Generally, this is bad advice. Let's look at A and B again.

Buyer A
Loan Amount: $150,000
Term: 30 Years
Rate: 8%
Monthly Payment: $1,101 per month
Tax bracket: 28%
Total Interest before Taxes: $246,233
Total Interest after Taxes: $177,288

Buyer B
Same terms as A, but pays an extra $100 per month that goes to reducing the amount of the loan.
Tax bracket: 28%
Loan paid off 7.5 years early
Total Interest before Taxes: $173,280
Total Interest after Taxes: $124,761

Again, it looks like B has an advantage — over $50,000 of interest saved. But . . .

Buyer A, rather than pay ahead on his mortgage, invests $100 each month in a stock mutual fund for thirty years and earns an average of 12 percent per year, the historical return in the stock market. This investment is done in a tax-deferred plan like an IRA or tax-deferred annuity.
Investment Return: $349,496
Total Return: $349,496 − 177,288 (after-tax interest) = $172,208

Buyer B has paid off his loan early, so he will have $1,200 to invest each month for 7.5 years. Again, A's early start is too much of an advantage.
Investment Return: $173,836
Total Return: $173,836 − $124,761 (after-tax interest) = $49,075

This time it's not even close. After thirty years A has a $123,000 advantage over B. This difference will continue to grow over time since A has a bigger amount to compound than B.

What is happening in these two examples? First, there is the importance of investing even small amounts for an extended period of time. This is the key to building up wealth. Second, the interest savings of a shorter mortgage are reduced by the fact that you already save money because the interest is tax deductible. A pays more interest than B, but some of the difference is returned to A through lower taxes.

Finally, there is the issue of looking at all financial decisions for their impact to your overall wealth. The interest you save by paying your mortgage ahead saves you less than 6 percent (depending on interest rates and your tax bracket) per year interest. If you make more than 6 percent after-tax with the money you're paying ahead, you'll make more money in profit than you'll save in interest.

Refinance and Invest

This strategy directly follows from the examples above. Whenever interest rates drop, there is a surge of homeowners looking to refinance their mortgages at lower rates. This is usually a sound financial decision. Unfortunately, most people don't get the full benefit from lowering the monthly housing expenses because they raise their expenses to match the newer and higher cash flow. Typically, if the payment difference after refinancing is substantial, people will use this difference to finance a major purchase such as a car or other consumer item.

Continued increases in one's standard of living, which usually are unnecessary, are folly. "Whoever loves money never has money enough; whoever loves wealth is never satisfied with his income. This too is meaningless. As goods increase, so do those who consume them. And what benefit are they to the owner except to feast his eyes on them?" (Ecc. 5:10-11) If your standard of living before the refinance was adequate, then a far better form of stewardship is to use your increased cash flow to increase your wealth or if necessary provide a more stable financial cushion. It is certainly more valuable to invest in material assets that will increase in value than to buy additional assets that will only depreciate.

For example, say that a person with a thirty-year fixed rate loan of $120,000 at 8 percent decides to refinance to take advantage of lower interest rates. The balance remaining on the original loan is $95,000 and at 6.5 percent interest rate, his or her payments will drop from $881 per month to $600 per month. This now reduces monthly living expenses by $281 every month. That could finance a beautiful new car, furniture, or an overseas vacation. It could also be invested for the next thirty years at an average of 10 percent per year and grow to $635,000! Even if you invested only half of the difference, it would still grow to $315,000. Naturally, you could use the other half to increase your insurance coverage, pay off other debts, or add to your emergency savings.

This same idea can work any time you obtain a lower rate of interest on borrowed money. You can refinance and invest the difference if you refinance your auto loan, for instance. The same would be true of lowering the rate on credit card debt although hopefully the difference will not matter much. The key is to look at refinancing as a way to increase wealth not increase lifestyle. Quite often we temporarily reduce our expenses only to later let the extra money "burn a hole in our pocket." The hole is usually filled with new loans, which traps us in a vicious debt cycle. As faithful financial stewards we should always look to fund an acceptable lifestyle and then create additional resources to fund the work of God's kingdom.

When You Should Reduce Your Mortgage

The only time people should consider a mortgage reduction strategy is if they are within ten to fifteen years of retiring. In this case, it makes some sense to pay off the home so that your housing cost in retirement is zero. Of course, this may be possible anyway if your house has appreciated to the point that you can pay off the loan by selling the house at retirement and buying another for the remaining cash.

Another instance where mortgage reduction is appropriate is if people feel they are incapable of earning anything more than the rate on CDs, money market funds, or other ultraconservative investments. If this is the case (and there is no reason why that should be!) one should seek professional money management advice through a stockbroker or a financial planner.

Finally, if you feel the psychological and spiritual benefits of having a debt-free home are important to you, that's what you should do. It's likely to be the wrong financial decision, and you are accountable for that decision. However, if your spirit is telling you to do something after study, prayer, and reflection, then that is the right decision. The bottom line is that, aside from spiritual reasons, I'm generally opposed to mortgage reduction strategies. Instead I'm totally in favor of investment

strategies. I don't believe there are any biblical commands, principles, or guidelines to own a debt-free home.

Should You Own a Home?

Many Americans believe the American dream is to own their
own home. No doubt this is primarily due to the psychological
benefits of owning the roof over your head. Safety and security
are at the base level of human needs, and home ownership is a
major factor in meeting those needs.

Part of the safety and security, though, come from the supposed financial benefits of owning your own home. Everybody
knows that owning a home is the best tax deduction, one that is
not the exclusive domain of the rich. Furthermore, everybody
knows that monthly rent payments go into someone else's
pocket while at least a portion of the monthly mortgage payment goes into your pocket. Then you get that tax break on the
piece going into the bank's pocket. Finally, everybody *knows*
that real estate *always* goes up in value, virtually assuring that
even the least savvy home owner can become a successful speculator. Alas, what everybody *knows* to be true is not necessarily
always the case. The financial *facts* of owning a home can often
be very costly fiction. In some cases, it can be financially more
rewarding to rent rather than buy!

The case for buying your own home is generally made on the
overly simplified comparison of rent payments versus a compa-
rable mortgage after the benefits of the tax deduction for mortgage interest. The thinking typically goes as follows: A person
earning $35,000 annually rents an apartment for $750 per
month, which represents 26 percent of his monthly salary. At
this salary level, 15 percent of income is paid in federal taxes.
However, since mortgage interest is deductible from income
tax, if the $750 paid in rent was instead a mortgage payment,
the actual cost of the home would be lower. In this example,
approximately 15 percent of the mortgage payment would be
"rebated" in a lower tax bill. The after-tax cost of a mortgage
would be $638 rather than the $750 for rent, a 15 percent
reduction.

What the typical home buyer does in this case is take out a

216

mortgage so that the monthly payments roughly equal the old rent. This is calculated according to the formula real estate professionals and financial advisers universally use:

$$\text{Rent} \div (1 - \text{tax bracket})$$

The result is a mortgage payment that will equal the old rent payments after the benefit of the interest tax deduction. In the above example, $750 \div (1 - .15) = $882. This is the size of a mortgage that is equivalent to $750 rent for $882, less a 15 percent tax break equals $750. The tax break generally allows individuals to own a superior dwelling to the one that they were renting.

Unfortunately, this simplified formula, which is probably the biggest argument in favor of the decision to buy a home, omits a number of crucial details. Careful consideration of a number of other relevant factors can actually tilt the scales in favor of renting rather than buying.

First, while paying rent puts money into the pocket of the property owner, paying mortgage interest puts money into the pockets of the bank. The portion of each payment that actually builds your equity by paying off the loan is very small in the early years of a home loan (your equity is the amount the house is worth less the balance owed on the loan. Any reduction in the loan balance increases your equity independent of any change in the home's value). The tax deduction helps, but as you can see, the savings are not significant, only 15 percent to 39.6 percent depending on your income level.

Second, property owners pay real estate taxes. As a homeowner, these taxes will be your responsibility. This obviously offsets some of the advantage of the tax deduction for mortgage interest.

Third, homeowners should anticipate higher home-related expenses. Maintenance and repairs are the owner's responsibility. A bigger dwelling usually means increased utility bills, especially if the rent previously covered them. Appliances may have to be purchased, and the empty space in a bigger house usually creates a desire for furnishings to fill it.

Finally, there is the problem of having "dead equity." The down payment needed to buy a house and the small amount each month that goes to paying off the loan is essentially tied up in a noninterest-bearing account with virtually no access, short of selling the house. Renters with the same amount of money could be investing this sum, not to mention that they have convenient access to this money. As we'll see, it is the investment potential of the down payment that is one of the crucial determinants of the relative advantages of renting versus buying.

As you can see, the "simple" decision is not so simple. However, all that I've discussed to this point are some of the disadvantages of buying. There are clearly advantages, or nobody would ever buy a home. First are the tax deductions given to homeowners. As we've stated, mortgage interest is tax deductible and so are property taxes. This helps minimize two of the disadvantages of buying. Second, a portion of your monthly mortgage payment goes into your pocket by building equity through the reduction of the loan.

Buying a Home

Let's look at a realistic example that shows how the advantages and disadvantages of home buying interrelate. This example will show that there are four major determinants in the value of home ownership, none of which have anything to do with tax breaks. They are resale value appreciation, size of down payment, investment return potential, and rate of increase in rent. While the example on page 219 is realistic, it is simplified to the extent that factors that have an immaterial impact on the overall outcome have been omitted.

To assess the value of home ownership we need to make three more assumptions. First, additional expenses associated with home ownership relative to renting amount to 1 percent of income. Next, the additional cost of homeowner's insurance is $50 per year. Finally, real estate taxes are assumed to be 1 percent per year of the assessed value of the house, which is 75 percent of the house's market value. It would be realistic to assume that these additional expenses would rise over time, adding further costs to owning a home. However, as they do not affect the analysis in a material fashion, they will be held constant.

Assumptions

Annual Income: $35,000
Federal Income Tax Bracket: 15%
Home Cost: $145,000
Down Payment: $14,500 or 10%
Mortgage Interest Rate: 6.5% on a 30-year fixed rate
Monthly Mortgage Payment: $825 or 28% of gross monthly income
Monthly Rent Payment: $750 or 26% of gross monthly income
Investment Return Potential: 12% annually (historical long-term stock market average)

Chart 8.1

An analysis of home ownership for thirty years under the above assumptions is as follows (negative numbers are payments to others; positive numbers payments to owner):

Outflows

Down Payment	+ 14,500
Mortgage Interest	-166,446
Additional Expenses	- 10,500
Insurance	- 1,600
Real Estate Taxes	- 32,625
Subtotal	**- 196,671**

Inflows

Interest Tax Deduction	+ 24,967
Real Estate Tax Deduction	+ 4,894
Equity Accumulation	+ 130,500
Subtotal	**+ 160,361**
Grand Total	**- 36,310**

Chart 8.2

Right away we can see that the tax advantages of home ownership do little to offset the big cost of mortgage interest. However, there is a major factor missing, home value appreciation, which is the most important determinant of the financial rewards of home buying. The first thing to realize about buying a house, is that if it does not appreciate in value over time, you will lose money. In this example, the resale value of the home would have to increase at a rate of just less than 1 percent per year to break even. While this specific amount cannot be generalized to every case, the principle almost always holds. If the house never sells for more than what you originally paid for it, you will not make up the cost of the interest on the loan, not to mention the other costs of owning a home.

As we saw in the real estate recession of the early 1990s, appreciation in resale value is far from guaranteed. Prior to this, it was widely assumed that real estate always goes up. Historically, real estate has been one of the best long-term investments. However, the assumption of permanently rising property values ignores several economic realities.

In real estate, all properties are not equal. Dwellings in rural and inner city areas have not experienced the same degree of price appreciation as suburban areas. Single family dwellings are generally more desirable than condominiums or multi-unit dwellings. There are also dramatic price differences because of national or regional location.

Perhaps the biggest factor in property prices is the degree to which an area is dependent upon one form of economic activity. For instance, the New York City area has finance, the Southwest has oil, Washington, D.C. has defense, the Northeast has high-technology, and the Midwest has autos. What we've experienced in the last decade is unforeseen downturns in the business activity that various regional economies depend upon. One result of this phenomenon is dramatic drops in property values due to these economic shocks. In many cases, property values have yet to recover to their pre-recession prices, not to mention their previous annual rate of increase.

Making a larger down payment can minimize the risk of no appreciation. A 20 percent down payment reduces the amount borrowed, resulting in lower interest expense. In this case, mortgage interest is reduced to $147,952, which in turn lowers the mortgage tax deduction to $22,193. The net result is a $17,490 loss before any increase in resale value as opposed to the $36,230 loss with a 10 percent down payment.

The only way to lower the cost of buying enough to make money without appreciation is to substantially increase your down payment. In this example, the specifics of which should not be generalized, it would take approximately a 30 percent down payment to break even with no appreciation in resale value.

However, larger down payments present several major problems. First, most people would never be able to save the money. Even if they could, they'd be better off buying as soon as possible if, in fact, home buying is better than renting. Second, large down payments create "dead equity." Money invested in your house does not appreciate like money invested elsewhere, even if elsewhere is only a bank account. Your house's resale value is independent of the money you put into it. As we saw in the discussion of mortgage reduction, that money is almost always invested better in other places. Furthermore, money in your house cannot be readily accessed unless you sell it — which isn't so ready — or you borrow against it, which not only defeats the point, but also costs money in closing costs and fees.

Therefore, the second major determinant of the value of buying versus renting is the size of the down payment. In general, smaller down payments are better to make if you are buying. This is true despite the fact that larger down payments reduce interest costs. Money that can be earned on other investments is likely to exceed what can be saved by reducing interest.

Why Taxes Don't Matter

One of the great misunderstandings about home ownership is the tax benefits. There are certainly tax savings that come from owning a house but they come at a high cost.

The tax deduction given to homeowners is based on the interest paid on your mortgage and real estate taxes. The cost of these items paid over thirty years almost always exceeds the cost of the home. The income tax deduction only saves you a portion of this cost. A homeowner can pay over five times more in interest and real estate taxes than they will save in income tax. In other words, for every dollar saved in taxes, nearly six dollars can be lost to the bank and local government.

For example, let's look at a $150,000, 8 percent, thirty-year mortgage. Monthly principal and interest payments on this loan will be $1,100.65. Assume real estate property taxes add another $125, making the total monthly payment for principal, interest, and taxes $1,225.65.

Over thirty years, you will have paid $441,234 for a $150,000 mortgage! This amount breaks down to $150,000 of principal paid to yourself in home equity and *$291,234* paid to the bank and the local government.

Uncle Sam wants to encourage you to buy a home so they will give you a tax break on the $291,234. But it's only a fraction of that amount, between 15 percent and 39.6 percent depending on your income. Therefore, you only "save" between $44,000 and $115,000. The rest, about $176,000 to $250,000, is greater than the orignal amount borrowed to buy the house. It cost up to $5.60 in expenses to save a dollar of income tax.

$150,000 Loan, 30 years, 8 percent
Total Principal Paid: $150,000
Total Interest and Real Estate Tax Expense: $291,234

Tax Bracket	Tax Deductions	After-Tax Expenses	Expense per $1 Tax Deduction
15%	43,685	244,549	5.60
28%	81,546	209,688	2.57
31%	90,283	200,951	2.23
36%	104,844	186,390	1.78
39.6%	115,329	175,905	1.53

Chart 8.3

What does all this mean? First, it means that the economics of home ownership cannot be justified on the basis of the tax breaks alone. The cost of those tax breaks in interest and real estate tax is far more than what is saved in income tax. The only true way to financially justify owning a home is to count on it appreciating in value. The experience of the last ten years shows that this is no longer always the case as it was in the past.

Second, the tax deductions for home ownership have the most benefit for high-income tax-payers. The lower your income level, the more risk you take of making a losing home investment. Most people fall into the lower two tax brackets. Based on financial considerations alone, a large number of homeowners should probably be renters. This concept will be seen now as we look at the cash inflows and outflows of renting.

Renting

The analysis of renting is simple. The only outflow we need consider is the rent payment itself. The inflow is what can be earned by investing what would have been a down payment on a house. The size of this inflow will be determined by the third major factor, the investment return potential. If you can invest money at a high enough rate of return, you may be better off doing so rather than depending on the appreciation of a home's resale value. To a large degree, resale values are out of one's control, which isn't necessarily true for a skillful investor.

If a potential home buyer invested the 10 percent down payment rather than buy a house, this amount will grow to $434,419 in thirty years at a 12 percent average annual rate. Investing a larger "down payment" naturally provides even greater benefits. A 20 percent down payment in our example, or $29,000, would grow to $868,838.

To make renting work out to an advantage, the potential investment return must be enough to offset the costs of renting. This is the last determinant of the rent or buy decision.

If rent never increases above the assumed $750 per month, this will amount to a $270,000 outflow over thirty years. Depending on the amount invested rather than used as a down payment for a house, the two "down payment" examples look like the chart on page 224:

	Invest $14,500 (10% "down")	Invest $29,500 (20% "down")
Rent	− 270,000	− 270,000
Investments	+ 434,419	+ 868,838
Total	+ 164,419	+ 598,838

Chart 8.4

Renting looks great, but an important part of the analysis is missing, which is the annual rate of increase of rent payments. This is the last determinant of the rent versus buy decision. It is crucial because it is so closely tied to the major factor of home resale value. Rents will probably increase at a rate very close to the rate of increase in property values. After all, from the standpoint of the landlord, the rental unit is a potential resale property. If it becomes worth more in resale, it is natural that it should be worth more in rental income.

If property values rise such that rents also rise, home buying will be a better financial decision than renting. This is true not only because the homeowner earns the appreciation on the home's value, but also because the homeowner has built-in rent control. Assuming the buyer has a fixed-rate mortgage, the housing expense is fixed. Unlike an owner, the renter may be exposed to constantly rising costs of living.

The Answer
Home buying will be a better decision than renting only if one can anticipate appreciation of property value in excess of the rate of increase in rents. The advantage is further enhanced by making a smaller down payment when buying a home. However, if your personal circumstances dictate buying a home in an area that may not experience any growth in value, you should strongly consider renting and investing until such time that anticipated rent increases no longer make this a viable option. In either case, you just look much deeper than the tax considerations of your decision, which only play a secondary role in the advantages of either case.

Probably the wisest move in buying a home is to buy less house than what is affordable. This will help you avoid being "house rich" but "cash poor." Real estate can be a good long-term investment, but others, such as stock mutual funds are better and easier to get in and out of. Home ownership is a great tax shelter, but there are many others with superior advantages, such as various retirement savings plans (see chap. 9). As we've seen, taxes are not a primary factor in the value of home ownership.

Too many people make their home their only financial asset. This could have serious implications in terms of meeting other major financial goals, like retirement planning. We'll have more to say about this in chapter 9. While a house should probably be your first major investment, it definitely should not be your last. To protect yourself and make your money grow, you will need to diversify your funds into other, more superior financial assets.

Buying less house than you can afford will allow you to do this. It may also allow you to enjoy a more interesting lifestyle and release more money into ministry.

Summary
1. Since debt is not a sin, you should not necessarily strive to be debt free.
2. Having debts, however, may be an indication of sin, especially covetousness.
3. Debt may indicate poor savings habits, which is unfaithful stewardship.
4. A "bad" debt is buying something you can't afford with money that you don't have; this is generally consumer debt.
5. A "good" debt is one that you can presently afford, makes economic sense, and you feel spiritually comfortable with.
6. Short-term mortgages and mortgage reduction strategies are usually poor financial decisions.
7. Refinancing and investing the difference is a wise move.
8. The decision whether to rent or buy a home should not be based on tax factors but primarily upon anticipated appreciation in property value.

9. Buy less house than you can afford. Don't be house rich and cash poor.

Notes

1. *Deuteronomy 15:7-8*
2. *Exodus 22:25; Leviticus 25:39; Deuteronomy 15:1-2*
3. *Proverbs 28:8; Ezekiel 18:10-13*
4. *Ezekiel 22:3, 12*
5. *Nehemiah 5:1, 5-7, 9-10*
6. *Deuteronomy 24:10-13*
7. *Exodus 20:15*
8. *James 4:13-14*

Chapter Nine

YOU MUST ESTABLISH FOR YOURSELF A FUTURE INCOME

GO TO THE ANT, YOU SLUGGARD;
CONSIDER ITS WAYS AND BE WISE!
IT HAS NO COMMANDER, NO OVERSEER OR RULER,
YET IT STORES ITS PROVISIONS IN SUMMER AND
GATHERS ITS FOOD AT HARVEST
(PROVERBS 6:6-8)

> Paul and Cathy are DINKS — dual income, no kids. They're in their thirties, earn good salaries, and are secure in their jobs. They're using a retirement plan with their employers and don't want to risk not having a sizable nest egg. So they're avoiding the stock market and are investing their money in CDs and Guaranteed Investment Contracts. Believe it or not, short of not saving at all, they're probably making a huge retirement planning mistake by being too cautious.

I look forward to Friday the way some people look forward to retirement" was the statement a friend once made to me. On the surface it's quite apparent that my friend didn't enjoy his job very much. However, at a deeper level there is something implied in the statement that is quite significant. There is the suggestion that my friend equates weekends with retirement in that everybody looks forward to a time when they don't have to work.

This attitude definitely explains the retirement planning phenomenon in America over the last forty years, particularly over the last twenty, as our work ethic has declined. Since we don't want to work, then it's obvious we need to plan how to accumulate enough money to support the leisurely lifestyle we're looking forward to.

This worldly view of retirement planning with an eye toward hoarding wealth to support a life of leisure is in direct conflict with God's principles on the subject. If we are truly living to please God, then our attitude toward retirement planning will be extremely different from the world's view.

People Were Created to Work

First of all, it is part of our human nature to work. "The Lord God took the man and put him in the Garden of Eden to work it and take care of it" (Gen. 2:15). God has instilled within us an innate knowledge that work is necessary and good. To not work is to create a void in our lives unintended by our Creator. Since we know that God loves us and desires only the best for us, we can further assume that work in some way contains blessings for us.

Apparently some benefits to work have nothing to do with our subsistence. Prior to the Fall, God met the physical needs of Adam and Eve in exchange for their care of the Garden of Eden.

However, once Adam and Eve sinned by eating from the forbidden Tree of the Knowledge of Good and Evil, humanity became cursed as a result of God's judgment. Part of this curse changed the nature of work. "By the sweat of your brow you will eat your food until you return to the ground, since from it you were taken; for dust you are and to dust you will return . . . so the Lord God banished him from the Garden of Eden to work the ground from which he had been taken" (Gen. 3:19, 23). Because of God's curse, people have to work to provide their own food and shelter.

Therefore, work is an avenue by which we do something pleasing to God and meet the needs that He once freely provided us. King Solomon, who perhaps more than any other person understood the value of work, wrote, "Then I realized that it is good and proper for a man to eat and drink, and to find satisfaction in his toilsome labor under the sun during the few days of life God has given him—for this is his lot" (Ecc. 5:18). Working is simply part of being human, and having a desire not to work is to want a life that is actually less, not more, than the life that God wants us to have.

Many times, God's blessings come in the form of removing dangers rather than bestowing gifts. Since we were created as working beings, the Bible specifically warns us of the dangers of idleness.[1] The concept of retiring to a life of leisure is clearly not biblical. Work, not leisure, is a vital part of life. God clearly wants us to be able to have time to relax and enjoy life, but the poverty that comes through laziness will not allow us to do that.

What Is a Productive Retirement?

It is not God's intent for us to store up enough money to have a self-possessed life of consumption. On the contrary, you should, "Make it your ambition to lead a quiet life, to mind your own business and to work with your hands" (1 Thes. 4:11). The scriptural view of retirement planning is to plan for a future of reduced income while still continuing to live a productive life. This raises two critical questions. First, what is a productive retirement? Second, how do we support ourselves without employment?

As to the first question of what is a productive life, we must not change our views simply because we are no longer employed. Good stewardship doesn't end in retirement simply because we have less income. Jesus said that the two central principles of our life are to " 'love the Lord your God with all your heart and with all your soul and with all your mind.' This is the first and greatest commandment. And the second is like it: 'Love your neighbor as yourself' " (Matt. 22:37-39). Employed or not, we must still seek to obey these commands. However, since we no longer work for earthly masters, we should strongly consider working, in a more direct fashion, for our Heavenly Father. Retirement is an opportunity to devote ourselves more fully to opportunities of ministry or witness to others. This is not to imply that your career prior to retirement was in work that was not pleasing to God. Since God created people to be working beings, all work is sacred. The point is that many people would love to have more time to devote to their favorite areas of ministry. Retirement affords us the time to do that.

However, can you financially afford to retire to a life of ministry? This is the second spiritual aspect of retiring, one that brings us back to the principle of saving money. Even the lowly ant knows enough to prepare for the times of reduced provision by living off the food it saved during the harvest time.[2] Similarly, we must be wise enough to save money in our peak earning years to support ourselves during our latter years of reduced income. God equates our failure to prepare for retirement with laziness and an intellect so lacking that it could learn from an ant. These words are obviously strong, and if you haven't yet started thinking about the financial ramifications of retirement, you should take these words to heart.

One of the things God wants us to avoid in our retirement years is to become a burden to others. We can become a burden if we have refused to save in preparation of caring for ourselves. "I will not be a *burden* to you. . . . After all, children should not have to save up for their parents, but parents for their children" (2 Cor. 12:14, italics added). Part of not being a burden is living in a productive, self-supporting manner so that you do not "eat anyone's food without paying for it. On the contrary, we worked night and day, laboring and toiling so that we would not be a *burden* to any of you" (2 Thes. 3:8, italics added).

This is not to suggest that you must continue being employed to pay for your daily bread. Rather it enhances the notion of living productively. If in retirement you are merely consuming the resources God allowed you to accumulate and not regenerating His kingdom in some manner, you are a burden to somebody. Even if you can support yourself, you should live to help remove the burdens of others. If not, you are misusing your life and its resources.

Hoarding for Retirement

While Scripture directs us to save enough to avoid imposing our needs upon others, we must guard against the preoccupation of saving as much as we possibly can. This attitude is becoming more and more universal today. Rather than save enough to meet specific financial goals, the objective now is to save as much as we can so that we can have the freedom to do whatever we want, whenever we want. This so-called "financial freedom" is what the Bible refers to as hoarding. To be financially free in the worldly sense is to not allow the quality of our fun to be dependent upon the quantity of our money. However, true financial freedom occurs only when the quality of our *life* is not dependent upon the quantity of our money. This can only occur when the quality of our life is determined in spiritual rather than monetary terms.

Hoarding occurs when we seek money for money's sake. The acquisition of wealth becomes not a means to an end but an end to itself. The Rich Fool (Luke 12:16-21) was preoccupied with accumulating and hoarding wealth. Jesus didn't think much of the Rich Fool's "early retirement" plans.

This man's retirement plans were foolish for three reasons. First, we are created to work in some useful capacity for God's glory. A goal of living to eat, drink, and be merry is not glorifying to God and not part of His plan. Second, money stockpiled over and above our own needs could be better used elsewhere. God would prefer that we seek His will to determine our own needs and to go about meeting those of others. However, occasionally He will take matters into His own hands. "To the man who pleases Him, God gives wisdom, knowledge and happiness, but to the sinner He gives the task of gathering and storing up wealth to hand it over to the one who pleases God" (Ecc. 2:26).

Finally, hoarding is foolish when it presumes upon the future. Despite our best efforts to plan it out, we cannot guarantee our future.[3] Even if we could guarantee it, we certainly shouldn't choose to place our hopes in something as transitory as money.[4] In any case, the Bible has a guarantee of its own, personally assured by the One whose promises have never failed.[5] Could this be why our paper currency says, "In God We Trust"?

Making a Career Goal out of Retirement
There is another unfortunate manifestation of our growing preoccupation with amassing great wealth for retirement. Today it

is completely acceptable to continue working in careers or jobs we detest simply to earn the retirement benefits. While this could be financially prudent, it is even more likely that happy people end up making more money—although ironically, they'd be satisfied with less—through their higher level of dedication. Obviously money isn't everything. In fact, King Solomon points out, "There was a man all alone . . . there was no end to his toil, yet his eyes were not content with his wealth. 'For whom am I toiling,' he asked, 'and why am I depriving myself of enjoyment?' This too is meaningless—a miserable business!" (Ecc. 4:8)

The concept of ensuring a great retirement to make up for all the years of sacrificial labor is indicative of a wrongful attitude toward work and life in general. God intends for us to get the maximum benefit from each moment as it occurs. We often crash and burn in the present while trying to navigate the future. Rather than trying to make up for a career of unhappiness in retirement, God would much rather us seek the daily blessings that come from fulfilling employment. "A man can do nothing better than to eat and drink and find satisfaction in his work" (Ecc. 2:24).

We know that any attempts to secure our future are very risky and in all likelihood made in vain. To willfully sacrifice your most productive years so you can "take life easy; eat, drink and be merry" like the Rich Fool is the height of foolishness. The future that you've sacrificed for each present day may never happen. Doesn't it make more sense to have a retirement plan that starts with having fulfilling employment every day?

This idea of self-deprivation for financial reasons raises another spiritual issue. To be a slave to a job that you detest can hardly be glorifying to God if it affects your job performance. Recent studies by labor psychologists suggest that not only does money not buy happiness, but also money as a sole reward for labor can actually be demotivating (*Washington Post*, 12/5/93). Natural motivators such as creativity and curiosity eventually lead to deeper levels of satisfaction with work. Desire for money replaces our natural motivators and becomes the object of our energies. However, psychologists are finding that it's an artificial and short-lived desire that ultimately results in lower levels of satisfaction and quality of work.

It's one thing to cost yourself the blessings God has in place for us through our labor. That's a personal choice that probably has no ramifications outside ourselves. God wants us to have His best, but we choose not to. That's fair enough. However, it's quite another thing to cost someone else their blessings through our poor witness. Many of us spend more of our waking hours at our place of employment than anywhere else. It is there that we'll see the most strangers, both to us and to our faith. What conclusions about God can they draw from our own attitude toward our work? To work in a manner that does not glorify God belies the notion that we should plan our retirement around a career that gets less than our best effort.

Retirement Planning: The World's Way versus God's Way

The world's method of planning for retirement is in direct opposition to the guidance provided to us in the Bible. The world is preoccupied with:

Guaranteeing the future. "Today or tomorrow we will go to this or that city, spend a year there, carry on business and make money" (James 4:13).

Hoarding money. "Then he said, 'This is what I'll do. I will tear down my barns and build bigger ones, and there I will store all my grain and my goods' " (Luke 12:18).

Living a life of leisure and consumption. "And I'll say to myself, 'You have plenty of good things laid up for many years. Take life easy; eat, drink, and be merry' " (Luke 12:19).

God is creative and intends for people to be productive, yet the world's way is destructive. Worrying about tomorrow gains nothing but loses today's blessings. Hoarding money for no real purpose prevents it from being used where it is really needed. Leisure consumes our wealth so that we cannot give elsewhere. God's retirement plan focuses on spiritual values rather than financial principles.

God's way to a vital, dynamic retirement is to

Make our plans according to God's will. "Commit to the Lord whatever you do, and your plans will succeed" (Prov. 16:3).

Save according to our needs as determined by God's specific will, not to fulfill our unknown future desires. "Go to the ant, you sluggard; consider its ways and be wise . . . it stores its provisions in summer and gathers its food at harvest" (Prov. 6:6, 8).

Enjoy ourselves through a lifetime of productivity instead of consumption. "Then I realized that it is good and proper for a man to eat and drink, and to find satisfaction in his toilsome labor under the sun during the few days of life God has given him—for this is his lot. Moreover, when God gives any man wealth and possessions, and enables him to enjoy them, to accept his lot and be happy in his work—this is a gift of God. He seldom reflects on the days of his life, because God keeps him occupied with gladness of heart" (Ecc. 5:18-20).

God's way is obviously the right way, but unfortunately it is very easy to fall into the world's mentality. The questions of life have difficult answers. At what point does prudent planning become an obsession with directing the future? How much savings is hoarding instead of reasonable preparation for an uncertain future? And at what point does enjoyment become self-indulgence?

Fortunately, God has given us the answer to all of these questions. Quite simply, it lies in our motivation. "But seek first His kingdom and His righteousness, and all these things will be given to you as well" (Matt. 6:33). When we seek God's will for our retirement years, He will guide us on a path that balances the conflicting desires.

Godly Retirement Objectives
Save enough money . . .

to meet your needs and not be a burden to others . . .

while you work in enjoyable areas of ministry or Christian
witness . . .
that are useful and productive to the kingdom of God . . .
glorifying God and demonstrating good and faithful stewardship.

The *Real* Economic Crisis

There is a potential economic crisis looming, but it's not the
one that people are expecting. Most people think our economic
system will eventually fail due to fiscal irresponsibility and poor
leadership on the part of our elected officials. In other words,
the problem is someone else's fault (this attitude conveniently
ignores the fact that these elected officials were elected by *us!*).
The economic catastrophe that is waiting to happen is the impact of the failure of Americans to properly plan for their
retirement.

The fact that this predicament exists is our fault, not the
government's. According to a study by the WEFA Group and
Arthur D. Little, 75 percent of Americans over twenty years old
will retire with less than half of the necessary funding in place
(*Barron's*, 7/12/93). This is a best-case estimate. Should either
the financial markets, the Social Security system, or employer
pension programs falter, the problem will be even worse. Given
their current troubled state, it is a certainty that both Social
Security and employer pensions — which were only meant to be
supplemental sources of retirement income, anyway — will un-
dergo major changes resulting in lower funding levels for future
retirees. There is no way the U.S. economy will not suffer when
three out of four people of the richest and most consumptive
generation of Americans live the last quarter of their life in
virtual poverty.

A complete discussion of the structural problems inherent in
the retirement system is beyond the scope of this book. However, it is simple to summarize the three major changes in retirement planning that confront all Americans.

The first is the movement of employers from defined benefit
plans to defined contribution plans. A defined benefit plan is
the traditional pension plan, where employees are paid a fixed

retirement income based upon their salaries and years of service. The employer sets aside enough money that, combined with professional investment management, will cover their obligations to future retirees.

On the other hand, in a defined contribution plan the employer makes a specified contribution to their employees' individual retirement accounts. The level of retirement income ultimately will be the responsibility of the employee. Basically this means that the employee, and not a professional pension fund money manager, is responsible for investing in such a way that an appropriate amount of funds exists at retirement.

The second trend is that defined benefit pension plans are increasingly becoming underfunded. In other words, many corporations do not have adequate funds today to pay all of the pension income they owe their employees. In fact, some American employees are working without a guarantee that their pensions will ever be paid. Although there is a government organization, the Pension Benefit Guarantee Corporation (PBGC), whose mission is to make good on failed pension payments, the gap between what companies promise to pay retirees and what they have in their plans was $38 billion dollars in 1992. This is up 31 percent from 1991 and is the fifth consecutive year that that gap has grown. Furthermore, the PBGC, which is funded by participating corporate contributors, itself has a $2.7 billion deficit. The PBGC is fine as long as most of the underfunded companies don't go belly up at once, which isn't likely unless there is a complete economic breakdown. Still, the problem is putting pressure on an already weak system. To make matters worse, U.S. government retirement programs for military and civilian employees are also underfunded by approximately $1 trillion (*USA Today*, 11/23/93).

Third, the Social Security system continues to struggle. When the system first began, workers rarely lived past sixty-five, so the Social Security Administration had short-lived obligations. In addition, since the ratio of workers paying into the system relative to those receiving money from Social Security was forty-two to one, the program was well funded. As life expectancy grew, the number of covered retired employees grew dramatically. The program has been forced to cover more people for a longer period of time so that now the ratio is three to one. As the baby boomers move into retirement, by the year 2020 the ratio is expected to go to two to one. It is safe to assume that the Social Security system will need some kind of reform in the not too distant future.

In truth, the problems outlined above should be secondary. Neither pension nor Social Security payments were meant to be the primary sources of retirement income. For the average retiree, these two sources of funds cover only approximately 40 percent of what is needed to maintain their preretirement lifestyle. The real issue is that the average American is doing nothing to cover the remaining 60 percent that is necessary. Through their own (in)actions, Americans are depending on two troubled secondary sources of funds to live off of during their retirement years.

To avoid an impoverished retirement, a dramatic reduction in lifestyle, or both, you will have to rely on your own savings, not the government's or your employer's. Unfortunately, the typical American has three problems.

First, Americans just don't save enough money. The United States has a much lower savings rate than any other developed country. In 1992, Americans had a savings rate of only 5 percent of after-tax income. This compares unfavorably to England and Germany, where savings rates exceed 12 percent, and especially Japan, where it's over 15 percent. When it comes to saving money, Americans start too late, assign it a low priority, and find it impossible when their consumptive lifestyle creates insurmountable financial burdens.

The second problem is that even when Americans save money, they save it in the wrong places. Managing your own money is easy once you've been taught what needs to be done and how to go about doing it. However, few Americans have ever received the training necessary to be successful money managers (until they read this book, that is!). The required skills are not part of the normal educational process. Unfortunately, the changes in the retirement system have made it necessary for Americans to do something they've not been prepared to do.

As a result, they are doing the job badly by investing too conservatively, a problem we'll explore in greater detail later in this
chapter.

Finally, two of the most important determinants of how
much money it takes to retire — life expectancy and inflation —
are out of the investor's control. There is no question that
Americans are living longer due to the advancements in medicine and the general trend of improved health conditions. When
retirement plans were first begun, the typical worker lived only
a few years after retirement. This is no longer the case. One out
of every five men and one out of every three women age sixty-
five will live to be eighty-five years old. Obviously the longer
one lives, the longer their savings must last to generate income.
The problem from the retirees' standpoint is that they don't
know how long they're going to live. Therefore, they don't
know how much they need to save.

The other planning problem is how to account for inflation.
One of the worst financial situations to be in is to have a fixed
income in the face of rising inflation. Inflation reduces the purchasing power of your money since your dollars buy less when
prices are rising. Chart 9.1 shows how the buying power of the
dollar has dropped due to inflation. Your money isn't worth

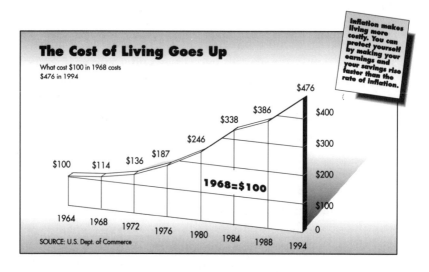

Chart 9.1

what it adds up to; it's worth what it will buy. If your income doesn't rise to match inflation, your standard of living is reduced. If your retirement savings don't grow as fast as inflation, you will have accumulated money in vain since the dollars won't buy any more than the original amount you started your savings with. Chart 9.2 shows how much more it costs to spend money after thirty years of inflation. Inflation must be accounted for in managing your retirement money, but like all other economic variables, it cannot be reliably predicted.

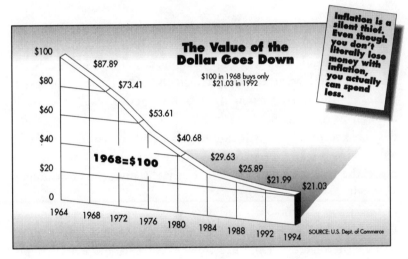

Chart 9.2

To summarize, Americans face a significant challenge. Faced with declining outside sources of retirement income, they must rely on their own ability to accumulate enough money for a comfortable retirement. Unfortunately, they lack both the skills and the discipline to do so. Furthermore, they must accumulate enough money to fund a potentially long life and offset unexpected rises in the cost of living. Sadly, few Americans will overcome these challenges and as a result will live the latter part of their life in increasing poverty.

Hopefully, this warning has aroused within you a sense of alarm. Statistically, it is highly likely that you are among the vast majority of those whose retirement years are in serious financial jeopardy.

How Much Do You Need to Retire?

Social Security and employer pensions were originally designed to supplement your retirement income. As much as 60 percent or more of your financial needs should be provided by your own accumulated savings. Your retirement nest egg needs to be big enough to accomplish two goals. First, it must provide regular withdrawals to meet living expenses for a number of years. Remember that it is quite possible that you will have a long retirement. You don't want your money to run out before you do!

Second, your nest egg must continue to grow, whether through interest, dividends, or appreciation, to replenish the retirement fund. This will help your money to last longer. Ideally, one would want to live exclusively off of the earnings of their accumulated principal, but few people will ever save enough to do this. As it is, the amount that is needed to fund a desirable retirement is shocking, although achieveable. If you're still a long way from sixty-five, there is plenty of time to acquire the necessary funds, with the right investment strategies that will be discussed later.

To show you how to estimate your own retirement needs, I've created a simple worksheet along with three tables at the end of the chapter. Let's use these tools to look at two hypothetical examples—a "good" start and a "bad" start—that will include the critical planning assumptions. The basic assumptions in the worksheet and all the examples are that (1) you will accumulate enough to produce 6 percent per year in income and never have to reduce the principal; (2) inflation will be at 4 percent a year, and thus the accumulated amount takes into account a higher cost of living at and throughout retirement.

Example A

This is a "good" planning example: a person, age twenty-nine earning $24,000 per year. Here are the assumptions used to project the retirement needs:

- Assume that 80 percent of current living expenses will be needed to maintain a preferred lifestyle.

Calculating Your Retirement Savings Needs

How much do you need to maintain your present lifestyle in retirement?

(1) Annual retirement expenses $19,200
(80% of current income)

(2) Retirement Income
    (a) Social Security $9,200
    (b) Defined Benefit Pension Plans $ 0
    (c) Other Income $ 0
        (postretirement income, rents, etc.)

(3) Total Income $9,200
(Add lines 2a, 2b, 2c)

(4) Retirement Gap $10,000
(Line 1 minus line 3)

(5) Total assets you'll need at retirement to eliminate $586,276
Retirement Gap
(Table 1, 36 years until retirement)

(6) Today's value of current retirement savings
    (a) Employer-sponsored plans (401K, 403B) $2,200
    (b) IRA's $ 0
    (c) Other investments $ 0
        (savings, CD's, stocks, bonds, mutual funds, etc.)

(7) Total savings $2,200
(Add lines 6a, 6b, 6c)

(8) Value of current savings *at retirement*
    (a) Factor from Table 2 (assume 11% return)   42.82
    (b) Multiply Line 7 by line 8a $94,204

(9) Total savings needed at retirement $492,072
(Line 5 minus line 8b)

(10) Factor from Table 3 (assume 11%) $ .003

(11) Annual savings needed to reach retirement goal $1,476
(Line 9 minus line 10)

(12) Annual savings through employer-sponsored $ 760
plans (assume 4% of gross salary)

(13) Annual matching funds through employer-sponsored $ 760
plans (assume employer matching = 200%)

(14) Your annual savings needed to reach retirement goal $ -44

Calculating Your Retirement Savings Needs

How much do you need to maintain your present lifestyle in retirement?

(1) Annual retirement expenses $34,000
(100% of current income)

(2) Retirement Income
(a) Social Security $11,500
(b) Defined Benefit Pension Plans $ 0
(c) Other Income $ 0
(postretirement income, rents, etc.)

(3) Total Income $11,500
(Add lines 2a, 2b, 2c)

(4) Retirement Gap $22,500
(Line 1 minus line 3)

(5) Total assets you'll need at retirement to eliminate $963,869
Retirement Gap
(Table 1, 28 years until retirement)

(6) Today's value of current retirement savings
(a) Employer-sponsored plans (401K, 403B) $10,000
(b) IRA's $1,000
(c) Other investments $ 0
(savings, CDs, stocks, bonds, mutual funds, etc.)

(7) Total savings $11,000
(Add lines 6a, 6b, 6c)

(8) Value of current savings *at retirement*
(a) Factor from Table 2 (assume 6% return)   5.11
(b) Multiply Line 7 by line 8a $56,210

(9) Total savings needed at retirement $907,659
(Line 5 minus line 8b)

(10) Factor from Table 3 (assume 6%) $ .015

(11) Annual savings needed to reach retirement goal $13,615
(Line 9 minus line 10)

(12) Annual savings through employer-sponsored $ 680
plans (assume 2% of gross salary)

(13) Annual matching funds through employer-sponsored $ 204
plans (assume employer matching = 30%)

(14) Your annual savings needed to reach retirement goal $12,731

- The employee is participating in an employer-sponsored retirement savings plan that matches 100 percent of their contribution. Current savings are $2,200 and payroll deductions into the plan are 4 percent of gross salary.
- Projected annual Social Security benefit is $9,200.

Example A needs over 580,000 to maintain his or her present lifestyle (line #5). The projected growth in current savings will contribute 94,000 of that (line #8b). The rest will come from the projected growth of future savings of $1,476 per year (line #11), half of which comes from the employer's retirement plan. The reason the annual savings needed on Line 14 is negative is that the current savings/investment plan will exceed the estimated need. This is a good plan!

Example B

This is a "bad" planning example: a person, age thirty-seven, earning $34,000 per year. Here are the assumptions used to project the retirement needs:

- Assume that 100 percent of current living expenses will be needed to maintain a preferred lifestyle.
- The employee is participating in an employer-sponsored retirement savings plan that matches 30 percent of their contribution. Current savings are only $10,000, not much after thirteen years of work, especially with employer matching funds.
- Payroll deductions into the plan are just 2 percent of gross salary.
- Projected annual Social Security benefit is $11,500.
- There is $1,000 in an IRA invested in a long-term bank CD.

Example B needs nearly $1 million to maintain his or her present lifestyle! This is what happens after nearly thirty years of inflation. B has another problem in that the investment strategy is too conservative. The projected investment return on Line 8a is only 6 percent. Therefore, the projected growth in current savings will only contribute $56,000 to the sizeable retirement need. A's $2,200 (Example A, line #6a) grows to almost twice that because of a more appropriate long-term investment approach. Since B is only saving $884 (line #12 + line #13) per year, which includes employer contributions, the rest of B's retirement fund must come from the projected growth of future savings of $12,731 (line #14) per year, most likely an impossible task.

Here is where better investing will help considerably. If B invests in a portfolio with a potential to grow an average of 11 percent per year, the annual need drops to $4,217. An earlier start would have also made a big difference. If B had managed to save $20,000, of which about $4,600 would have been the employer's, and could see it grow at 11 percent annually, the additional yearly savings declines to $2,558. However, with this set of assumptions, typical for many future retirees, this is still an example of a bad plan.

Go through the worksheet yourself and get a quick, basic idea of what your retirement planning needs are. You should especially experiment with percentage of Annual Retirement Expenses (Line 1) and different investment return assumptions (Line 8a, Line 10).

This short and simplified worksheet is useful to get you thinking about your retirement planning needs. However, being simplified, it omits a number of crucial assumptions that can have a dramatic affect on the results. I recommend that you call T. Rowe Price (1-800-638-5660), one of the major mutual fund companies, and ask for their Retirement Planning Kit. It will take about an hour of your time to complete the forms. It is well worth the effort. One of the inputs you'll need is an estimate of your future Social Security Benefits, which you can get from the Social Security Administration (1-800-772-1213) by asking for Form SSA-7004, Request for Personal Earnings and Benefit Estimate Statement. Within four to six weeks of returning this form back to the SSA, you'll get a statement that contains your estimated monthly benefits in today's dollars.

Another input you'll need in order to complete the T. Rowe Price workbook is your projected pension benefits, which you can get from your company's employee benefit office. Ask whether your pension is adjusted for inflation after retirement. Your employer may also give you your projected Social Security benefits, but they will be related to your current job. The same would be true of your pension benefit if you've changed jobs.

Calculating Your Retirement Savings Needs

How much do you need to maintain your present lifestyle in retirement?

(1) Annual retirement expenses $_____
(70–100% of current income)

(2) Retirement Income
 (a) Social Security $ _____
   (call Social Security Administration,
   1-800-772-1213, ask for Request for
   Personal Earnings Benefits Estimate Statement)
 (b) Defined Benefit Pension Plans $ _____
 (c) Other Income $ _____
   (postretirement income, rents, etc.)

(3) Total Income $ _____
(Add lines 2a, 2b, 2c)

(4) Retirement Gap $ _____
(Line 1 minus line 3)

(5) Total assets you'll need at retirement to eliminate $ _____
Retirement Gap
(Use Table 1)

(6) Today's value of current retirement savings
 (a) Employer-sponsored plans (401K, 403B) $ _____
 (b) IRA's $ _____
 (c) Other investments $ _____
   (savings, CD's, stocks, bonds, mutual funds, etc.)

(7) Total savings $ _____
(Add lines 6a, 6b, 6c)

(8) Value of current savings *at retirement*
 (a) Factor from Table 2 $ _____
 (b) Multiply line 7 by line 8a $ _____

(9) Total savings needed at retirement $ _____
(Line 5 minus line 8b)

(10) Factor from Table 3 $ _____
(same as line 8a)

(11) Annual savings needed to reach retirement goal $ _____
(Line 9 minus line 10)

(12) Annual savings through employer-sponsored plans $ _____

(13) Annual matching funds through
employer-sponsored plans $ _____

(14) Your annual savings needed to reach retirement goal $ _____

Finally, you'll want to have the status of all of your retirement savings accounts such as tax-deferred savings plans, Individual Retirement Accounts, deferred annuities, and so on.

How to Get There, Part 1

The single most important step you can take in your retirement saving effort is to start saving *now*. Remember, it takes time not money to make money. Time is your greatest ally in achieving your investment goals. You must save early and often, even if it is in small amounts. It is not the amount of savings that matters. It is time in combination with the right investment strategies that will help you reach your goals. You don't have to work to make a lot of money when your money can work for you—if you give it enough time to do its job.

A 1988 survey by the Investment Company Institute found that 90 percent of retirees agreed that it is best to start your retirement saving right when you enter the workforce. I completely agree with this philosophy. On the other hand, I vehemently dispute the notion that you should not begin your retirement savings until you are debt-free including your home mortgage. We have already seen in chapter 8 that in most cases paying off a mortgage early is a poor financial decision. I believe to delay funding retirement is even more disastrous. The benefits of starting early are too great to pass up and the costs of waiting are too considerable to bear.

For example, here are three different ways to retire with $500,000, each assuming a conservative long-term investment return of 9 percent per year:

(1) Invest $2,090 each year between the ages of 25 and 34, *and none thereafter;*
(2) Invest $8,080 each year between the ages of 45 and 65;
(3) Invest $26,100 each year between the ages of 55 and 65.

The advantages of an early start should be readily apparent. Time makes your money work for you rather than you having to work for your money. Look at how the power of time multiplies your money:

246

Age	25–34	45–65	55–65
Money Accumulated	$500,000	$500,000	$500,000
Money Invested	$ 20,900	$169,680	$287,100
Investment Earnings	$479,636	$330,257	$212,473
Multiplication of Money Invested	**22.9 times**	**1.9 times**	**0.7 times**

Chart 9.3

The earlier you start, the harder your money works. In Example 1, only $20,900 had to be invested to become a half-million dollars. The original investment grew nearly twenty-three times. In Example 2, by waiting until age 45 to start saving, eight times more money needs to be saved since it only has time to be multiplied 1.9 times. Example 3 is a financial horror story. To reach $500,000, $26,100 each year must be saved, quite a formidable task for all but the very wealthiest families. At 55, you have to do all the work, since your money is barely working.

There is another significant advantage to starting early. Not only does your money work harder, but also it's easier to put your money to work when you start early. It is certainly true that the average American both earns more and saves more as they get older. However, by starting to save early, one needs to set aside a much smaller percentage of their income. This can be seen using the examples above along with 1987 data from the U.S Bureau of Labor Statistics (BLS):

Ages	Income	Savings	Savings %	Funding	Income %
25–34	$27,835	$1,145	4%	$ 2,090	8%
45–64	$33,990	$2,702	8%	$ 8,080	24%
55–64	$31,038	$2,430	8%	$26,100	84%

Chart 9.4

Despite the fact that both income and savings rise with age, it is easier to save money for retirement when you are young.

Using the above example, a person age twenty-five can accumulate $500,000 by investing $2,090 each year until they are only thirty-four. This will require them to save 8 percent of their annual income for a period of ten years. A person who waits until age forty-five must save $8,080 each year until retirement to achieve the same results. This will make them save 24 percent of their annual income for twenty years. Even though they are making more money, the higher salary will not make up for the necessary increase in savings. At age fifty-five, the required savings rate becomes a virtual impossibility.

Chart 9.4 also illustrates one of the problems discussed earlier in the chapter. As you can see, regardless of the age-group the savings rate needed for retirement exceeds the savings rate of the average American. While the numbers above are based upon a unique example of three ways of saving $500,000, it still highlights the issue that Americans simply consume too much of their income to accumulate wealth. Furthermore, it emphasizes the point that the earlier you start to save, the less you'll have to cut your expenses to reach your financial goals.

Someone could make the weak argument that by waiting until forty or forty-five years of age to start retirement savings, one could have eliminated their home mortgage and substantially increase their ability to save money. We can extend the examples above to accommodate this possibility, again using the BLS data:

Ages	Income	Savings	Savings %	Funding	Income %
25–42	$27,835	$ 1,145	4%	$ 2,090	8%
45–64	$33,990	$10,860	32%	$10,860	32%

Chart 9.5

The average forty-five to sixty-four year old uses 24 percent of his or her income on housing. Let's assume that this proportion of income represents mortgage payments and that by age forty-five an individual has the mortgage paid off. Then let's assume that what was being used for the mortgage can now be invested. As you can see in chart 9.5, 24 percent of an average income of $33,990 adds $8,158 per year to savings bringing total annual savings to $10,860. Finally, let's assume that the entire annual savings is invested to build a retirement fund and earns 9 percent per year until age sixty-five. Does waiting until you can invest a meaningful amount make a difference?

This strategy will result in accumulated savings of $671,000 as shown in chart 9.6. However, an investor who starts early can easily surpass this amount. In this case, $2,090 invested per year between the ages of twenty-five and forty-two will become over $680,000.

Age	25–42	45–64
Money Accumulated	$682,883	$671,944
Money Invested	$ 37,620	$228,060
Investment Earnings	$645,263	$443,884
Multiplication of Money Invested	17.2 times	1.9 times

Chart 9.6

It Takes Time, Not Money, to Make Money!

Once again, early starters see their money work harder, multiplying their original investment seventeen times. The late start/debt-free investors' money failed to multiply two times. In addition, early starters in this example now have the next twenty-three years to worry about paying off the mortgage and be debt-free by retirement.

The above examples use data of average Americans and may not be representative of your specific financial situation. In any case, it is the principles behind the examples, not the examples themselves, that are crucial to grasp. The most powerful retirement savings tool that you will ever have is time. Save early, save often, and remember—*It takes time, not money, to make money!*

How to Get There, Part 2
The principles above only work if you have the right investments. Those advisers who advocate becoming mortgage-free

before investing for retirement *prove* their point by showing that you can save more in mortgage interest than what can be earned investing. This is only true if you select poor investments. In chapter 8, we saw the wisdom of investing rather than accelerating your mortgage payments. This wisdom assumes that you will select the right investments.

One thing that putting time on your side accomplishes is that it allows you to benefit from growth-oriented investments that involve greater than average risk but offer much higher potential returns. Extending your time horizon gives you better odds of surviving extreme price volatility and recovering from short-term losses. In fact, with a long enough time horizon, you can virtually eliminate all investment risk.

I've studied the return on the Dow Jones Industrial Average (DJIA) since its inception in 1897. The DJIA is an index that represents the stock-price movement of thirty of the country's largest and most financially stable companies. These are the so-called "blue-chip" stocks favored by conservative, prudent investors. One thousand dollars invested in these stocks thirty years ago would be worth nearly $1.8 million today for a compound annual return of 10 percent. This is substantially greater than the return on any other class of financial investments, including bonds, real estate, or precious metals. However, the concern of investors who have avoided the stock market is that stock prices move up and down in a largely unpredictable fashion. Since they quite logically want to avoid losing any portion of their retirement savings, they don't want to take any chances with the stock market's volatility.

In any one year or even three-year period, the stock market can be very risky. In the 1973–1974 market decline, the DJIA dropped 31 percent. Many lower quality stocks dropped two to three times that much. During the Depression years of 1929–1932, the stock market dropped nearly 70 percent! However, by extending your investment time horizon, the risk of investing in stocks disappears. While the odds of losing money in any one year is about 30 percent, the longer you invest, the lower the likelihood of losing money. Based on the stock market's complete history, if you hold a portfolio of quality companies for five years, the chances of losing money drop in half, to 15 percent. The exciting truth for long-term investors is that over any twenty-year period, including the Depression and twenty-one other recessions, the stock market has never declined! The chart below shows the odds of losing money and the best and worst compound returns for various holding periods.

	Hold Stocks For:						
	1 Yr.	3 Yrs.	5 Yrs.	10 Yrs.	20 Yrs.	30 Yrs.	40 Yrs.
% of Losing Periods	31%	23%	15%	4%	0	0	0
Largest Compound % Gain	37%	26%	18%	15%	13%	13%	12%
Largest Compound % Loss	-43%	-30%	-14%	-1%	+.1%	+1.2%	+3.5%

Chart 9.7

There are two important facts to glean from this table. First, the longer you hold stocks, the lower the risk of losing money, until it disappears. The stock market has not gone down over any twenty-year time period. Even if you invested money on the eve of the Great Depression in 1929 and suffered through the market's most devastating losses, you still doubled your money by 1949 and tripled it by 1951! The losses suffered in 1973–1974 were made up by 1976, and your money was doubled by 1983 and tripled by 1986. The bottom line is that there is no reason to fear stock investing for retirement since the time when you need the money is typically more than twenty years away.

The second key fact is that the market actually gets more predictable over longer periods of time. As you can see in chart 9.7, in any one year the market has gone up as much as 37 percent and dropped as much as 43 percent. For three-year periods, the variation narrows but still ranges from +26 percent to -30 percent. However, look what happens for longer holding periods. The range between the best ten years and the worst ten years shrinks from +15 percent to -1 percent and is little changed for longer periods. What is uncertain on a daily or even annual basis becomes predictable over the long haul.

In essence, the two biggest fears investors have regarding the stock market, volatility and risk of loss, really do not exist for long-term investors. Retirement savings is a long-term process. Over the long-term, stock investing offers the greatest returns with virtually no risk. Furthermore, it is the only investment that has provided returns significantly above inflation, which is critical to the preservation of purchasing power.

Retirement Investment Strategy

Any prudent retirement plan will emphasize long-term investing in the stock market. In preceding chapters we have learned about the key ingredients to a successful investment plan: investing according to personality; diversification; Regular Investment Plan; the 3-Stage Strategy; and the Constant Ratio Plan. These strategies stress the two primary factors in your retirement plan's success: time until retirement and risk tolerance. Time until retirement plays a role because you will have to modify your portfolio objectives over time as you close in on retirement day. Your risk tolerance is your ability to accept uncertainty and price changes in your investments. As we saw in chapter 4, there are basically four temperament types, two of which are suited for moderate to high-risk investments and two that are more comfortable with less risk.

Average Americans invest too conservatively to reach their retirement goals. Statistics show that there is far too much money parked in fixed-income investments, such as money market funds, CDs, and Guaranteed Investment Contracts (GICs). Very little money is invested for growth in the stock market. Fixed income investments are fine for capital preservation and, in some cases, a modest amount of growth. However, they are completely inappropriate as the sole vehicle for long-term capital accumulation.

At a minimum, individual investors should model themselves

after professionally managed pension funds. Pension funds must have money available each year to meet their pension income obligations. They cannot afford to lose much money for extended periods of time. Furthermore, they have a legal and fiduciary responsibility to invest conservatively. With all those restrictions, the average pension fund portfolio still has more than half of their assets invested in stocks. Individuals, on the other hand, have barely more than 20 percent of their retirement funds in stocks despite being able to invest with far fewer obligations and restrictions. They need to be more aggressive.

If an aggressive investment approach scares you, go back to the Retirement Worksheet and see what a difference the higher projected returns make. Study and become comfortable with each of the components of P.I.ST.O.L. in chapter 7. Then review the statistics on the long-term risks of investing, which are few to none barring a complete financial meltdown. Using my P.I.ST.O.L. strategy further reduces investment risk. Read my optimistic thoughts (not predictions!) about the future in chapter 6. Pray some more. I'm assuming that's where you started. If not, shame on you! If being a stock investor under these circumstances still scares you, please pray some more. My prayer for you will be that God will show you clearly what He would have you do in terms of stewardship in this critical area. Many Americans are failing to plan for retirement, and given their direct access to the greatest source of wisdom, Christians should not be among them.

How to Get There, Part 3

After determining your best investment strategy, you must turn your attention to tax-deferred savings plans. Tax-deferred investment vehicles allow your money to grow faster because you don't have to pay taxes on the earnings and gains you make as your money accumulates. Depending upon your income level and tax situation, tax deferral can be a signficant advantage, as you can see demonstrated in chart 9.8. We'll look at two of the most popular tax-deferred savings vehicles: employer sponsored plans, such as 401K or 403B, and the Individual Retirement Account, commonly known as an IRA. We'll also take a brief look at a new and very popular tax-deferred investment, the variable annuity.

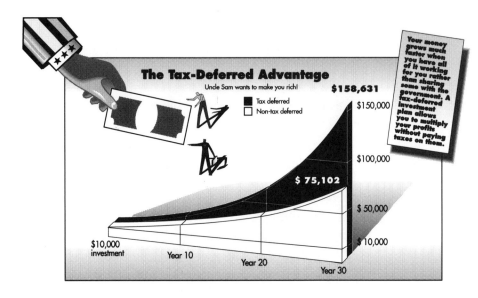

Chart 9.8

Employer Sponsored Plans

Employer sponsored plans, also known as 401K or 403B, tax-deferred savings (TDSPs), or defined contribution plans, are part of the corporate movement away from traditional defined benefit pension plans. In a defined contribution plan, an employer promises to contribute a sum of money toward an employee's retirement rather than a lifetime income based upon service and salary. The size of the retirement pension paid out becomes the ultimate responsibility of the employee.

In these plans, employees make regular contributions to their pension fund through payroll deductions. Some portion of the employees contribution is matched by the employer. The employees' taxable income is reduced by the amount they contribute. A choice of investments is offered for employees to choose from, and the earnings in the account accumulate free of taxes until the money is withdrawn.

TDSP's Are Probably the Greatest Financial Tool Ever Invented!

They say that there is no such thing as a free lunch or a money tree. A TDSP is both! You save your own money. The government will give you money for saving your own money. Your employer will give you money for saving your own money, and the government won't even ask for a piece of that—at least for a long time. Your money will make money, and the government won't even ask for a piece of that either—at least for a long time. Is this a great country or what?

To get maximum benefit out of a TDSP there are some easy guidelines to follow. First, you *must* participate. According to Hewitt Associates, a benefits consulting firm, 28 percent of eligible workers do not participate in their 401K plans (*Washington Post*, 1/10/93). There is virtually no excuse for this. This is the best personal financial tool ever invented. It should be your first choice for retirement savings, and as we've seen earlier in this chapter, it makes the most sense to start saving in one today.

Second, contribute as much as you possibly can, and then try to put in even a little bit more. This is the best money you will ever save in your entire life. This is the free lunch and the money tree, an instant return just for saving money. The more money you put in, the more your employer adds to it and the bigger the tax break you get. This is how the tax break works. If you contribute $2,000 per year, you have reduced your taxable income by $2,000. In other words, if you earn $35,000, the IRS will tax you as if you earned $33,000. This will save you money each payday as your payroll withholding will be based on a lower salary. You'll also save money at tax time. If you're in the 15 percent tax bracket, this $2,000 you've saved for retirement has also saved you $300 in federal income taxes for the year; the savings would be $560 if you're in the 28 percent bracket. These tax savings do not include those from state taxes, just another institution waiting to give you money for saving your money. If saving money was a good idea in biblical times before TDSPs were available, is there any excuse for not saving money this way now?

Third, you must make wise investment choices. Most participants invest far too cautiously for retirement. As a result, most TDSP money can be found in fixed income investments, especially Guaranteed Investment Contracts. There is not nearly enough invested in stock mutual funds. We've already seen that over the long term there is little to fear about the stock market. TDSPs make the fear factor even less because much of the money that's invested was contributed by your employer. In a way, you're actually in the market with someone else's money. This makes the odds even less — and they are close to zero anyway — that you will lose *your* money in the stock market. TDSPs are also a great way to implement P.I.ST.O.L.

If it is offered under your plan, one investment that you should be cautious of is company stock. The mistake that is commonly made is to invest too much of your retirement plan in company stock. Even if your company is in great financial shape, it is far too risky to commit a significant amount of money to any one investment. The amount invested in company stock should be considered part of the growth portion of your portfolio. Including contributions of stock by your employer, company stock should amount to no more than 10 percent of your overall retirement assets.

The only disadvantage of TSDPs is that early access to your money can be costly. The IRS is willing to give you the tax breaks only as long as you use the money for retirement. Withdrawals of your money before age fifty-nine and one-half are usually considered additional income and will cost you regular income tax plus a 10 percent penalty on the amount withdrawn. However, many TDSPs will allow you to borrow against them, although I'm not a big fan of that unless it's an emergency. Furthermore, after a few years, all the money you've been given by your employer or saved in taxes will likely be much greater than the tax penalties for early withdrawal. Even with the possibility of tax penalties, the TDSP is the single greatest financial vehicle ever created — and it's available for people like us.

Individual Retirement Accounts

IRAs are a misunderstood financial tool. It is not an investment, but a special account that offers tax advantages and a variety of self-selected investments. In an IRA, you will choose and in some cases manage your own investments. The contributions you make to the account may be fully, partially, or nontax deductible depending on your income, access to other retirement plans, and marital status. Like the TDSP, the earnings you make within your account accumulate tax-free until you withdraw the money. There are similar penalties for early withdrawal as with the TDSP.

The basic advantages of IRAs is the same as that provided by TDSPs — tax-deferred growth of savings. While there is no limit to what you can contribute to an IRA, your contribution may not be tax-deductible. Like everything else with the IRS, there are many rules for IRA contributions. If you decide to contribute above the tax-deductible limits set by the IRS, you will have to track these additional contributions through an annual maze of IRS forms until you retire. Your money will still grow tax-deferred. However, TDSPs offer better tax advantages, employer matching, and much higher contribution limits. Therefore, it is best to fund an IRA only after you are contributing the maximum amount possible to your TDSP.

Variable Annuities

A complete discussion of annuities is beyond the scope of this book. Were it not for the incredible success — from a sales standpoint — of one annuity product, the variable annuity, I wouldn't have included it at all. However, the variable annuity combines aspects of long-term investing with tax advantages. Therefore, it is appropriate to briefly point out the similarities and differences between them and TDSPs and IRAs. A variable annuity (VA) is a contract with a life insurance company that requires you to make lump-sum or periodic payments into an account that will be invested in stock and/or bond mutual funds. While there is no limit to the size of your contributions, they are not tax deductible. Like a TDSP or an IRA, the investment choices are left to the individual. Also like TDSPs and IRAs, the money invested in an annuity will grow without any tax liability, a very attractive feature. At age fifty-nine and one-half, you can begin receiving distributions from the annuity.

There are penalties for early withdrawal of funds from an annuity.

Variable annuity products have some obvious advantages, which helps explain the boom in their sales to the public. They are also highly complex investment vehicles and are not suited to everybody. A variable annuity should be bought only as part of your entire financial plan. Therefore, you need to totally understand your overall financial plan before investing in one. Because of their complexity, you should consider them only with the assistance of a qualified professional who fully understands your complete financial situation. Here are some other variable annuity shopping guidelines:

- Because the contributions are not tax deductible, you should consider a VA only after you are maximizing your contributions to TDSPs and IRAs. This normally means that VAs would appeal only to high income individuals.
- Watch out for expenses. Studies have shown that the average VA has annual expenses so high that they completely outweigh the advantages of tax deferral! You can expect front-end commissions (loads), surrender charges, insurance company expenses, mutual fund management expenses, annual record and maintenance fees, and death benefit expenses. As always, when the financial services industry moves a lot of a product, you can be sure it's because they're making a lot of money selling it. Shop around and compare costs before you buy.
- If you're up to the task of buying a VA on your own, two low-cost plans are available directly from Scudder (Scudder Horizon Plan; 1-800-225-2470) and Vanguard (Vanguard Variable Annuity Plan; 1-800-662-7447)
- With expenses levels so high, you must compensate by investing aggressively to have any meaningful chance of making your money grow. Allocate a higher percentage than usual of your portfolio to growth mutual funds.
- Because of high expenses, it makes sense only to have a large VA account. This will make the annual fixed costs smaller on a percentage basis. Many VAs have rather high-minimum in-

vestments anyway, especially relative to the ease of opening an IRA or investing in a TDSP.

- Again, unless you're smart enough to do this yourself—not an easy task—deal only with an experienced, qualified professional who is looking at a VA as a supplement to existing retirement and other financial plans.

What to Do If You Haven't Started Your Retirement Savings

Hopefully, you haven't waited too long to start saving. Unless you have fifteen to twenty years before retirement, you will have to regularly set aside a substantial portion of your income to accumulate a meaningful amount. Even then, there is a good chance that you will have to invest more aggressively than otherwise would have been necessary with an early start. The combination of higher-risk portfolios and investing larger sums of money lowers the odds of success.

That's another advantage to an early start. Investing early will allow you to invest more conservatively and increase your odds of accumulating the sum you need. Using the 3-Stage Strategy, a late start saver will have to construct a higher-risk Stage 1 portfolio and stay within both the Stage 1 and Stage 2 portfolios much longer than an early starter.

There are alternatives to not meeting your retirement fund objectives. You will have to accept a lower standard of living than you initially had planned, one that may actually decrease each year depending on cost of living increases. You may also be forced to supplement your income by working more than you had planned. These may or may not be desirable options, but you may have to consider them as part of your retirement planning now if you've started thinking about retirement investing too late.

Retirement Planning Summary

1. Lower high-cost debt. It's tough to earn a higher rate of return on your investments than the cost of consumer debt.
2. Start your retirement savings first but still have a goal of owning your home debt-free by retirement.
3. Take full advantage of tax-advantaged investments.

4. Adjust your budget to increase your savings, especially into employer-sponsored savings plans (401K, 403B).
5. Emphasize growth investments. Cash is trash! Use the 3-Stage Strategy to control risk.
6. Start today! The early bird catches the worms.

Notes
1. *Proverbs 24:32-34*
2. *Proverbs 30:25*
3. *James 4:14-16*
4. *Proverbs 23:5*
5. *Proverbs 11:28*

Table 1: Total Assets Needed at Retirement

Income Shortfall:	Years between Now and Retirement									
	4	8	12	16	20	24	28	32	36	40
$5,000	58,493	68,428	80,052	93,649	109,556	128,165	149,935	175,403	205,197	240,051
$7,500	87,739	102,643	120,077	140,474	164,334	192,248	224,903	263,104	307,795	360,077
$10,000	116,986	136,857	160,103	187,298	219,112	256,330	299,870	350,806	410,393	480,102
$12,500	146,232	171,071	200,129	234,123	273,890	320,413	374,838	438,507	512,992	600,128
$15,000	175,479	205,285	240,155	280,947	328,668	384,496	449,805	526,209	615,590	720,153
$17,500	204,725	239,500	280,181	327,772	383,447	448,578	524,773	613,910	718,188	840,179
$20,000	233,972	273,714	320,206	374,596	438,225	512,661	599,741	701,612	820,787	960,204
$22,500	263,218	307,928	360,232	421,421	493,003	576,743	674,708	789,313	923,385	1,080,230
$25,000	292,465	342,142	400,258	468,245	547,781	640,826	749,676	877,015	1,025,983	1,200,255
$27,500	321,711	376,356	440,284	515,070	602,559	704,909	824,643	964,716	1,128,581	1,320,281
$30,000	350,958	410,571	480,310	561,894	657,337	768,991	899,611	1,052,418	1,231,180	1,440,306
$32,500	380,204	444,785	520,335	608,719	712,115	833,074	974,579	1,140,119	1,333,778	1,560,332
$35,000	409,450	478,999	560,361	655,543	766,893	897,156	1,049,546	1,227,821	1,436,376	1,680,357
$37,500	438,697	513,213	600,387	702,368	821,671	961,239	1,124,514	1,315,522	1,538,975	1,800,383
$40,000	467,943	547,428	640,413	749,192	876,449	1,025,322	1,199,481	1,403,223	1,641,573	1,920,408
$42,500	497,190	581,642	680,439	796,017	931,227	1,089,404	1,274,449	1,490,925	1,744,171	2,040,434
$45,000	526,436	615,856	720,464	842,842	986,005	1,153,487	1,349,416	1,578,626	1,846,770	2,160,459
$47,500	555,683	650,070	760,490	889,666	1,040,783	1,217,569	1,424,384	1,666,328	1,949,368	2,280,485
$50,000	584,929	684,285	800,516	936,491	1,095,562	1,281,652	1,499,352	1,754,029	2,051,966	2,400,510

Table 1

Table 2: Factor to Value Current Assets at Retirement

Projected Years between Now and Retirement

Return:	4	8	12	16	20	24	28	32	36	40
6%	1.26	1.59	2.01	2.54	3.21	4.05	5.11	6.45	8.15	10.29
9%	1.41	1.99	2.81	3.97	5.60	7.91	11.17	15.76	22.25	31.41
11%	1.52	2.30	3.50	5.31	8.06	12.24	18.58	28.21	42.82	65.00
12%	1.57	2.48	3.90	6.13	9.65	15.18	23.88	37.58	59.14	93.05

Table 2

Table 3: Annual Savings Needed to Reach Asset Goal

Years between Now and Retirement

	4	8	12	16	20	24	28	32	36	40
$25,000	5,387	2,186	1,169	695	436	282	186	124	84	56
$50,000	10,774	4,372	2,338	1,391	873	565	373	249	167	113
$75,000	16,160	6,558	3,507	2,086	1,309	847	559	373	251	169
$100,000	21,547	8,744	4,676	2,782	1,746	1,130	745	497	334	226
$125,000	26,934	10,931	5,845	3,477	2,182	1,412	931	621	418	282
$150,000	32,321	13,117	7,014	4,172	2,619	1,695	1,118	746	501	339
$175,000	37,707	15,303	8,184	4,868	3,055	1,977	1,304	870	585	395
$200,000	43,093	17,489	9,353	5,563	3,492	2,260	1,490	994	669	452
$225,000	48,481	19,675	10,522	6,259	3,928	2,542	1,676	1,119	752	508
$250,000	53,868	21,861	11,691	6,954	4,365	2,825	1,863	1,243	836	565
$275,000	59,254	24,047	12,860	7,650	4,801	3,107	2,049	1,367	919	621
$300,000	64,641	26,233	14,029	8,345	5,238	3,390	2,235	1,492	1,003	678
$350,000	75,415	30,605	16,367	9,736	6,111	3,955	2,608	1,740	1,170	791
$400,000	86,188	34,978	18,705	11,127	6,984	4,520	2,980	1,989	1,337	904
$450,000	96,962	39,350	21,043	12,517	7,857	5,085	3,353	2,237	1,504	1,017
$500,000	107,735	43,722	23,382	13,908	8,730	5,650	3,726	2,486	1,672	1,130
$600,000	129,282	52,466	28,058	16,690	10,476	6,780	4,471	2,983	2,006	1,356
$700,000	150,830	61,211	32,734	19,472	12,222	7,910	5,216	3,480	2,340	1,582
$800,000	172,377	69,955	37,411	22,253	13,968	9,040	5,961	3,977	2,674	1,808
$900,000	193,924	78,700	42,087	25,035	15,714	10,170	6,706	4,475	3,009	2,033
$1,000,000	215,471	87,444	46,763	27,817	17,460	11,300	7,451	4,972	3,343	2,259

Assumed Return in Retirement

Return%	10%
Years	4

Table 3

263

Chapter Ten

WEALTH IS MORE
THAN MONEY

BUT SEEK FIRST HIS KINGDOM AND HIS
RIGHTEOUSNESS, AND ALL THESE THINGS
WILL BE GIVEN TO YOU AS WELL
(MATTHEW 6:33)

Ray and Chris were successful professionals with sizable and growing incomes. They never thought of themselves as materialistic. They had always been generous givers and considered their use of money to be reasonable and not extravagant. However, their view of money and possessions was biased by the fact that they always had money and possessions. It wasn't until Ray left his career to start his own business that they got a more balanced view of themselves. Going without money taught them to find value in other things. As they transferred control of their life from their money to their faith in God they learned something very powerful. In the face of declining financial assets, their life became richer and happier than they ever thought possible.

A company called Sonlight Marketing makes an imitation dollar bill with a provocative message on the back. It reads:

Money Will Buy:

A bed BUT NOT sleep.
Books BUT NOT brains.

Food BUT NOT appetite.
Finery BUT NOT beauty.
A house BUT NOT a home.
Medicine BUT NOT health.
Luxuries BUT NOT culture.
Amusement BUT NOT happiness.
A crucifix BUT NOT a savior.
A church pew BUT NOT heaven.
What money can't buy, Jesus can give free of charge.

It Is OK to Have Money

The chuch has historically had an aversion to money because of its worldly connotations: greed, hedonism, abuse, and so on. Therefore, Christians have become indoctrinated not to allow ourselves to think unnecessarily about money. Our attitude has been to ignore, hate, or feel guilty about having financial wealth. Nowhere in the Bible does it indicate that these are correct attitudes. Neither does it say that wealth in and of itself is bad. God often bestows prosperity and financial blessing upon people according to His sovereign will. In fact, many of the great biblical patriarchs were very wealthy:

Abraham
"Abram had become very wealthy in livestock and in silver and gold" (Gen. 13:2).

Job
"[Job] owned seven thousand sheep, three thousand camels, five hundred yoke of oxen and five hundred donkeys, and had a large number of servants. He was the greatest man among all the people of the East" (Job 1:3).

Solomon
"I will also give you wealth, riches and honor, such as no king who was before you ever had and none after you will have" (2 Chron. 1:12).

It is critical to our understanding of money to know that no wealthy person was ever rebuked for having money. For instance, in the story of the Rich Young Man (Matt. 19:16-22), it was not his substantial wealth that was the issue but his attachment to it. He arrogantly claimed that he had followed all the commandments.[1] His braggadocio rang hollow when asked to further demonstrate his commitment to God by selling all that he had. Jesus answered, "If you want to be perfect, go, sell your possessions and give to the poor, and you will have treasure in heaven. Then come, follow Me" (v. 21). Jesus was not advocating disinvestment as a universal principle for salvation. Rather, it was the young man's attachment to his money that Jesus was rebuking.[2]

Compare Job's response to losing his family and wealth.[3] He praised God![4] God eventually doubled the wealth Job previously had, so He obviously has no aversion to money.[5]

Likewise, the Rich Fool (Luke 12:16-21) was not rebuked for his substantial assets. Jesus' contempt was for the fool's preoccupation with self.[6] Jesus was attacking the fool's vain attempt to make his wealth support a self-serving, consumptive lifestyle.

It is because of the preoccupation with money that Jesus said, "Indeed, it is easier for a camel to go through the eye of a needle than for a rich man to enter the kingdom of God" (18:25). Time and again, Jesus warned of the judgment on the rich that would come from the preeminent position of money in their life. Preeminence is a position reserved only for God. It was this attitude that Abraham, Job, Solomon, and other rich figures were praised for. Their wealth did not have an adverse impact on their relationship with God. Desire for Him and His ways was greater than their desire to amass and protect wealth.

Abraham
"And the Scripture was fulfilled that says, 'Abraham believed God, and it was credited to him as righteousness,' and he was called God's friend" (James 2:23).

Job
"Then the Lord said to Satan, 'Have you considered My servant Job? There is no one on earth like him; he is blameless and upright, a man who fears God and shuns evil' " (Job 1:8).

Solomon

"God said to Solomon, 'Since this [wisdom and knowledge] is your heart's desire and you have not asked for wealth, riches or honor' " (2 Chron. 1:11).

Jesus said, "I have come that they may have life, and have it to the full" (John 10:10). The original Greek word for "full," translated as "more abundantly" in the King James Bible, implies extraordinary, overflowing, surplus, to unusual excess. While Jesus had no specific aversion to wealth, He did say that the good life has nothing to do with money. We know this to be true through the story of Solomon.

The Vanity of Solomon

King Solomon had it all. He had intellect, power, money, fame, and reputation. He indulged himself in every possible human pleasure — wine, women, music, and the arts. He became learned in many fields of study: architecture, gardening, cattle breeding, art collecting, musicianship, philosophy, and formal religion. Near the end of this life of unequaled accomplishment, Solomon summed his life up by saying, "Meaningless! Meaningless! . . . Utterly meaningless! Everything is meaningless . . . I hated life . . . All of it is meaningless, a chasing after the wind" (Ecc. 1:2; 2:17).

Solomon devoted his life to the pursuit of pleasure, and since he had been equipped with God-given wisdom, he was uniquely qualified to achieve the desires of his heart. Yet in spite of his saying, "I denied myself nothing my eyes desired" (v. 10), his quest ended in abject failure. His life embodied Jesus' teachings on wealth, that life without God is an empty, vain pursuit. Wealth ultimately disappoints, and no amount of money can provide the security and satisfaction that exists in a personal relationship with God.

Solomon wrote the Book of Ecclesiastes so that its readers would avoid the same futile lifestyle he earnestly sought. Through his leadership, Jerusalem's prosperity was at its peak, but Solomon wanted his people to understand that money and possessions are fleeting and eventually meaningless.[7] His goal was to direct them to seek God's will as the only sound basis for living and to turn them away from the empty pursuit of wealth. Solomon's admonitions carry so much weight because of his unique experience in having it all. Nobody has ever had more, yet for all of his God-given wisdom, he couldn't handle it. If the smartest and richest man ever couldn't handle life without God, what chance do we or anyone else have?

Solomon's message to a prosperous and self-sufficient Jerusalem 3,000 years ago is still timely. Today, the very attitudes toward money that Jesus warned against are seen as the necessary attributes of financial success. Covetousness is called aspiration, hoarding is called prudence, and greed is called ambition. The attitudes our culture value most in its pursuit of excellence are those that exalt self. Christians, on the other hand, are asked "to put off your old self, which is being corrupted by its deceitful desires" (Eph. 4:22) and "whatever you do, do it all for the glory of God" (1 Cor. 10:31).

The Futility of Money

Why did Solomon say the pursuit of worldly pleasure is meaningless? The key to an extraordinary life of overflowing excess is to give up your life in exchange for spiritual wealth. A preoccupation with money shows that we do not understand what an abundant life is. If we did, we would not be concerned with what our money will do for us but with what it can do for others. Ultimately, money can do little for us. It can fulfill only our shallow, base desires.[8] Our money is meaningless because we have deeper desires that money cannot satisfy, desires that only our Creator understands.[9]

No wonder the pursuit of money is foolish and meaningless. We don't know ourselves well enough to know what it is we really want in life, and yet we try to satisfy our needs anyway. As a result, we ignore the promise of Philippians 4:19; "And my God will meet all your needs according to His glorious riches in Christ Jesus"; and so we put our trust in money. By putting money first we implicitly say that God can't take care of us the way *we* want Him to.

When God won't take care of us according to our naive whims, we quickly turn to another god — money — to meet our demands, which we call needs. In doing so, we continue a pattern of behavior seen by the Israelites in the desert when they felt abandoned by God.[10] The calf they created to worship was made of gold, humanity's most enduring symbol of wealth. It's ironic that what means so much to us means so little to God. Heaven is made such that "the street of the city was of pure gold" (Rev. 21:21). We repeatedly choose to turn away from God for something that in His eyes is like dirt, fit only for walking on. Although God would let us walk on gold, on Mount Sinai He told Moses, "Take off your sandals, for the place where you are standing is holy ground" (Ex. 3:5). Quite apparently, God and people have different views of wealth. Indeed, God never sees wealth in material terms.

"For where your treasure is, there your heart will be also" (Matt. 6:21). To both the Jews and the Greeks, the term "heart" figuratively referred to the mind, the intellect, and one's religion. According to a study, 50 percent of people's non-sleeping time is spent thinking about money. This means that God must share the other 50 percent with our remaining concerns. "In his pride the wicked does not seek Him; in all his thoughts there is no room for God" (Ps. 10:4). Since money dominates our thoughts, it is our treasure. How much more of our heart could be devoted to God if we could live as Paul instructed Timothy, "If we have food and clothing, we will be content with that" (1 Tim. 6:8).

Jesus warned us against greed and the intense desire to accumulate more things. "Then He said to them, 'Watch out! Be on your guard against all kinds of greed; a man's life does not consist in the abundance of his possessions' " (Luke 12:15). If life did consist of one's possessions, then we would be in for a lifetime of disappointment. To be sure, occasional, brief bursts of happiness may interrupt these disappointments, but like a spoonful of sugar, the moment provides its sweetness and then quickly fades away.

The Key to an Abundant Life
Complete satisfaction with our outward prosperity can never be achieved. Limits to our wealth give birth to coveting the things

that we don't have. However, even limitless wealth cannot ultimately satisfy, which Solomon discovered.[11] Our material desires always grow faster than our financial affluence, and the results are disastrous.[12] The godly person prospers inwardly rather than outwardly. Even though the Apostle Paul was not as wise as King Solomon, he found the key to inner prosperity. "I know what it is to be in need, and I know what it is to have plenty. I have learned the secret of being content in any and every situation, whether well fed or hungry, whether living in plenty or in want" (Phil. 4:12). Apparently, Paul found a satisfaction in life that was not predicated upon his financial condition. In fact, it had absolutely no bearing on his outlook on life whatsoever!

What is this "secret of being content in any and every situation"? It is a willingness and ability to create a lifestyle that allows us to generously meet the needs of others. This lifestyle is the key that unlocks the abundant life in Christ. When we uncomplicate our lives by stripping away our worldly desires, we can live a truly contented life and pursue godliness — the true wealthy lifestyle. The world may equate money with happiness, "But godliness with contentment is great gain. For we brought nothing into the world, and we can take nothing out of it" (1 Tim. 6:6-7). "The fear of the Lord leads to life: Then one rests content, untouched by trouble" (Prov. 19:23). "Moreover, when God gives any man wealth and possessions, and enables him to enjoy them, to accept his lot and be happy in his work — this is a gift of God. He seldom reflects on the days of his life, because God keeps him occupied with gladness of heart" (Ecc. 5:19-20).

To obtain this abundant life with "so much blessing that you will not have room enough for it" (Mal. 3:10), you are advised to "store up for yourselves treasures in heaven" (Matt. 6:20) through commitment, sacrifice, and perseverance. In fact, faithful stewardship and the proper use of our earthly possessions store up heavenly treasure. When used wisely, earthly wealth is merely a tool that results in limitless heavenly wealth "where moth and rust do not destroy, and where thieves do not break in and steal" (Matt. 6:20). This wealth is described as "a rich store of salvation and wisdom and knowledge" (Isa. 33:6). This implies eternal fellowship with God, the originator of salvation, wisdom, and knowledge. Moreover, I believe it includes eternal fellowship with all those people who were brought into a closer relationship with God by the use of our money. "I tell you, use worldly wealth to gain friends for yourselves, so that when it is gone, you will be welcomed into eternal dwellings" (Luke 16:9). Unlike worldly wealth, which is of finite worth and reluctantly shared, God's wealth is freely given and beyond value.

At all times, we must remember that what we have is not our own. It's not as if what we put in the collection plate on Sunday is God's and the rest is ours. *All* that we have is a gift from God, given according to our ability to manage it. We must focus our attention on the Giver rather than the gift. "Keep your lives free from the love of money and be content with what you have, because God has said, 'Never will I leave you; never will I forsake you'" (Heb. 13:5). Our true wealth is in God's grace, not God's gifts.

The One Thing Money Can't Buy

We can buy anything we want if we have enough money, except for the single most important thing. We cannot buy ourselves. Our lives have already been bought at a price we can't afford. The only Person who could meet the price of our salvation paid that price on a cross 2,000 years ago. Ironically, the one thing we can never afford — eternal life — can be ours free of charge. What then can be the value of money when it can't buy the one thing we value most, and yet that thing we value most can be had without any money? Wealth can have any value only when it is used to express our gratitude for sharing in the greatest wealth of all.

"Now all has been heard; here is the conclusion of the matter: Fear God and keep His commandments, for this is the whole duty of man. For God will bring every deed into judgment, including every hidden thing, whether it is good or evil" (Ecc. 12:13-14).

Notes

1. *Matthew 19:20*
2. *Matthew 19:22*
3. *Job 1:15-17, 19*
4. *Job 1:20-21*
5. *Job 42:10*
6. *Luke 12:17-19*
7. *Psalm 103:15-16*
8. *Revelation 3:17*
9. *Psalm 139:1-6*
10. *Exodus 32:7-8*
11. *Ecclesiastes 5:10-11*
12. *1 Timothy 6:9-10*

Epilogue

My life, rather my approach to life, has changed dramatically from the time that this book was started. This has had a profound effect on what you are reading now. This book started out being an investment book with some spiritual guidance. It turned out to be—I hope—a spiritual book with some investment advice.

An extremely gifted missionary to Africa once told me that the most serious spiritual issue facing Americans is materialism. I couldn't agree more. Materialism is a very clever form of spiritual warfare in that we always see it as someone else's problem. Materialism blinds us to the truth of how we manage our resources to our own benefit rather than to the benefit of others. We see what we can do with our money as being limited by how much we have instead of how we decide to use it. If we could only see how our materialism keeps a distance between us and God's heavenly riches.

My wife and I fell prey to materialism. We didn't know it until most of our material was consumed in the first years of my leaving a successful career to become self-employed. During this time, we lived on an austerity budget, consumed much of our savings, and finally, sold the house we were supposed to own "forever."

Things are still tight, though there is finally some room in our budget above basic living expenses. We rent a beautiful home in a nice neighborhood that's neither as beautiful a home or as nice a neighborhood as the one we used to own. However, we have found ourselves "filled with an inexpressible and glorious joy" (1 Peter 1:8).

Without the blinders of materialism, which we didn't think we had in the first place, we have found that joy is not found in fancy clothes, nice houses, club memberships, a big retirement account, and so on. Those things can definitely make a person very happy and I would love to have them. But if they come at the expense of our relationship to God, we'll pass.

We couldn't have made that statement when we had all of our material things. Now that we've lived some time without them, we've had a chance to compare. If you're willing to replace your devotion to materialism with a serious devotion to God, you'll wonder why it took you so long. Your ability to satisfy against God's ability is no contest.

The tools in this book will help you have more money and more material. But it's the principles behind the tools that will give you far more than all the money in the world can buy. God's Word guarantees it and we're living proof of it.

For Further Reading

Newsletters
The Linder Letter
1-800-742-9804
$39 per year, 12 monthly issues
The Linder Letter is written to provide novice and small investors ongoing guidance on investing. It's excellent! (I know— Prov. 16:18: Pride goeth before destruction.)
Ray can also be reached on-line on Compuserve: 74743,372

Planning Resources
T. Rowe Price Retirement Planning Kit
T. Rowe Price College Planning Kit
Free: 1-800-638-5660
These tools are excellent but require lots of time to work through. They are the best I've seen.

Charles Schwab Guide to Retirement
Charles Schwab Guide to College
Free: Available in the lobbies of their nationwide offices. Easier to use than the ones above, but not as complete.

Social Security Administration
Form SSA-7004
1-800-772-1213
Contact to get estimate of future Social Security Benefits.

Saving Money
Tightwad Gazette (Amy Dacyczyn)
Book $9.99, Villiard Books (have seen at Crown Books)
Newsletter $12 per year, R.R. 1, Box 3570, Leeds, Maine 04263
Some of her money saving hints border on the absurd, but she knows more ways to stretch a dollar than everyone else combined.

Cut Your Bills in Half
by the Editors of Rodale Press.

Another good book on money saving hints (have seen at Crown Books).

Books on Investing and Financial Planning
Making the Most of Your Money, Jane Bryant Quinn
The most complete book on personal finance I've come across. 934 pages!

How to Master Your Money, Ron Blue
An excellent, basic book on financial planning from a Christian perspective. Highly recommended.

Winning on Wall Street, Martin Zweig
For the serious do-it-yourself investor, this easy to follow book explains how a wide variety of market statistics can be used to make reasonable forecasts of the stocks market. The author is one of America's leading money managers and one of my investing role models.

Getting Started in Mutual Funds, Alan Lavine
This is one of the best introductory books on mutual fund investing, although I could be biased. The author, a nationally syndicated columnist, asked me to write two chapters of this book.

The All-Season Investor, Martin Pring
For more advanced investors who want to further their understanding of how the economic/business cycle affects the financial markets.

Credit/Debt Management
Improving Your Credit and Reducing Your Debt
Gail Liberman and Alan Lavine
Another winner co-authored by Alan.

Bankcard Holders of America
524 Branch Drive, Salem, VA 24153
(703) 389-5445

This is a consumer advocacy group that publishes a newsletter and lots of other key information on how to manage and reduce your credit card debt. Highly recommended.

Speaking/Seminars/Workshops

Ray loves to talk (and talk . . . and talk . . .) about money and he's very good at it! For information on contacting Ray to speak at your event, call 1-800-742-9804.